Sri Lanka
a travel survival kit

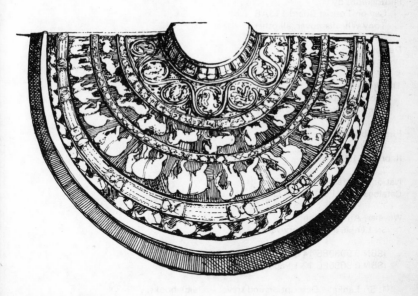

Moonstone — beautifully carved "doorsteps" found on many ancient Sinhalese religious buildings.

Sri Lanka — a travel survival kit

Published by
Lonely Planet Publications
PO Box 88, South Yarra
Victoria 3141, Australia

Typeset by
Lonely Planet Productions

Printed by
Colorcraft, Hong Kong

Illustrations by
Peter Campbell

Photographs by
Ceylon Tourist Board 113AB
Tony Wheeler cover, all others

Design by
Andrena Millen

Thanks to
Faber & Faber for permission to quote two lines on page 147
from *The Story of Ceylon*

First Published
February 1980
Reprinted 1981

National Library of Australia
Cataloguing in Publication Data

Wheeler, Anthony Ian
Sri Lanka, a travel survival kit

ISBN 0 908086 14 8
ISBN 0 908086 12 1 Paperback

1. Sri Lanka — Description and travel — Guide-books.
I. Title.

915.49'304'3

DISTRIBUTION

Ask your local bookshop to order Lonely Planet travel guides from one of our distributors below. If you have any trouble write to us directly in Australia — we'll rush copies to you as fast as the mail can carry them:

Lonely Planet Travel Guides

Other Lonely Planet travel guides include *Kathmandu & the Kingdom of Nepal* — "the best little modern guide to the mountain kingdom". *Trekking in the Himalayas* — now including day-by-day route reports of all the major treks. *Papua New Guinea* — *a travel survival kit* — explore the "last unknown". *New Zealand* — *a travel survival kit* — both islands of the "land of the long white cloud". *Africa on the Cheap* — even the countries to avoid. *Australia* — *a travel survival kit* — the

complete guide to down-under. *Hong Kong & Macau* — so much more than duty free shopping. *South America on a Shoestring* — at last we tackle Latin America with our biggest guide yet. *Across Asia on the Cheap* — with a "bad news on Iran & Afghanistan" supplement. *Burma* — *a travel survival kit* — one of the most fascinating countries in the region. *Europe* — *a travel survival kit* — this one is available only in Australasia. *South-East Asia on a Shoestring* — the most popular guide to the region.

Lonely Planet

A few short years ago Maureen and I made a lengthy overland trip and turned the info we'd gathered into the first edition of *Across Asia on the Cheap*. Since then we've kept on moving and managed to gather an enthusiastic band of fellow travellers around us to produce the Lonely Planet travel guide series.

We're still a very small organisation but we're very proud of our guide books — because what we publish comes from people who've been there and found out for themselves. Not from glossy travel brochures.

Tony

THANK YOUs

Particular thanks for information go to the Sri Lankan Tourist Board, to Tony and Lena Cansdale, Lorne Goldman, Martin and Pauline Hall, Bob Stevens and Sheila Tyrrell, Hardy (who climbed Adam's Peak with us) and to the many other people both travellers and Sri Lankans who made our visit to the resplendent island so enjoyable.

A WARNING & A REQUEST

Things change — prices go up, good places go bad, bad places go bankrupt, and nothing stays the same. So if you find things better, worse, cheaper, more expensive, recently opened or long ago closed please don't blame me but please do write and tell me. The letters we get from "our" travellers out there on the road are some of the nicest things about doing these guides for a living. As usual the best letters will score a copy of the next edition (or any othe LP guide if you prefer).

Contents

cover picture is of the beach at Tangalla

Introduction

It's easy to think of Sri Lanka as just an offshoot of India — a miniature, tropical island India where the people are Buddhist, not Hindu, and there aren't so many of them. It's a total misconception for Sri Lanka is nothing like India. It's a totally different place and enormously appealing. In fact it's hard to disagree with Marco Polo's impression that this is the finest island in the world — for no matter what you want Sri Lanka is likely to have it. Beaches? — the coastal stretch south of Colombo has beach after beach as beautiful as anywhere in the world. Culture? — try the Kandyan dances or the demon mask dances for size. Ruins? — if you like ruins you'll find your fill in the ancient cities of Anuradhapura and Polonnaruwa. Scenery? — head for the hill country where the heat of the plains and the coast soon fade away. Wildlife? — they say you can see leopards in the national parks, I did! All this comes with friendly people, good food, pleasant places to stay, absurdly low costs and in a handy, compact package. Sri Lanka? — I love it.

CEYLON OR SRI LANKA?
Changing the country's name from Ceylon to Sri Lanka caused considerable confusion but in actual fact it has always been known to the Sinhalese (the people of Sri Lanka) as Lanka or to the Tamils as Ilankai. Indeed the two thousand year old Hindu epic, the *Ramayana*, tells of Rama's beautiful wife being carried away by the evil king of Lanka. Later the Romans knew it as Taprobane and the Moslem traders talked of the island of Serendib from which was derived the word serendipity — the faculty of making happy and unexpected discoveries by accident. The Portuguese called it Ceilao, a corruption of the native name Sinhala-dvipa. In turn the Dutch altered this name to Ceylan and the British to Ceylon. In 1972 the name was officially altered to the original Lanka with the addition of Sri which means "auspicious" or "resplendent".

On leaving the Island of Andoman and sailing a thousand miles, a little south of west, the traveller reaches Ceylon, which is undoubtedly the finest Island of its size in all the world.

Marco Polo

Facts about the Country

HISTORY

Sri Lanka is definitely one of those places where history can be said to fade into the mists of legend. Is not Adam's Peak said to be the very place where Adam set foot on earth, having been cast out of heaven? Isn't that his footprint squarely on top of the mountain to prove it? Or is it Buddha's, visiting an island half way to paradise? And isn't Adam's Bridge (the chain of islands linking Sri Lanka to India) the very series of stepping stones which Rama, aided by his faithful ally the monkey god Hanuman, skipped across in his mission to rescue Sita from the clutches of the evil demon Rawana, king of Lanka, in the epic Ramayana?

It is probable that the story of the Ramayana actually does have some frail basis in reality for Sri Lanka's history recounts many invasions from the south of India. Perhaps some early, punitive invasion provided the background for the story of Rama and his beautiful wife, a story which is recounted over and over again all around Asia. Whatever the legends the reality points towards the Sinhalese people first arriving in Sri Lanka around the 5th or 6th century BC and gradually replacing the original inhabitants, the veddahs, who still linger on in remote parts of the island.

In the centuries that followed more settlers came in from India and the kingdom of Anuradhapura developed in the dry northern plain region of the country. Later other kingdoms rose up in the south and west coast regions but Anuradhapura remained the strongest. At this time, around the third century BC, the great Buddhist-Emperor Ashoka reigned in India and his son, Mahinda, came to the island with a retinue of monks to spread the Buddha's teachings. He soon converted the king and his followers to Buddhism and his sister planted a sapling of the sacred bo-tree under which the Buddha attained enlightenment in Boah-Gaya in northern India. It can still be seen flourishing in Anuradhapura today. Buddhism went through a rejuvenation in Sri Lanka and it was here that the Theravada, Hinayana or "small vehicle" school of Buddhism developed and later spread to other Buddhist countries. Even today the Buddhists of Burma, Thailand and other Theravada school countries look to Sri Lanka for spiritual leadership.

Buddhism gave the Sinhalese people a sense of national purpose and identity and also inspired the development of their culture and literature — factors which were to be important in the tumultuous centuries that followed. Although Anuradhapura was the centre of Sinhalese kingdoms for over a thousand years, from around the 4th century BC to the 10th century AD, it suffered repeated invasions by the Pandyan and later Chola kingdoms of south India. Each time some Sinhalese leader arose to repel the invaders; one of the most famous being Dutugemunu (around the first century BC) and later Vijayabahu (1055-1110 AD). The repeated invasions took their toll and Vijayabahu decided to abandon Anuradhapura and move his capital south to Polonnaruwa. Today the majestic ruins of his earlier capital are not the only reminders of this period of Sri Lankan history. Scattered throughout the country are enormous "tanks", artificial lakes developed for irrigation purposes in the dry regions of Sri Lanka. Even today they would be enormous engineering feats.

Polonnaruwa survived as a Sinhalese capital for three more centures after the fall of Anuradhapura and provided two other great kings apart from Vijayabahu. His nephew Parakramabahu (1157-1186 AD), not content with Vijayabahu's expulsion of the Cholas, carried the war to south India and later followed this military feat with a daring raid on Burma. Internally he indulged in an orgy of building at his capital and constructed many new tanks around the country. But his warring and architectural extravagances wore the country out and probably shortened Polonnaruwa's lifespan. His successor, Nissankamalla (1187-1196) was the last great Polonnaruwa king. He was followed by a series of weak rulers and once more Sri Lanka was subject to invasions from south India. Another Tamil (south Indian) kingdom rose in the north of the island, tanks were neglected or destroyed, malaria started to spread due to the neglect of the irrigation system and finally, like Anuradhapura before it, Polonnaruwa was abandoned.

The centre of Sinhalese power now shifted to the south-west of the island and between 1253 and 1400 AD there were five Sinhalese capital cities. During this period Sri Lanka also suffered from attacks by Chinese and Malyasians as well as the periodic incursions from the south of India. Finally the most powerful invaders of all, the colonial European powers, arrived on the scene in 1505.

At this time Sri Lanka had three main kingdoms — Jaffna in the north, Kandy in the central highlands and Kotte, the most powerful, in the south-west. In 1505 Lorenco de Almeida arrived in Colombo, established friendly relations with the King of Kotte and gained for Portugal a monopoly on the spice and cinnamon trade which would soon become of enormous importance in Europe. Attempts by the kingdom of Kotte to utilise the strength and protection of the Portuguese only resulted in Portugal taking over and ruling not only their regions but all the rest of the island apart from the central highlands around Kandy. Remote and inaccessible the kings of Kandy were always able to defeat attempts by the Portuguese to annex them and on a number of occasions drove them right back down to the coast.

Portuguese rule was characterised by European greed, cruelty and intolerance at its worst but attempts by the kingdom of Kandy to enlist Dutch help in expelling the Portuguese only resulted in the substitution of one European power for another. In 1656, just 151 years after the first Portuguese contact, the Dutch took control over the coastal areas of the island. In many ways the 140 years of Dutch rule were a carbon copy of the Portuguese period for the Dutch too were involved in constant, and unsuccessful, attempts to bring the highland power of Kandy under their

An Execution by an Eliphant.

One of many fascinating illustrations from Robert Knox's 1681 book *An Historical Relation of Ceylon.*

control. The Dutch were much more interested in trade and profits than the Portuguese who also had a strong interest in spreading their religion and extending their physical control. They also indulged their national penchant for canal building and you can still find many canals in Sri Lanka today, particularly around Negombo.

The French revolution resulted in a major shake-up amongst the European powers and in 1796 the Dutch were easily supplanted by the British who also managed to subdue the kingdom of Kandy and became the first European power to control the whole island. Until 1802 the British administered Sri Lanka from Madras in India but in that year it became a Crown Colony and in 1818, three years after the incorporation of Kandy, a unified administration for the entire island was set up.

In 1832 sweeping changes in property laws opened the doors to British settlers — at the expense of the Sinhalese who did not have clear title to their land, in British eyes. Soon the country was dotted with coffee, cinammon and coconut plantations and a network of roads and railways were constructed to handle this new economic activity. English became the official language and remained so until 1956 when it was replaced by Sinhala, nevertheless English is still widely spoken today.

Coffee was the main cash crop and the backbone of Sri Lanka's economy but a disastrous leaf blight virtually wiped out the coffee business in the 1870s and the plantations quickly switched over to growing tea or rubber. Today Sri Lanka is the world's largest tea exporter but tea production is subject to considerable price fluctuations on the international market and the taking over of privately owned British tea plantations has often resulted in drastically lowered yields. Rubber is grown as an intermediate crop — between the high country tea plantations and the low country coconut belt. The arrival of rubber in Sri Lanka has a distinct flavour of Victorian industrial espionage. Little more than 100 years ago rubber was a Brazilian monopoly but in 1876 Sir Henry Wickham quietly departed from the Amazon with 700,000 rubber tree seeds. They were whisked across the Atlantic and taken to Kew Gardens in London, where all the flowers had been removed from the greenhouses in readiness for this illicit crop. A rubber tree nursery of 2000 plants was set up 30 km from Colombo in the Heneratgoda Botanical Gardens and all the rubber trees in Sri Lanka, and later Malaysia, came from this first planting. You can still see the very first rubber tree planted in Asia and there is another grove of these original trees at the Royal Botanical Gardens at Peradeniya, near Kandy. Today Sri Lanka and Malaysia produce 70% of the world's natural rubber.

The development of the plantations had a secondary, yet equally important, effect upon the country. The British were unable to persuade the Sinhalese to work cheaply and willingly so they imported large numbers of Tamil labourers from south Inida. The natural enmity between the Sri Lankans and the south Indians was exacerbated by this additional Tamil influx and it remains a serious problem to this very day. Attempts by the Sinhalese to repatriate the "plantation Tamils" are considerably confused by the fact that there are many other Tamils who are descendants of the Tamil invaders of a thousand or more years ago.

Between the first and second world war political stirrings started to push Sri Lanka towards eventual independence from Britain — but in a considerably more peaceful and low-key manner than in India. At the close of WWII it was evident that independence would come very soon, in the shadow of Sri Lanka's larger neighbour. In February 1948 Sri Lanka, or Ceylon as it was still known at that time, became an independent member of the British Commonwealth. The country had emerged in remarkably good shape from WWII and the Sinhalese politicians were confident that the path ahead would be a smooth one, now that the "colonial yoke" had been cast aside.

The first independent government was formed by D S Senanayake and his UNP (United National Party). His main opponents were a mixed bag of Communists, Marxists and Bolsheviks and the Tamil parties either from the north of the country or the tea plantations. Sri Lanka's transition to independence went through very smoothly and at first everything else went smoothly too. The economy remained strong; tea prices, already running at a high level from WWII, were further bolstered by the Korean conflict. The government concentrated their energies on improving social services and keeping the opposition as weak as possible. Disenfranchising the plantation Tamils certainly helped the latter programme.

In 1952 D S Senanayake was killed in an accident and was followed by his son Dudley Senanayake. His first, of four, periods as Prime Minister was very short. One of the first moves following independence was to institute a policy of providing a free ration of rice to every Sri Lankan and also to heavily subsidise imports of this important staple. World-wide the price of rice had started to escalate and since minimal progress had been made in improving production rates the balance of payments started to run the wrong way. An attempt in 1953 to increase the price of rice resulted in mass riots, a large number of deaths and the declaration of a state of emergency. Dudley Senanayake resigned — he was not to be the last Sri Lankan leader to be brought down by the "rice issue".

Sir John Kotelawala took his place; since he just happened to be Dudley Senanayake's uncle the degree of nepotism in the UNP had by now resulted in the nickname of the "Uncle Nephew Party". Kotelawala was forceful but often careless and made many enemies both within Sri Lanka and abroad; not least being Nehru, leader of India. In 1956 he went to the polls and to his surprise was stunningly defeated, retaining only eight seats in the 101 member Parliament. The new leader was Solomon Bandaranaike, until his resignation from the UNP in 1951 he had been the only member of the UNP cabinet who was not related to Senanayake!

Bandaranaike's MEP (Mahajana Eksath Peramuna) coalition defeated the UNP primarily on nationalistic issues. Nearly 10 years after independence English remained the national language and the country continued to be ruled by an English speaking elite. The MEP's first moves included elevation of Sinhala to the role of national language and recognition of Buddhism as the national religion. The Tamils were caught in the middle of this English-Sinhala and Christian-Buddhist disagreement. The Tamils now put their weight behind the Federal Party, pressed for a degree of autonomy in the heavily Tamil areas in the north and east and bitterly opposed the position of Sinhala as the national language. Substituting a Sinhala letter for a Roman letter on car licence plates was just one government decision which led to considerable violence. When Bandaranaike tried to ease back on the Sinhala language decision and assure the Tamils that they would still have "reasonable use" of their own language the "Sinhala only" lobby turned on him, backed up by the opportunistic UNP which had been so strongly opposed to the substitution of Sinhala for English in the first place.

Inevitably this inter-communal bickering, fanned on by the opportunism of the political parties, led to violence, deaths and another state of emergency.

Sri Lanka's major Sinhala-Tamil difficulties really date from this time although they had clearly been simmering long before. Undeterred by these difficulties Bandaranaike set out on a huge programme of nationalisation and the setting up of state monopolies. The most visible of these is the Ceylon Transport Board (CTB) which took over every private bus line in the country and has managed to make bus travel an uncomfortable and thoroughly chaotic experience anywhere in the country. He soon came into outright conflict with the still privately run press which proved to be just as opportunistic as the opposition parties. In 1958 Phillip Gunawardhene, his right-hand man, left the MEP to join the opposition SLFP (Sri Lanka Freedom Party) but before he could accomplish very much there, Bandaranaike was assassinated by a Buddhist monk in late 1959. To this day Bandaranaike is looked up to as a national hero who brought the government of Sri Lanka back to the common people and it was this creation of a national sentiment which was his main accomplishment.

The MEP soon ran into trouble without Bandaranaike and in the 1960 elections, only a few months after his death, Dudley Senanayake came back to power. The SLFP ran a narrow second to the UNP but in the Tamil dominated north the Federal Party held a majority. The UNP did not, however, hold a clear majority and a second election in mid-1960 swept the SLFP, now led by Mrs Sirimavo Bandaranaike, widow of the late Prime Minister, back into power. She was the first woman Prime Minister in the world. Strong arm tactics on the Tamils, and a continuing state of emergency in the north, kept the racial pot from boiling over and she pressed on with her husband's nationalisation policies and at least temporarily soured relations with the US by taking over the oil companies. Sri Lanka had earlier decided to follow an even-handed foreign relations policy and had enjoyed friendly relations with China, which purchased a large part of the country's rubber output. Meanwhile the economy was running from bad to worse and an attempt by the Finance Minister (yet another Bandaranaike, the UNP was not the only party to play the nepotism game) to abolish the rationed rice policy led to massive opposition and his resignation. In 1962 a plot was uncovered to overthrow the government by force.

In late 1964 the SLFP were defeated in Parliament and in the following election in 1965 Dudley Senanayake scraped back into power with the support of the Federal Party. As was by now becoming usual in Sri Lankan politics his policies turned out to have more bark than bite and his reluctance to turn back the clock on the SLFP's nationalisation programme soon lost him much of his support. Nevertheless he managed to survive his full five year term and led the UNP to a massive defeat in 1970. Major issues were unemployment, the cost of living, the poor state of the economy, the bungled development of the Mhavali irrigation project and, once again the rice issue. Mrs Bandaranaike was again in power but in turn squandered her huge majority by failing to come to grips with the disastrous economic conditions and in 1971 an outright insurrection broke out, led by students and young people under the banner of the JVP (People's Liberation Army). The JVP had supported Mrs Bandaranaike's election but were bitterly disappointed by her reluctance to confront the country's problems. Poorly organised they were quickly defeated by the army but at enormous cost both in property and lives. North Korea was accused of aiding the revolt and their diplomats were booted out of the country.

The revolt did hand the government a mandate to make sweeping changes including a strengthened armed forces, a new constitution, abolition of the upper house (the Senate) and the changing of the country's name from Ceylon to Sri Lanka. Nevertheless the economy continued to deteriorate and attempts to continue the free importation of rice at all costs led to drastic shortages of almost everything else. Long queues became commonplace at shops all over the country and in the 1977 elections the SLFP (in its new guise of the ULF -- the United Left Front) went down to a stunning defeat at the hands of the UNP. Politics in Sri Lnaka seems to be a continued succession of either shaky victories or stunning defeats!

J R Jayewardene, the new leader of the UNP, appears determined to follow a more pragmatic path than his predecessors. The institution of a free trade zone is one of the more visible signs of the attempt to lure back some of the foreign investment which was so comprehensively chased away by Mrs Bandaranaike. Efforts to improve rice production also enjoy a high priority but the Tamil question continues to bedevil the government.

PEOPLE

Sri Lanka today has a population of around 14 million, the resulting population density of around 200 people per square km is one of the highest in Asia. Like many other Asian countries Sri Lanka has suffered from explosive population growth over the past few decades. Approximately 70% of the population live in the rural areas and another 10% or so work on the great plantations.

The Sinahalese people, originally settlers from India, constitute about 70% of the population. They speak Sinhala, are predominantly Buddhist and have a reputation as an easy-going, warm hearted people. Like the Hindus of India the Sri Lankans have a developed caste system although it is of nowhere near the same overall importance.

The Tamils are the second largest group, constituting about 20% of the population. Tamils will often claim that the actual percentage is rather higher and that there is a Sinhalese plot to underestimate their numbers in order to maintain Sinhalese superiority and control. There is considerable animosity between the Sinhalese and the dourer, hard working Tamils although these days it is generally kept under tight control. Many Tamils have been living in Sri Lanka since the series of Tamil-Sinhalese wars and invasions of a thousand or more years ago. But there are also a great number of "plantation" Tamils who were brought over by the British to work on the tea plantations. Attempts by the Sinhalese to disenfranchise or repatriate these Tamils has caused considerable bitterness. The Sri Lanka Tamil population is concentrated in the east and north, particularly around Jaffna. They are predominantly Hindu, speak Tamil and caste distinctions are more important than amongst the Sinhalese although nowhere near as important as in the north of India.

The remaining 10% (actually a bit less) of the population is composed of a number of elements. The Burghers are Eurasians, primarily descendants of the Portuguese and Dutch, more frequently the former than the latter. For a time, even after independence, the Burghers had a disproportionate influence over the political and business life of Sri Lanka but growing Sinhalese and Tamil nationalism has reduced their advantage and many Burghers have moved abroad. Nevertheless names like Fernando, de Silva or Perera are still very common. There is also a small Moslem community described as either Ceylon Moors, Indian Moors or Malays. The Ceylon Moors date from Portuguese times and were probably the descendants of Arab or Indian Moslem traders. The Malays generally came with the Dutch from Java while the Indian Moors are more recent arrivals from India or Pakistan. There are also smaller Chinese and European communities and a small, down-trodden group of low-caste south Indians brought in to perform the most menial tasks. In the more remote parts of the country there are still a few groups of veddahs, the aboriginal people who inhabited Sri Lanka long before the Sinhalese came on the scene.

Westerners interested in assuming more permanent residence in Sri Lanka may be interested in the government's policy — if you can prove you have a regular external income the government will allow you to settle in Sri Lanka. The longest resident westerner under this programme is science fiction author Arthur C Clarke.

ECONOMY

Prior to independence it was a constant source of complaint that the British had forced upon Sri Lanka a typical colonial economy. All effort was concentrated upon a limited number of commodities whose production was probably more beneficial to the coloniser than the colonised. It's a sad reflection on the government bungling that Sri Lanka has been subject to that — 30 years after independence — tea, rubber and coconuts are still overwhelmingly the mainstays of the economy.

Tea remains the single largest export by a very large margin. Despite Sri Lanka's abundant fertility it is still unable to produce sufficient rice and other staples to feed its population and a large part of the import bill is devoted to food. It is hoped that with the completion of major new irrigation projects the rice production shortfall will be dramatically reduced. Similarly the island has a long coastline and is surrounded by waters teeming with fish yet is unable to provide sufficient fish; large quantities are imported either fresh or canned. This despite large sums of money spent on a national Fisheries Corporation.

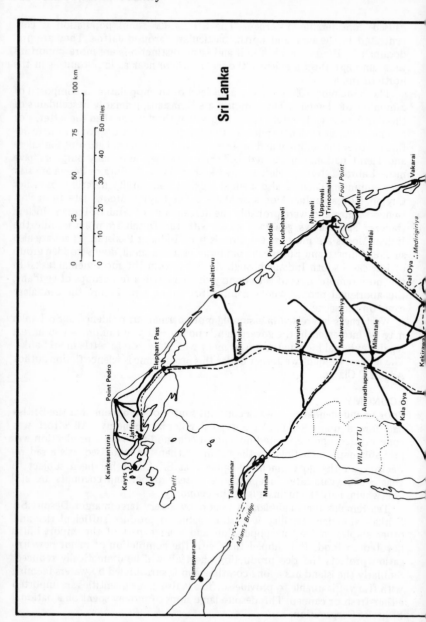

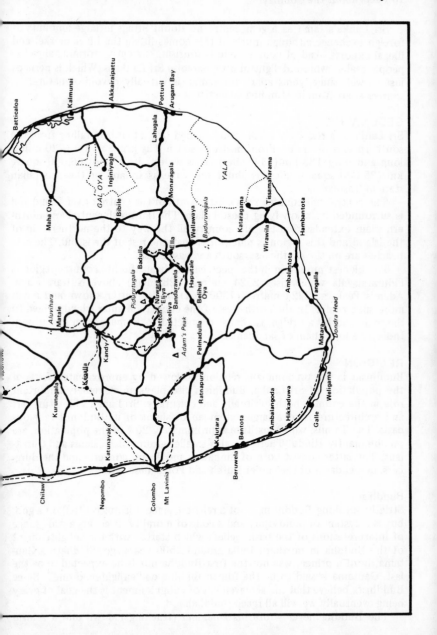

Sri Lanka's fame as a gem centre no doubt brings in large amounts of foreign exchange although much of this comes in via the black market and illegal exports. And of course there is tourism, currently storming ahead as people realise what a delightful little paradise Sri Lanka is. Which is perhaps just as well since, gems apart, Sri Lanka is virtually devoid of natural resources apart from its stunning attractiveness.

GEOGRAPHY
Sri Lanka is a relatively small island shaped like a teardrop falling from the southern end of India. From north to south it is just 353 km (220 miles) long and only 183 km (114 miles) at its widest. Its area of 66,000 square km (25,000 square miles) is about the same as Ireland or the Australian state of Tasmania.

The central hill country rises a little south of the centre of the island and is surrounded by a low-lying coastal plain. The flat north-central and northern plain extends from the hill country all the way to the northern tip of the island and this region is much drier than the rest of the island. The best beaches are on the south-west, south and east coasts.

The highest mountain in the spectacularly beautiful hill country region is Piduratalagala which rises 2524 metres (8281 feet) above Nuwara Eliya. Adam's Peak, at 2224 metres (7300 feet), is far better known and much more spectacular. In the north-west of the country Mannar Island, joined to the mainland by a bridge, is almost connected to Rameswaram in southern India by a long chain of sandbanks.

RELIGION
Buddhism is the predominant religion, followed by approximately 70% of the population of Sri Lanka. Buddhism also plays an extremely important role in the country both spiritually and culturally. Sri Lanka's literature, art and architecture is to a large extent an offshoot of its Buddhist religious basis. The Tamils, who constitute approximately 20% of the population, are predominantly Hindu. There are also smaller groups of Moslems and Christians. The latter consist both of Sinhalese and Tamil converts and the Burghers, descendants of the earlier Dutch and Portuguese settlers.

Buddhism
Strictly speaking Buddhism is not a religion, since it is not centred on a god, but is a system of philosophy and a code of morality. It covers a wide range of interpretations of the basic beliefs which started with the enlightenment of the Buddha in northern India around 2500 years ago. Siddhartha Gautama, born a prince, was not the first Buddha nor is he expected to be the last. Gautama is said to be the fourth Buddha or "enlightened one". Since Buddhists believe that the achievement of enlightenment is the goal of every being eventually we will all reach Buddhahood.

The Buddha never wrote his *Dhamma* (teachings) down and a schism later developed so that today there are two major schools of Buddhism. The *Theravada*, *Hinayana*, "doctrine of the elders" or "small vehicle" holds that to achieve *nirvana*, the eventual aim of every Buddhist, you must "work out your own salvation with diligence". In contrast the *Mahayana*, or "large vehicle", school holds that their belief is enough to eventually encompass all mankind and bear it to salvation.

The *Mahayana* school have not rejected the *Theravada* teachings but claim that they have extended it; the *Theravada* see the *Mahayana* as a corruption of the Buddha's teachings. It is true that the *Mahayana* offer the "soft option", have faith and all will be well, while the *Theravada* is more austere and ascetic; harder to practise. In the Buddhist world today *Theravada* Buddhism is practised in Sri Lanka, Thailand and Burma. *Mahayana* Buddhism is followed in Viet Nam, Japan and amongst Chinese Buddhists. The "large" and "small" vehicle terms were coined by the *Mahayana* school. There are also other, sometimes more esoteric, divisions of Buddhism such as the Hindu-Tantric Buddhism of Tibet, also practised in Nepal, or the Zen Buddhism of Japan.

The Buddha taught that life is suffering and that although there may be happiness in life this was mainly an illusion. To be born is to suffer, to live and toil is to suffer, to die is to suffer. The cycle of life is one of suffering but man's suffering is caused by his ignorance which makes him crave things which he feels could alleviate his pain. This is a mistake for only by reaching a state of desiring nothing can man attain true happiness. To do this one must turn inward, master one's own mind and find the peace within.

Buddha preached the four noble truths:

1. all life is suffering
2. this suffering comes from selfish desire
3. when one forsakes selfish desire suffering will be extinguished
4. the "middle path" is the way to eliminate desire

The middle path to the elimination of desire and the extinction of suffering is also known as the "eight-fold path" which is divided into three stages: *Sila* — the precept, *Samadhi* — equanimity of mind, *Panna* — wisdom and insight. The eight "right" actions are:

1. right speech
2. right action
3. right thought
4. right exertion
5. right attentiveness
6. right concentration
7. right aspiration
8. right understanding

This is an evolutionary process through many states of spiritual development until the ultimate goal is reached — death, no further rebirths, entry to *nirvana*. To the western mind this often seems a little strange — for us death is the end, not something to be looked forward to but something to be feared.

Buddha taught that all things are part of the whole, that there is no part of man which is called the soul: "In the beginning is the One and only the One is. All things are one and have no life apart from it; the One is all things and incomplete without the least of them. Yet the parts are parts within the whole, not merged in it."

Supreme enlightenment is the only reality in a world of unreality, the teachings continue. All else is illusion and there is no unchanging soul which is reborn life after life, but a consciousness which develops and evolves spiritually until it reaches the goal of *nirvana* or oneness with the all. *Karma* is central to the doctrine of rebirth, but this is not "fate" as it is sometimes described. *Karma* is the law of causation, each rebirth results from the actions one has committed in the previous life, thus in Buddhism each person is alone responsible for their life. The Buddha did not claim that his way was the only way, since in the end all beings will find a path because the goal is the same for all.

Ashoka, the great Indian emperor who was a devout Buddhist, sent missions to all the known world and his son Mahinda brought Buddhism to Sri Lanka. It took a strong hold on the country almost immediately and Sri Lanka has been looked upon as a centre for Buddhist culture and teaching ever since. It was in Sri Lanka that the *Theravada* school of Buddhism first developed and was later passed on to other countries.

Buddhism emphasises love, compassion, gentleness and tolerance and this tolerant outlook on other religions has often resulted in Buddhism being absorbed into other religions, as eventually happened with Hinduism, or absorbing already extant beliefs. The personal experience one has of Buddhism remains the same from country to country despite local adaptations, changes, amalgamations and inclusions — it's an overriding impression of warmth and gentleness; a religion practised by friendly people who are always eager to explain their beliefs.

Books
If you'd like to read more about Buddhism a good book to start with is Christmas Humphreys' *Buddhism* (Pelican paperback London, 1949). There are many books on Buddhism available in Sri Lanka, a particularly good place to look is the Buddhist Publication Society which is located by the lakeside in Kandy.

FESTIVALS & HOLIDAYS
Sri Lanka has a wide variety of festivals and holidays related to the Buddhist, Hindu and Christian religions. Many of the holidays are based on the lunar

calendar so they vary in date from year-to-year by our Gregorian calendar. In addition every full moon day is a holiday, whether it coincides with some other holiday or not. The tourist office has a colourful brochure describing the many festivals.

January On the full moon day in January the Duruthu Perahera is held at the Kelaniya temple in Colombo. Second in importance only to the huge Kandy Perahera, this festival celebrates a visit by the Buddha to Sri Lanka. On January 14th the Thai Pongal harvest festival is held by Hindus in honour of the Sun God.

February Independence Day, celebrating independence from Britain, features parades, dances, processions and national games all over the country on February 4th. In late February or early March the Hindu festival of Mahasivarathri commemorates Parvati, the consort of Lord Shiva, in her winning of the god. The usually uninhabited islands of Kachchaitivu and Palaitivu off the Jaffna Peninsula are the scene for Roman Catholic festivals at churches consecrated to St Anthony.

March An Easter passion play is performed on the island of Duwa off Negombo.

April A month of festivals and holidays with both the Sinhala and Tamil new years falling in April. This is an occasion for hospitality and it also coincides with the end of the harvest season. The new year also marks the start of the south-west monsoon and the end of the pilgrimage season to climb Adam's Peak.

May Workers' Day falls on May 1st as in other parts of the world and May 22nd is celebrated as Republic Day but Wesak is the important holiday in this month. This two day holiday over the full moon day in May celebrates the birth, enlightenment and death of Lord Buddha. Villages are decorated with huge panels showing scenes from the Buddha's life, puppet shows and open air theatre performances take place. The temples are crowded with devotees bringing flowers and offerings. High point of the Wesak festivities are the lighting of countless paper lanterns and oil lamps which turn the whole island into a fairyland.

June The full moon day in June celebrates the festival of Poson when Mahinda, the son of Ashoka, brought Buddhism to Sri Lanka. Anuradhapura and Mihintale, where Mahinda met and converted the Sinhalese king, are the main sites for this celebration. Thousands of white-clad pilgrims climb the staircase to the summit of Mihintale.

July In late July or early August fire-walking ceremonies take place at

Udappu and Mundel. The annual pilgrimage from Batticaloa to Kataragama also starts at this time. The important Kandy Esala Perahera and the Vel festival take place in late July or early August. The Catholic festival of Madhu on July 2nd commemorates the meeting in the jungle of two parties of Portuguese and Sinhalese Catholics fleeing from Dutch oppression to the safety of the Kingdom of Kandy.

August At the full moon in the Sinhalese month of Esala the huge Kandy Esala Perahera, the most important and spectacular festival in Sri Lanka, takes place. This great Perahera or procession honours the Sacred Tooth Relic of Kandy. The festival continues for ten days and nights with peraheras from the four principal devales or shrines. Thousands of dancers, drummers and temple chieftans take part in the parade which also features 50 or more magnificently decorated elephants including the most splendid of them all, the mighty Maligawa Tusker which carries the golden relic casket. Smaller peraheras are held at other locations around the island.

The Hindu festival of Vel is held in Colombo at the same time. The gilded chariot of Skanda, the God of War, complete with his ayudha (weapon) the vel (trident) is ceremonially hauled from the Hindu temple in Sea St, Pettah to the kovil at Bambalapitiya. Other important Hindu festivals are held in and around Jaffna and at Kataragama where Hindu devotees put themselves through the whole gamut of ritual masochism. Skewers are thrust through their tongues and cheeks, others tow heavy carts or suspend weights from hooks piercing their skin. The grand finale is the fire-walking ceremonies as the devotees prance barefoot across beds of red-hot embers.

September Bandaranaike Commemoration Day takes place on September 26th.

October The Hindu festival of Deepavali, the festival of lights, takes place in late October or early November. Thousands of flickering oil lamps celebrates the triumph of good over evil, the return of Rama after his period of exile and welcomes Lakshmi, the Goddess of Wealth. The Moslem festival of Id-ul-Fitr also takes place at this time.

December The pilgrimage season to climb Adam's Peak starts during this month. The full moon day commemorates Sangamitta, Ashoka's daughter who accompanied Mahinda to Sri Lanka and brought a sapling from the sacred Bo-tree. The tree grown from that original sapling still stands in Anuradhapura over two thousand years later.

LANGUAGE
It's very easy to get by in Sri Lanka with English. Although Sinhala is now the official national language English is still widely spoken and in all the major centres you'll have no problem finding somebody who can understand

you. If you get off the beaten track you'll quickly find that knowledge of English fades away so it's nice to know at least a few words of Sinhala — it's pleasant to be able to greet people in their own language anyway. Remember that Sinhala is not the only local language, a substantial minority also speak Tamil.

The Sinhalese alphabet has about 50 letters in it so you're unlikely to find yourself able to read signposts in a short stay in Sri Lanka! One considerable achievement of the post-independence Sri Lankan governments has been excellent progress in the educational field — today Sri Lanka has a very high, by Asian standards, literacy rate. Sinhalese is somewhat simplified by the use of many "eka words". *Eka* is used more or less similarly to the English definite article "the", *ekak* is used like "a" or "any". English words for which there is no Sinhalese equivalent have often been incorporated straight into Sinhalese with the simple addition of *eka* or *ekak*. Thus if you're in search of a telephone it's simply *telifoon ekak* but if it's a specific telephone then you want *telifoon eka*. Similarly specifically English definitions of people have been included in Sinhala simply by adding *kenek* — if you hire a car the driver is the *draiwar kenek*.

A simple Sinhalese phrasebook is a cheap item to pick up in Colombo. Look for *Say it in Sinhala* by J B Disanayaka (Lake House, Colombo, 1974).

Greetings and Civilities In common with many other Asian countries our multitude of greetings — hello, good morning, how are you, goodbye — simply don't exist. Saying *aaibowan* more or less covers them all. Similarly there isn't really a Sinhalese word for "thank you". You could try *bohoma stutiy* but it's a rather awkward thing to say — better to smile. Appreciation of a meal could be covered by *bohoma rahay* which serves as appreciation and a compliment — sort of "that was good". *Hari shook* covers our expressions like "wonderful, terrific" or even "fine".

Personal Terms Again, as in some other Asian countries, the word "you" is studded with pitfalls — in Sinhalese there are over 20 different ways to say "you" depending on the other person's age, social status, sex, position and even (as in French and German) how well you know him. It's best to simply avoid saying you! The word for Mr is *mahatteya* and Mr Jayewardene is Jayewardene mahatteya since the word comes after the name, not before. Similar Mrs is *noona*. Any non-eastern foreigner is defined as white so a male foreigner is a *suda mahatteya*.

Useful Words & Phrases

		really?	habatta?	eggs	bittara
yes	ou	room	kaamare	vegetables	eloolu
no	naa	bed	anda	fish	maalu
OK	hari	food	kaama	hoppers	aappa
	honday	tea	tea	bank	bankuwa

post office	tapal kantooruwa
certainly, of course	nattan
really?	habaata
wait a minute	poddak inna
so so?	itin itin?
this/that	mee/oya
what/where	mokadda/koheda
what is this?	mee mokadda?
how much?	kiiyada?
my name is.....	ma-ge nama....
what is this?	meeka mokadda?
when is the bus?	bas-eka kiiyata da?
where is the hotel?	hootale koheda?
how much is this?	meeka kiiya da?

Two useful little Sinhalese words are *da* and *ge*. *Da* turns a statement into a question — thus if *noona* means a lady then *noona-da* means "this lady?" or "is this the lady?". *Ge* is the Sinhalese equivalent of apostrophe s, thus "Tony's book" in Sinhala would be *Tony-ge pota*. *Ta* is like the English preposition to — if you want to go "to the beach" it's *walla-ta*.

1	eka	6	haya
2	deka	7	hata
3	tuna	8	ata
4	hatara	9	namaya
5	paha	10	dahaya
100	siiya	1000	daaha

Place Names Sri Lanka's often fearsome looking place names become much simpler with a little analysis. *Pura* or *puram* simply means town — as in Ratnapura (town of gems) or Anuradhapura. Similarly *nuwara* means city and *gama* means village. Other common words that are incorporated in place names include *gala* or *giri* (rock or hill), *kanda* (mountain), *ganga* (river), *oya* (large stream), *ela* (stream), *tara* or *tota* (ford or a port), *pitiya* (park), *watte* (garden), *deniya* (rice field), *gaha* (tree), *arama* (a park or monastery) and *duwa* (an island). Not surprisingly many towns are named after the great tanks — *tale*, *wewa* or *kulam*. The same word can appear in Sinhala, Sanskrit, Pali and Tamil! Finally *maha* means great. Put it all together and even a name like Tissamaharama makes sense — it's simply "(King) Tissa's great park".

Facts for the Visitor

VISAS & VISA EXTENSIONS

If you are from Britain, Ireland or Canada you can stay for up to six months without a visa. If you are from Australia, New Zealand the USA or most western European countries you can stay for up to one month without a visa. A number of other countries also fall into these categories but others must have a visa, obtained from a Sri Lankan consular office or through a British office if there is no Sri Lankan office in the country concerned. Irrespective of visa requirements an initial stay of 30 days is usually permitted and this can be extended in Colombo. The office is at the Department of Immigration and Emigration (Unit 6), Galle Back Rd, Colombo 1 (tel 29851). Follow the sign for "Registration for Indian Nationals (People of Indian Origin)"! You usually have to leave your passport and application form here and come back in a couple of hours but the procedure is generally quite straightforward. There is a Rs 2 charge for the extension for most nationals and if you're wondering what all those kids are doing hanging around outside the windows they've got the Rs 2 stamps which you must have to pay the extension charge. You can either walk back to the post office or pay their small markup!

Non-commonwealth citizens have another hurdle to leap before getting an extension beyond 30 days. They have to register at the Aliens Bureau, 4th floor, New Secretariat Building, Colombo 1. Whatever your nationality you must either have an onward ticket or "sufficient" foreign exchange before being allowed to enter Sri Lanka. On the ferry from Rameswaram this problem was handled with typical Indian panache — if you didn't have "sufficient" funds they simply insisted that you buy a return ticket on the ferry.

Some relevant Sri Lanka consular offices abroad include:

Australia	High Commission of the Republic of Sri Lanka, 35 Empire Circuit, Forrest, Canberra, ACT 2603
Canada	High Commission of the Republic of Sri Lanka, Suites 102-104, 85 Range Rd, Ottawa 2
Federal Republic of Germany	Embassy of the Republic of Sri Lanka, 53 Bonn, Bad Godesberg, Rolandstrasse 52
India	High Commission of the Republic of Sri Lanka, 27 Kautilya Marg, Chanakyapuri, New Delhi 21 also in Madras and Bombay

Indonesia	Embassy of the Republic of Sri Lanka, 35 Jalan Diponegoro, Jakarta
New Zealand	Trade Commission of the Republic of Sri Lanka, 3rd floor, Huddart Parker Building, Wellington
Singapore	Trade Commission of the Republic of Sri Lanka c/o MS US de Silva & Sons, Nos. 12-13 Collier Quay, Singapore
Thailand	Embassy of the Republic of Sri Lanka, 28 Soi Asoke, Bangkok
United Kingdom	High Commission of the Republic of Sri Lanka, 13 Hyde Park Gardens, London W2
USA	Embassy of the Republic of Sri Lanka, 2148 Wyoming Avenue, Northwest, Washington 8, DC 20008 also in New York, Chicago, Seattle, New Orleans and Los Angeles

MONEY

A$1 = SL Rs 17.1		NZ$1 = SL Rs 15.1	
US$1 = SL Rs 15.2		DM1 = SL Rs 8.6	
£1 = SL Rs 33.1		S$1 = SL Rs 7.1	

The Sri Lankan unit of currency is the rupee (Rs) divided into 100 cents (c). There are coins of 1, 2, 5, 10, 25 and 50c and of 1 rupee. Notes come in Rs 2, 5, 10, 50 and 100 denominations. The usual two Asian rules apply to Sri Lanka's currency:

First there is never enough change. Breaking Rs 100 notes can often be difficult and even smaller amounts can be hard to find change for. Remember that "no change" may mean "I don't want to part with my change" just as much as "I don't have any". When you change foreign currency insist on breaking down some of your Rs 100 notes. The Sri Lankan change problem is compounded by a severe shortage of coins smaller than 25c. Bus conductors in particular never seem to have 5c or 10c coins (deliberately one feels) so 40c fares always get rounded up to 50c, 60c fares to 75c and so on.

The second rule is never to accept very dirty or torn notes. Actually this is less of a problem in Sri Lanka than many other Asian countries but a secondhand looking note is always difficult to dispose of except to a bank.

On arrival in Sri Lanka you are given a currency declaration "D form" in which you are supposed to enter all the currency or travellers' cheques you have brought with you. Each time you change money the bank enters the transaction on the form and at the end of your stay the amount you have left is supposed to tie up with your form. Naturally this would be impossibly time consuming to check so at the end of your stay the form is simply collected and probably consigned to the waste paper basket — if you didn't (like me) lose it on the last day!

The form does have a few more important roles to play though. First of all you cannot change money without it (legally at least) so don't lose it. If you want to change unspent rupees back you'll need the form to prove they were changed officially in the first place. If you ask for a visa extension you'll need to produce your form to prove that you have been exchanging a "reasonable" amount of money during your stay.

Although the form is not checked on departure it is wise to fill it in reasonably accurately. If you filled in your US dollars and pounds sterling but forgot to enter your Deutsche marks it's conceivable you could come across some backwoods bank where an officious clerk might refuse to exchange them since they were not on the form.

Travellers' cheques get a better rate of exchange than cash in Sri Lanka and the rate is said to vary slightly from bank to bank. Daily rates for major currencies are shown in the *Ceylon Daily News*. Banking hours are 9 am to 1 pm on Mondays and to 1.30 pm on other weekdays. In Colombo there is a special Bank of Ceylon counter which is open from 8 am to 8 pm every day of the week at the Ceylon Intercontinental Hotel in Fort. There is another long hours counter for the benefit of tourists at 91 York St but this is only open until 4 pm. That's where I lost my D form!

COSTS

Sri Lanka is a pleasantly cheap country to visit. Getting around by public transport is very cheap, accommodation is low priced and so is food. Compared to India you'll find many things are about half the price — even the major Sri Lankan soft drink brand costs about 50% of the price for Indian soft drinks and the bottle is twice as large. If you are a real shoestring traveller you would probably find it quite easy to live in Sri Lanka for under Rs 50 a day (say $3). Dorm beds are available in hostel style places for Rs 10 or less all over Sri Lanka — a cheap single can be as low as Rs 15 or even less. A standard rice and curry meal in a local "boutique" (restaurant) will only cost Rs 2 to Rs 3. And you'd have to have endurance (and a long day) to spend Rs 10 on a day's bus travel. That would still leave money over for other day-to-day expenditure and things like hiring bikes, buying stamps and so on.

On the other hand for Rs 150 to 200 a day a couple could do it in some comfort. You could stay in better rooms — usually with your own bathroom, fan and often mosquito nets. You could travel 2nd class rail, only resorting to buses when you had to. Plus making occasional jaunts by taxi. You could eat more expensively, have a few flashy meals, enjoy a bottle of beer now and then.

CLIMATE

Sri Lanka is a typically tropical country in that there are distinctly dry and wet seasons but the picture is somewhat complicated by the fact that it is subject to two monsoons. From May to July the southwest monsoon brings rain to the southern and western coastal regions and the central hill country. From December to January it's the northeast monsoon that blows — bringing rain to the north and east of the island. This peculiar monsoon pattern does have the distinct advantage that it is always the "right" season somewhere on the island. If it is raining on one coast you simply have to shift across to the other.

In the low-lying coastal regions the temperature is uniformly high year round — Colombo averages 27°C. The temperatures rapidly fall with altitude so if you don't feel like cooling off in the sea you have simply to go up into the hill country. At Kandy (altitude 305 metres) the average temperature is 20°C and at Nuwara Eliya (at 1890 metres) you're down to 16°C. The climate is generally a sort of eternal spring up in the hills but you should come prepared for chilly evenings.

The highest temperatures usually come in March to June but the mercury rarely climbs above 35°C. November to January is usually the coolest time of the year. The sea can be counted upon to remain at around 27°C year round although it is much less suitable for swimming during the monsoon period when it can be choppy and murky.

There is also an inter-monsoon period in October and November

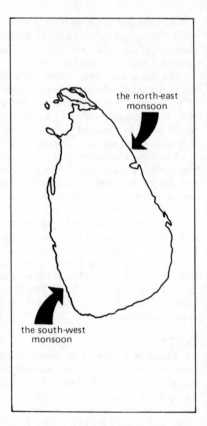

the north-east monsoon

the south-west monsoon

when rain and thunderstorms can occur in many parts of the island. The south, south-west and central highlands are much wetter than the dry central and north-central regions. In the latter area annual rainfall averages only 100 cm (40 inches) and the many "tanks", built over a thousand years ago to provide irrigation water, indicate that this is by no means a new problem. In the wetter part of the country the annual rainfall reaches 400 cm (150 inches) or more per year.

BOOKS & BOOKSHOPS

Sri Lanka is well endowed with bookshops, particularly in Colombo. Three of the best bookshops there are H W Cave & Co on Sir Baron Jayatilaka Mawatha, Fort, K V G de Silva across the road in the Times Building and the Lake House Book Shop at 100 Sir Chittampalam Gardiner Mawatha, Colombo 2 which all have good stocks of new books. The most interesting finds are likely to turn up in second-hand bookshops like Ashoka Trading, 183 Galle Rd, Colombo 4, which has a marvellous collection of tatty old books where you're quite likely to find something interesting. K V G de Silva at 415 Galle Rd, Colombo 4 also deals in secondhand books but a notch up-market from Ashoka Trading.

History There is nothing very recent on Sri Lanka so while it is easy to find out about the pre-European history of the island or the fortunes of the various European powers, you won't find too much on recent political events. *The Story of Ceylon* by E F C Ludowik (Faber, London, 1962) and *The Modern History of Ceylon* by the same author (Praeger, New York, 1966) provide a good introduction to Ceylonese history. *Sri Lanka in Transition* by W M K Wijetunga (Lake House Bookshop, Colombo, 1974) is a cheap and concise paperback that provides a readable description of the country economically and culturally and covers the turbulent post-WWII history almost up to the present day.

Guidebooks

There are a couple of well produced guidebooks readily available in Sri Lanka. *The Moonstone Guide to Ceylon (Sri Lanka)* by Mervyn Fernando and Harrison Peiris (Mervyn Fernando, Colombo, 1972) provides a handy, pocket size description of all the places of interest around the country and also covers other general information. *Handbook for the Ceylon Traveller* (Studio Times Publications, Colombo, 1974) does much the same but in rather greater (and more poetic!) detail. The weighty British publications *Murray's Handbook to India* (ed by Professor L F Rushbrook Williams, John Murray, London, 1975) devotes 40 pages to the island.

General

If you can find a secondhand copy, *An Historical Relation of Ceylon* by Robert Knox (Tisara Prakasakayo, Colombo, 1966), is a fascinating book to read. Robert Knox was an Englishman, captured near Trincomalee and held captive by the King of Kandy for nearly 20 years. His captivity was relatively loose and he had considerable freedom to wander around the kingdom and observe its operation. When he eventually escaped and returned to England his description of the kingdom of Kandy became an instant best-seller. It's equally readable today and far and away the best book on pre-European Ceylon.

Ceylon, History in Stone by R Raven-Hart (Lake House, Colombo, 1973), is a much more modern description of a lengthy visit to Sri Lanka. *Sri Lanka* by Akira Uchiyama (Kodansha International, Tokyo, 1973) is another of the Japanese "This beautiful world" series with plenty of pretty photographs.

Maps Fairly good standard maps are readily available from the Survey department's Map Sales Branch on Lower Chatham St, Fort (tel 31083).

NEWSPAPERS & MEDIA

Sri Lanka has a number of daily and Sunday English language papers. The main English daily is the *Ceylon Daily News* which gives a good coverage of local and international news. Others are the *Sun* and the *Mirror*. *Time* and *Newsweek* are readily available and their newstand price is considerably lower than in neighbouring India. Radio Ceylon broadcasts news and other programmes in English.

FILM

Don't count on buying film in Sri Lanka. It even makes film prices in India look cheap! If film is available at all (and what is available is generally courtesy of some visitor who has managed to bring sufficient to sell) you can expect to pay 2½ to four times the price in the west or places like Singapore. I saw 35 mm Kodachrome 64 (36 exposure) priced from US$13 to US$20. The special "foreign currency only" shop in Colombo Fort by the lighthouse (supposedly set up only for tourists) was asking a rip-off US$17. A good place if you're desperate, both from the supply and the price point of view, is Millers on the corner of Mudalige Mawatha and York St in Fort. It had the widest range of film and the lowest prices I came across.

PHOTOGRAPHY

Permits are required to take photographs at a number of places in Sri Lanka. For Polonnaruwa, Sigiriya, Anuradhapura and Mihintale the permits are free and available either from the archaeological offices at the sites or from the Commissioner of Archaeology, Sir Marcus Fernando Mawatha, Colombo 7 — that is directly opposite the museum in Colombo. If possible I would advise that you get the permit in Colombo — just in case you arrive in one of the ancient cities on a holiday or when everybody is out to lunch, that happened to me at Sigiriya. You are often asked to show your permit. At certain other sites permits are obtainable only at the place, and cost money. They are Aukana (Rs 15), Kandy (Rs 15 still, Rs 50 movie, Rs 25 tape recorder — but nobody seems to be too concerned, about still cameras anyway), Dambulla (Rs 25). There are also smaller fees (just Rs 2) for taking photographs in certain museums (Colombo, Kandy, Ratnapura, Anuradhapura Folk Museum) but for the archaeological museums you must obtain a permit from the Commissioner of Archaeology.

HEALTH
Vaccination certificates for smallpox, cholera and yellow fever are required if you are arriving from or have recently visited an "infected" area. I think cholera and smallpox vaccinations are wise precautions for any Asian traveller. Visitors to Sri Lanka should also take precautions against malaria — a weekly malarial tablet, prescribed by your doctor, is the usual answer. Tap water is not drinkable in Sri Lanka and a little care with food quality is a good idea but overall Sri Lanka is a remarkably healthy country and if you're only slightly careful you should suffer no stomach problems.

POST
The GPO in Colombo is on Janadhipathi Mawatha in Fort, just down from the lighthouse. It has an efficiently run Poste Restante and there is often a tourist only stamp counter so you can avoid the crush. Aerograms cost Rs 1.75, postcards cost Rs 1.50 to the UK or USA, Rs 1.25 to Australia. Stamp collectors should head for the Sri Lanka Philatelic Bureau, 4th floor, Ceylinco House on Janadhipathi Mawatha, Fort where they will find a wide selection of first day covers and stamp packs.

ELECTRICITY
230-240 volts, 50 cycles, alternating current.

BUSINESS HOURS
The working day is usually 8 am to 4.30 pm.

TIME
Sri Lankan time is 5 hours 20 minutes ahead of Greenwich Mean Time. When it is 12 noon in Sri Lanka the time is 6.40 am in London, 1.40 am in New York, 10.40 pm the previous day in San Francisco and 4.40 pm in Sydney. Make allowances for summer time changes in the west.

INFORMATION
The Ceylon Tourist Board has its office at the Travel Information Centre, 25 Galle Face Centre Rd, Colombo 3 (tel 32178 & 31951 extension 264). That is actually in the Samudra Hotel, facing across the Galle Face. The tourist office is friendly and reasonably informative. Amongst the various brochures and maps they put out the most useful is the *Welcome to Sri Lanka* booklet with a host of addresses, information sources, accommodation details and recommended itineraries. The colourful *Sri Lanka Information* booklet is a good appetiser should you need any urging to set out to see more of the "resplendent island". There is a second tourist office situated in the United Services Library Building by the lakeside in Kandy and there is also an airport desk open for flight arrivals and departures at the airport at Katunayake.

Overseas offices are located in:

Australia	Ceylon (Sri Lanka) Tourist Board, 1st floor, 110 Bathurst St, Sydney 2000
Federal Republic of Germany	Ceylon (Sri Lanka) Tourist Board, 6000 Frankfurt Kaiserstrasse 13 (tel 280010, 283750)
Thailand	Ceylon (Sri Lanka) Tourist Board, 4th floor, British Airways Building, 133/19 Gaysorn Rd, Bangkok (tel 2525888, 2525891, 2518062, 2515989)
USA	Ceylon (Sri Lanka) Tourist Board, Room 820, 2007 Wilshire Boulevard, Los Angeles, California 90057 (tel 484 0577)
	Ceylon (Sri Lanka) Tourist Board, Suite 308, 609 Fifth Avenue, New York, NY 10017 (tel 935 0369)

CONSULATES & EMBASSIES

Some of the relevant consulates and embassies in Colombo are:

Australia	High Commission, 3 Cambridge Place, Colombo 7 (tel 96464, 96465, 96466)
Burma	Embassy, 53 Rosmead Place, Colombo 7 (tel 91964, 94077)
Canada	High Commission, 6 Gregory's Rd, Colombo 7 (tel 95814, 95815, 95817)
Federal Republic of Germany	Embassy 16 Barnes Place, Colombo 7 (tel 95814, 95815, 95816, 95827)
India	High Commission, 3rd floor, State Bank of India Building, 18-3/1 Sir Baron Jayatilaka Mawatha, Colombo 1 (tel 21604, 22788, 22789)
Netherlands	Embassy, 1st floor, Baur's Building, Upper Chatam St, Colombo 1 (tel 29834, 32594)
Thailand	Embassy, 10 Sir Ernest de Silva Mawatha, Colombo 7 (tel 27280)
United Kingdom	High Commission, Galle Rd, Colombo 3 (tel 27611-5)
USA	44 Galle Rd, Colombo 3 (tel 26211, 26218)

ACCOMMODATION IN SRI LANKA

There is quite a selection of places in Sri Lanka which I will arbitrarily divide into several categories. The tourist office's *Welcome to Sri Lanka* booklet lists accommodation in all the various brackets all around the country — but does not cover every establishment, particularly at the bottom end of the market and in the more out-of-the-way locations. Also worth looking for is the booklet produced by the Travellers' Halt network of low price hostels.

Guest Houses These are often the best deals in Sri Lankan accommodation. They're more-or-less rooms with local families, sometimes just a couple of rooms in the house are rented out like English bed-and-breakfast places. Other times they're like small hotels. You'll find some very cheap places to stay in this category plus some in the medium price bracket and even the occasional more expensive place. In the family style guest houses you'll also often find very good food — better Sri Lankan food, in fact, than almost any of the restaurants and better than a lot of the more expensive hotel restaurants.

Rest Houses Originally established for the use of travelling government officials they're now mainly used by foreign visitors — or at least the rest houses in the tourist centres are. Small town rest houses are still principally for government people. There are rest houses all over the country, many being the only regular accommodation in smaller or out-of-the-way centres. Although they vary widely in standards and prices (some are even privately run these days) many of them are the most pleasant accommodation in town — attractively old fashioned, well kept and usually very well situated. This last virtue particularly applies in the ancient cities where the rest houses were the first on the scene and usually the only places actually within the precincts of the ruins. Later regulations have required that modern buildings be put up in adjacent "new town" areas. Prices in the rest houses vary from the medium price range to the bottom end of the upper price range. A room-only double will generally cost in the Rs 75 to Rs 125 bracket.

Other Government Accommodation A step down from the rest houses are the archaeological bungalows, circuit bungalows and the like. They're intended very much for government officials but may be open to visitors if there is space. Facilities and standards are much simpler and you'll usually have to provide your own bed sheets or even food. Prices are also lower — as little as Rs 10 for a double. Don't count on them though — apart from some of the archaeological bungalows or the wildlife park cottages accommodation is often only available if you have written and applied far in advance.

Travellers' Halts All over the country you'll find the traveller's halts, a loosely organised network of places for the shoestring travellers. If you're backpacking around Asia they're a good place to start looking. Their actual connection is no more than one recommends another and they all appear in a jointly produced booklet listing their locations.

Economy Hotels Throughout most of Sri Lanka you can find a reasonable double room for Rs 20 while Rs 30 to Rs 40 will generally get you a very pleasant room, often with attached bathroom. For the really economy minded travellers dorm beds are available at the rock bottom places for Rs 10 or less per night.

Medium Price Hotels A nightly cost of Rs 50 to Rs 125 will get you into a superior place — you should definitely expect your own bathroom and a fan. This category will include the more expensive guest houses and almost all of the rest houses.

Expensive Hotels Double rooms costing more than Rs 125 are in the expensive category in Sri Lanka. You have to get to really flashy places in the big centres (Colombo or the major beach resorts) to be paying over Rs 200 for a double (say US$15) although major "international standard" hotels will cost US$30 and up.

FOOD & DRINK

Sri Lanka does not have one of the great Asian cuisines but it's certainly quite enjoyable and the food quality is generally quite high. If you insist on eating just like back at home the Sri Lankans also manage to make a very reasonable stab at cooking "English style" — unlike some nationalities who are most definitely best left to their own cuisines. A Sri Lankan taste treat not to be missed though, is fruit. Sri Lanka rates right up there with the best places in south-east Asia when it comes to finding the knock-out best of tropical fruits.

Food

Like many other aspects of Sri Lankan life the food is closely related to that of India — but rice and curry Sri Lankan style still has many subtle variations from the Indian norm. Curries in Sri Lanka can often be very hot indeed but adjustments will often be made to suit sensitive western palates! If you find you have taken a mouthful of something that is simply too hot, relief does not come from a gulp of cold water. That's like throwing fuel on a fire. Far better is a fork of rice or better still some cooling curd (yoghurt) or even cucumber. That's what those side dishes are for. Of course if it's not hot enough the solution to that is there too — simply add some *sambol*, a red hot grated coconut, chilly and spice side dish.

Sri Lankan rice and curry usually consists of a variety of small curry dishes — vegetable, meat or fish. Surprisingly, for the amount of rice eaten in Sri Lanka, the rice is not always so special. Sri Lankan rice often seemed, to me, to have a very musty, "old" taste to it. Certainly not of the same standard as Thai rice. The spices used to bring out the subtle flavours of Sri Lankan curry, and remember that "curry powder" is purely a western invention, are all from Sri Lanka. It was spices, particularly cinnammon, that first brought Europeans to the island and even today a selection of Sri Lankan spices is a popular item to take home when you leave.

The usual Indian curry varieties are also available of course — south Indian vegetarian *tali* or the delicate north Indian *biriyani*. From the northern Jaffna region comes *kool* a boiled, fried and then dried in the sun, vegetable combination.

Naturally Sri Lanka has a wide variety of seafood — they do excellent fish and chips in many coastal towns, Negombo is famous for its prawns and in Hikkaduwa and Trincomalee (to name but two places) I had delicious steamed crab for under US$1. In the south of the island a very popular fish dish is *ambul thiyal* which is usually made from tuna and translates literally as "sour fish curry".

Moving through the day there are a number of Sri Lankan specialities starting with hoppers which are usually a breakfast or evening snack. A string hopper is a tangled little circle of steamed noodles, use them as a curry dip, they cost about 15c each. Or try a hopper which is rather like a small pancake (30c) but if you then fry an egg into the middle of it you have an egg hopper (Rs 1.25). Another rice substitute is *pittu* — a mixture of flour and grated coconut which is steamed in a bamboo mould so it comes as a cylinder.

At lunchtime my favourite Sri Lankan meal was a plate of "short eats" — a selection of assorted goodies, spring rolls, vegetable patties, meatballs and other snacks is placed in the middle of the table. You eat as many as you feel like and the bill is added up from how many are still left. At the Pagoda Tea Room in Colombo Fort, a favourite place for short eats, they even follow it up with what I suppose you could call "short desserts".

The Sri Lankans also have lots of ideas for desserts, such as watalappam a Malay originated egg pudding. Curd and treacle, which often seems to get mis-spelt to "curd and tricle" is the not-to-be-missed dessert — nice at any time of the day. Curd, yoghurt, is made from buffalo milk — it's rich and tasty but certainly does not come in a handy plastic container. A street stall curd container is a shallow clay pot, complete with a handy carrying rope and so attractive you'll hate to throw it away. The treacle (*kitul*) is really palm syrup, another stage on from toddy! If it's dried into hardened blocks you have *jaggery*, an all purpose Sri Lankan candy or sweetner.

Like the Indians the Sri Lankans waste no opportunity to indulge their sweet tooth — sweets are known as *rasa-kavili*. You could try *kavun* a spiced, flour and treacle batter cake fried in coconut oil. Or *aluva* — rice flour, treacle and cashew nut fudge. Coconut milk, jaggery and cashew nuts gives you dark and delicious *kalu dodol.*

Fruit

I'll always carry one taste from my first foray around south-east Asia — after you've tried rambutan, mangosteens, jackfruit and durians how could anybody live with boring old apples and oranges again? Well, if you're already addicted Sri Lanka is a great place to indulge. If you've not yet developed a taste for tropical fruits then it's a great place to become addicted. Just a few favourites:

Rambutan The name, it's a Malay word, means spiny and that's just what they are, large walnut or small tangerine size and covered in soft red spines. You peel the spiny skin off to reveal a very close cousin to the lychee. The cool and mouth watering flesh is, unfortunately, often rigidly attached to the central stone.

Pineapple In season Sri Lanka seems to be afloat in pineapples. They're generally quite small and very thirst quenching. In Colombo there will be a stall virtually every 50 metres where you can get a whole quarter of a pineapple for half a rupee — less than US5c.

Mangosteen One of the finest tropical fruits, the mangosteen is about the size of a small orange or apple. The dark purple outer skin breaks open to reveal pure white segments shaped like orange segments — but with a sweet-sour flavour which has been compared to a combination of strawberries and grapes. Queen Victoria, so the story goes, offered a considerable prize to anybody able to bring a mangosteen back intact from the east for her to try.

Mango The Sri Lankans claim that is is the mango which grows best on their island. It comes in a large variety of shapes and tastes although generally in the green skinned, peach textured variety like that found around Jaffna Sri Lanka's mango-capital.

Custard Apple The custard apple that grows in Australia is not the real thing (to my Asian-inclined tastes) whereas the Sri Lankan variety definitely is. Actually there are a number of custard apple types with a variety of flavours. It's the refreshing slightly lemon/tart flavour which I love. Outwardly custard apples are quite large (say the size of a grapefruit but more pear shaped). The thin skin is light green and dotted with little warts but a custard apple isn't ready for eating until it has gone soft and squishy and the skin is starting to go grey-black in patches.

Jackfruit This enormous fruit (watermelon size but it hangs from trees) breaks up into hundreds of bright orange/yellow segments with a slightly rubbery texture. It's also widely used as a vegetable, cooked with rice or curries.

Coconut The all-purpose coconut provides far more food value than the obvious coconut itself would suggest. But for a refreshing drink you can't go far wrong with a *thambili*, the golden king-coconut. All over Sri Lanka there will be some lad sitting with a huge pile of coconuts, machete at the ready to provide you with a thirst-quenching Rs 1 drink.

Other There is a wide variety of bananas which are often referred to as plantains. Or pawpaws, that best known of tropical fruits with the golden orange, melon like flesh — a delicious way to start the day with a dash of lemon. Or woodapples, a hard wooden-shelled fruit which is used to make a delicious drink or creamy dessert topping. Or melons, passion fruit, avocados, jambus (like little pink, crispy pears) and many others I've still got to discover. Not to mention the famous durian — a big, green hand-grenade of a fruit which breaks open to reveal a smell like a disgustingly blocked up sewer! But what a taste!

Drinks

As in most Asian countries you're advised not to drink water unless you're certain that it has been carefully boiled. Of course you've got no way of telling if that really has been done should a restaurant tell you so. Plus you get awful thirsty at times so you may just have to take the risk.

Safe substitutes? Well there's Sri Lanka's famous tea although, unfortunately, it's another place which is famous for the quality tea it produces but is generally unable to make a decent cup of it! A cup of Sri Lankan tea may not be as bad as the horrible "mixed" tea (tea, milk and too much sugar all brewed up together) the Indians specialise in but it is still too often an over-strong, over-stewed concoction.

The other side of the drinks menu will usually be labelled "cool drinks", which doesn't necessarily mean they're cool at all. It simply means they're the sort of drinks which could (if there was a fridge, if it worked, if they cared to use it) possibly be served cool! There'll be excellent lime juice, made from the usual questionable water, and a range of soft drinks. Coca Cola is widely available in Sri Lanka but is usually two to three times as expensive as local brands. Most widespread of the Sri Lankan soft drinks is Elephant House — a wide variety of flavours (but no cola), generally quite palatable, big 400 ml bottles and very cheap at Rs 1.25 to Rs 2.00 depending on where you buy it.

Alcoholically there are two Sri Lankan beer brands, both brewed in Nuwara Eliya in the hill country. Cost per "big" bottle is anything from about Rs 7 to Rs 9 on up towards Rs 20 in deluxe hotels. It's OK but will certainly win no prizes from any beer fancier.

Sri Lanka also has two extremely popular local varieties of intoxicating beverage. Toddy is a natural drink, a bit like cider, produced from one or other of the palm trees. Getting the tree to produce toddy is a specialised operation performed by people known as "toddy tappers". Your typical toddy tapper will have as many as 100 trees in his territory and his daily routine involves tightroping from the top of one tree to another on shaky ropeways to remove full buckets of toddy, lower them to the ground and replace them with empty buckets. Toddy tapping is not a particularly safe occupation although fewer toddy tappers manage to fall out of the trees than you'd expect. Fermented and refined toddy becomes arrack. It's produced in a variety of grades and qualities -- some of which are real fire-water. Proceed with caution! The town of Kalutara, 40 km south of Colombo on the way to Bentota and Beruwela, is the toddy and arrack capital of Sri Lanka. Annually Sri Lanka produces five million gallons of toddy and 7½ million bottles of arrack.

THINGS TO BUY
Sri Lanka has a wide variety of very attractive handicrafts on sale, most of which you can find in shops and street stalls in Colombo although you will, naturally, find greater variety "at source". Whatever you do, don't miss the government run Laksala in Colombo. Here you will find a very representative collection of items from all over the country — generally of good quality and at reasonable prices. Even if you do intend to look for some particular item elsewhere in the country the Laksala will give you a good idea of what to look for and how much to pay.

Masks Sri Lankan masks are a very popular collectors' item for visitors. They're carved at a number of places, principally along the south-west coast, but the town of Ambalangoda, slightly north of Hikkaduwa, is the mask carving centre. There are a number of mask specialists here but, surprisingly, I thought some of the "pupils" had better masks than the "masters". The Laksala in Colombo is a good place to get an initial impression of styles, qualities and prices but there is not the variety here that you will find in Ambalangoda. If you'd like to know a lot more about masks there are some expensive coffee-table quality books and a rather haphazard booklet: *The Masks of Sri Lanka* by M H Goonatilleka (Department of Cultural Affairs, 1976) — it's very scathing on the "tourist" masks which are all you really see in Sri Lanka today, outside of museums.

There are two basic types of masks. One is the *kolam* mask, the name literally means a mask or form of disguise and these masks are used in rural dance-dramas where all the characters wear masks. The other type is the devil dancing-mask where the dancers wear masks in order to impersonate disease causing demons and thus exorcise these demons. *Kolam* masks generally illustrate a set cast of characters but although these masks are still made for dance performances, and even some new characters have been introduced, they are not produced for tourist consumption. Basically the masks you see on sale are all of two devil styles. One is the cobra king where the demonic face, complete with protruding eyeballs, lolling tongue and

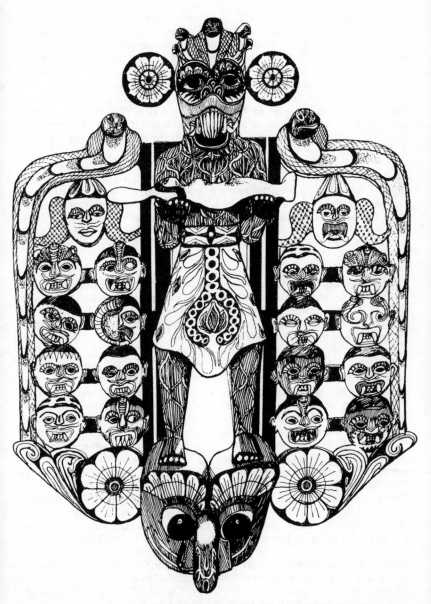

18 demons mask

pointed teeth, is topped with a "coiffure" of writhing cobras. The other masks you will see on sale, but much less frequently, are the "18 disease" masks. A demon figure, clutching one or more victims and often with another clenched in his teeth, is flanked by 18 faces representing the whole gamut of diseases which the dances can exorcise. The whole ensemble is bordered by two cobras and others sprout from the demon's head.

Touristic or not the masks are remarkably well made, low in cost and look very nice on the wall back home. I've got one. They're available from key ring size for a few cents up to high quality (and large size) masks at Rs 300, Rs 1000 or even more. The majority of them are in the Rs 75 to Rs 200 bracket.

Batiks The Indonesian art of batik making is a relatively new development in Sri Lanka but one they had taken to with alacrity. You'll see batiks made and sold in many places around the island but the best ones, in my opinion, were the batik pictures from Fresco Batiks on the Peradeniya road outside Kandy. Batik pictures start from as little as Rs 40 for a little one, up to Rs 1000 or more for a good big one. Batik is also used for a variety of clothing items.

Leather You can also find some very low priced and quite reasonable quality leatherwork — particularly shoulder bags. Look in the Laksala in Colombo Fort or in other leatherwork shops and shoe shops around Fort. There is a Ceylon Leather Products Corporation with sales outlets in the YMBA building in Fort and on the Galle Rd at Kollupitiya.

Gems Sri Lanka's famous gemstones remain one of the most important (and interesting!) cornerstones of the economy. Initially gems were found mainly around Ratnapura and this remains one of the most important areas for gemming, but they are now also found in many other localities. In Colombo you can inspect and purchase gems at the State Gem Corporation's showroom at 24 York St, Fort or at their branch offices in the Lanka Oberoi Hotel, the Hotel Inter-Continental, at the Katunayake airport or at the Bentota resort. The People's Bank also has a Co-operative Gem Society with showrooms at their bank offices in Ceylinco House, Fort and in Ratnapura. Plus, of course, there are countless private gem dealers and showrooms. In Ratnapura everybody and his brother is a spare-time gem dealer! All gems purchased from the State Gem Corporation are guaranteed and they will also test, free of charge, any gem you care to bring in to them. For more information on gems see the section under Ratnapura in the Hill Country.

Other There are countless other purchases waiting to tempt your travellers' cheques out of your moneybelt. The ubiquitous coconut shell is carved into all manner of souvenirs and useful items. Like the Thais and Burmese the Sinhalese also make lacquerware items like bowls and ash trays — layers of lacquer are built up on a light framework, usually of bamboo strips. There is much interesting antique jewellery but modern jewellery is often not terribly exciting. Modern reproductions of antique Dutch furniture are very popular. Coir, a rope fibre made from coconut husks, is made into baskets, bags, mats, and many other useful items. All the usual travellers'-style clothes are available, particularly in Hikkaduwa. Tortoiseshell and ivory are best left on the backs of turtles or in the tusks of elephants.

WHAT TO BRING

Not too much! Apart from up in the hill country, where the temperatures can sink surprisingly low at night, Sri Lanka is definitely a place for high-summer gear only. In the hill country, and Nuwara Eliya in particular, you'll need a sweater or light coat for the evenings. If you intend to make the pre-dawn ascent of Adam's Peak you'll need all the warm gear you can muster — wearing a T-shirt, shirt, sweater and ski-jacket I still found it bitterly cold until the sun rose when the temperature became comfortable almost immediately.

The usual Asian rules of decorum apply — one should be decently dressed if you do not wish to risk offending the locals. Shorts, particularly on women, are really only for the beach. Of course on the beach almost anything goes — at centres like Hikkaduwa you can forget about bikini tops, they're a rare sight. If you're a snorkelling fan then bring your mask and snorkel along with you. It's easy enough to rent them in Hikkaduwa but not so simple in other beach centres.

You'll find all the usual Asian ethnic gear on sale in Sri Lanka, particularly at Hikkaduwa, so if you want a new blouse, shirt, T-shirt, lightweight trousers or whatever you'll have no problem. Maureen went out one morning in Hikkaduwa to buy a top and was amazed to find everything about five sizes too large. "Ah," said the shopkeeper, "German ladies' bus comes today," indicating fisherman-like what size she expected the average "German lady" to be.

Sri Lanka is not as staunch as Burma in insisting that visitors barefoot-it in Buddhist temples but you should be prepared to discard your footwear so it makes more sense to wear sandals or thongs than shoes when you're out sightseeing. Some sort of head cover is also a wise precaution when you're exploring the ruins in the dry, hot, ancient cities area of Sri Lanka.

Soap, toothpaste (some terrible brands) and other general toiletries are fairly readily available but, like India, toilet paper can be very hard to find. When you do locate it the cost/quantity ratio is much better than in India but I suggest that you stuff a number of rolls into your baggage — if you're staying at the cheaper hotels where toilet paper is a luxury not regularly provided. That is a very useful way of ensuring that you have enough room in your baggage to put all the items you'll inevitably end up buying — toilet paper is very light but kind of bulky!

THINGS I DON'T LIKE ABOUT SRI LANKA

Even Paradise can't be perfect so here are 10 things I dislike about Sri Lanka —
some of course are mere minor irritations: 1. The buses I've already gone on
about at length. 2. Mosquitoes deserve a paragraph too. 3. Why is every
single Sri Lankan drinking straw about an inch shorter than every single Sri
Lankan soft drink bottle? Could someone please show one of the straw
manufacturers what a bottle looks like? 4. Sri Lankan matches are every bit
as terrible as their Indian counterparts — I once used 18 matches to light
one mosquito coil! Matches seem a very simple thing to make properly. 5.
Sri Lankan rice often has a very musty, unpleasant taste and smell — strange
in a country where rice is a staple food. 6. The shortage of coins smaller
than 25c seems to be an excuse for everybody to round every price up to
the nearest 25c — always up never down. 7. The tourist office's generally
excellent literature is very fond of admonishing you not to miss seeing X
(or Y or Z) then giving you a map that doesn't show where X (or Y or Z)
is. And locally nobody will have ever heard of it. 8. The Sri Lankans sometimes appear to have a total disdain for any sort of mechanical maintenance,
particularly with plumbing where, when the toilet ballcock fails (which Sri
Lankan toilet ballcocks do with quite amazing frequency) the usual answer
is to turn the water off completely rather than try to fix it. Or bicycles —
they will quite happily attempt to rent you a bicycle with absolutely no
brakes at all. A Sri Lankan bicycle that has one brake working at about 20%
efficiency is reckoned to be in perfect shape. 9. Kids reciting that standard
litany: "give me school pen, bon bons (sweets/toffees), money". Who was
it started them off on this demanding things game? 10. And this is probably
the worst — the amazing amount of food that appears to get wasted in Sri
Lanka. In any but the most basic tea houses ordering curry and rice produces
twice as much curry and three times as much rice as I could ever eat. I
thought at first it was just my western inability to consume rice the way
Asians do until I started to notice Sri Lankans also leaving the table with
half the food still there. Perhaps it goes back to the kitchen, (or gets served
up to the next diner) but it sure looks wasteful.

Getting There

You can fly to Sri Lanka from almost anywhere in the world with a number of scheduled or charter carriers. At the moment air fares world-wide are in a considerable state of confusion — half of them are going up due to fuel cost increases, the other half coming down due to new budget, advance purchase or whatever, fares. The figures that follow should all be interpreted accordingly but they are as accurate as I could make them. Regular economy fares can be bought up to the time of departure, have no minimum/maximum stay requirements and usually (but not always) permit stopovers en route. Economy excursion fares generally have a minimum and maximum stay requirement and do not permit stopovers. Advance purchase and budget fares usually require that you pay for the ticket some stipulated period in advance and that once paid for the ticket cannot be changed without a penalty. From Asian neighbours there are direct flights from Singapore, Bangkok, Kathmandu and three Indian cities. In 1978 and 1979 flights to and from India were somewhat chaotic due to the dramatic and colourful collapse of Air Ceylon. Indian Airlines are over-crowded at the best of times and having to handle Air Ceylon's share of the market certainly caused some problems. In late '79 Air Lanka, under the management of super-efficient Singapore Airlines, took to the air and over-crowding should be a thing of the past.

These days there are no regularly scheduled shipping services to Sri Lanka although it is still a fairly regular stop for cruise ships. There is a three times weekly ferry service between Rameswaram at the southern end of India and Talaimannar, except during the height of the monsoon.

From Europe

British Airways have two direct flights a week to Colombo from London. The regular one-way economy fare is £425. There is a minimum 28 day, maximum 90 day economy excursion fare available for £613 which permits one stopover but is open to UK residents only. Or you can get there on an advance purchase APEX fare — tickets must be purchased 30 days in advance, the usual cancellation rules apply and one-way fare is £304. Return the fare is £575 and the minimum/maximum stay requirements are 14 days/90 days. Air Lanka are also supposed to be connecting London and Colombo twice each week. There are many European charter flights to Sri Lanka — particularly from Germany, Switzerland and the Scandinavian countries. And of course Aeroflot, in their single minded quest for foreign currency, offer knock down fares between Sri Lanka and Europe. British package tours range from around £500 to £600 for a two week beach and tour combination.

From Australia

One-way economy fare from the Australian east coast to Colombo is A$711 or there is a 20 day minimum, 45 day maximum excursion fare for A$1000. KLM, Garuda and Lufthansa now have direct flights to Colombo but with other airlines, including Qantas at present, you must change at Singapore. This is not the cheapest way to fly to Sri Lanka from Australia though — for A$820 you can take a 60 day excursion to Madras in India and then add on a Madras-Colombo-Madras fare. You save around A$100 and also get up to 60 days instead of up to 45 days. Of course, Australia's crazy airline regulations being what they are, it's illegal to advertise this fare combination but there is nothing to stop you asking for it. Package tours from Australia range from around A$1250 to A$1450.

From New Zealand
One-way fare from New Zealand is NZ$854 (plus the government travel tax). The return fare, on a 20/90 day excursion, costs NZ$1223, again plus the travel tax. Flights will involve an aircraft change in Singapore.

From the USA
Because of recent sweeping changes on north Pacific fares the story from the US is currently rather confused. One-way economy fares are US$1253 from New York or US$1036 from Los Angeles but the new budget one-way from Los Angeles to Singapore is only US$468 and tacking on a Singapore-Colombo one-way at around US$240 would get you there for over US$300 cheaper. There is also an excursion fare out of Montreal, Boston and New York for US$894 return. See your travel agent!

From Asia
Air fares from Singapore and Bangkok (business being business) may not have too close a relation to what "the book" says. Count on around US$190 from Bangkok or US$240 from Singapore. From Kathmandu the fare will be about US$150. India has been the most difficult Asian neighbour to connect with due to the shortage of space but this will probably ease now that Air Lanka is airborne. After currently due increases the fares to Colombo are expected to be about US$60 from Madras (seven Indian Airlines, four Air Lanka flights per week), US$44 from Tiruchirapalli (three times weekly) and US$40 from Trivandrum (twice weekly).

The Rameswaram-Talaimannar Ferry Service
Rameswaram is the final south Indian town from where Adam's Bridge points the way across to Sri Lanka. Three times a week a ferry service makes the short, 3½ hour, crossing from here to Talaimannar in Sri Lanka. The service is suspended during the worst of the monsoon — usually November and December. At that time the always overcrowded air services simply become even worse.

To get to Rameswaram means rail — it's actually an island connected to the mainland by a rail-only causeway. A road bridge is a future possibility, meanwhile cars intended for shipment to Sri Lanka have to be loaded on to the train at Mandapam where the road ends. You can rail to Rameswaram direct from Madras or pick the train up further along the route. The daily services from Madurai take an agonisingly slow six hours to get to Rameswaram. The 6 am departure cannot be counted upon to get you to Rameswaram in time if you travel down on the day of the ferry departure. Which means you virtually have to take the 10.45 pm train from Madurai and arrive in Rameswaram a little before dawn. There is virtually no accommodation in Rameswaram, particularly the night before a ferry departure, so it is no use arriving a day early.

From the railway station to the ferry terminal is only a few minutes walk — say Rs 3 by a horse cart. You can get tickets for the ferry and for the Sri Lankan train from Talaimannar at the railway station booking office starting at 7 am. The ferry costs:

	From Rameswaram	From Talaimannar
upper deck	I Rs 50	SL Rs 97
lower deck	I Rs 35	SL Rs 68

It's equally easy to get your tickets at the terminal after the doors are opened at 8 am. When the terminal gates are swung back the usual mad stampede takes place as everybody rushes in to do battle with Indian bureaucracy. It's really no use hurrying because the whole business is going to take a long time no matter what. Plus lucky westerners get precedence over the Indians and Sri Lankans who have to wait until the tourists have all been processed. Buying your ferry ticket is the first operation once you get inside. Afterwards it goes like this:

1. Fill in a form for the Shipping Corporation of India stating that should the Sri Lankan immigration authorities not want you — due to your lack of finance, lack of airline tickets to far-away-places, "hippy" characteristics, or whatever, you'll quietly turn around and come back to Rameswaram.

2. Show that you have US$500 or an airline ticket from Sri Lanka to your home country or purchase a return ticket to Rameswaram.

3. Pay Rs 2 "port charges".

4. Have your name checked in a huge ledgerbook listing, one suspects, all the possible foreign undesirables wishing to escape from India. This takes a long time as there is only one big book to check everybody from and you're searched for under both Christian name and surname.

5. Wait — you can change back Indian Rs to dollars while you wait.

6. Go through customs, after first queueing up to have your number of bags entered on a form. The number one question from the customs officials is "do you have any opium or contraband?"

7. Another lengthy queue to have your passport stamped out.

If you were at the ferry terminal entry gate at 8 am it could well be after 11 am by the time you've finished all this. There is no suitable dock facility at Rameswaram so to get out to the ferry you have to transfer in a creaky, old wooden lighter which is towed out two or three at a time. Cars for shipping to Sri Lanka are brought out precariously balanced on two lighters lashed together side-by-side. It's great entertainment, but not for the car owners.

The *Ramanujam* is an elderly ship (built in 1929) but in reasonably good shape. Even the toilets are fairly clean! The upper deck is definitely a little more comfortable and commodious than the lower deck, but it isn't just comfort that makes it worth laying out the extra Rs 15 for the upper deck. At the other end the uppers are let off the ferry (to do battle with Sri Lanka's bureaucracy) first and this can be very important.

Finally, if things have gone pretty smoothly and everybody has got through the paperwork OK, you sail at around 2 pm. There's quite a good canteen where you can get a pleasant banana-leaf wrapped biriyani for Rs 2.75, a tali for Rs 2.50. The trip across is straightforward, perhaps a bit uncomfortable if it's close to the monsoon season. If the departure has been delayed at all, which is quite likely since simply loading all the passengers on by lighter takes a long, long time, you may not arrive in Talaimannar until after dark.

●

Well I would too! It's rather absurd that one of the most difficult countries to jet to or from should be the closest neighbour India. There are far too few flights between the two countries since Indian Airlines were the only carrier allowed to carry passengers on this route following the demise of Air Ceylon. Indian Airlines' chaotic booking system (IA is really Indian Railways airborne) hardly helps and the end result is people are pushed onto the ferry which at peak times can't cope. Getting to the ferry terminal at Talaimannar involves a long (usually overnight, crowded and sleepless) train journey and once there you will find virtually nothing apart from the railway platform and the ferry pier — certainly nothing much by the way of accommodation. So if the ferry is full all you can do is sit and wait for a couple of days until it returns from India. Wouldn't you storm it?

Hippies storm Indo-Ceylon ferry

About 100 foreigners, described by the Police as hippies, stormed the Indo - Ceylon ferry at Talaimannar yesterday after they had been told there was no room for them.

Police said last night that 250 persons bound for India were shut out for want of space. The hippies who had boarded the ferry, were later ordered ashore by the Police.

●

After docking at Talaimannar the Sri Lankan immigration officials come aboard and start the lengthy process of checking the passengers through.

Upper deck gets cleared first — this is the main reason for opting for the more expensive tickets. Once off the ship you have a long stroll down the pier to the customs hall and the railway terminal.

Here there's a small Catch 22 — at the entrance to the hall you must pay Rs 2 per person in port charges. But the currency exchange counter is on the railway platform — on the other side of the customs hall. And it is illegal to bring Sri Lankan currency into Sri Lanka! Since it is quite a hassle to go through customs, change money without a currency form, then go back through customs, the best advice is to ignore illegality and bring at least a little Sri Lankan currency with you. At Rameswaram you're offered a good rate for changing Indian rupees into the Sri Lankan variety.

Having surmounted this small problem you'll be whisked through customs, handed a currency control form and you're in Ceylon. If you want your first Sri Lankan journey to be a comfortable one you've now got to be very fast. Don't change money, don't join the queue for railway tickets. Instead go to the office behind the ticket counter and ask for a sleeping berth booking. There are only a dozen or so berths, half the people on the boat would like one (if they knew about them), so getting one is a matter of getting quickly off the boat, quickly through customs and wasting no time changing money. If you are lucky and can get one you'll find a berth the best Rs 15 (2nd class) investment you can make in Sri Lanka. Booking note in hand you can now change money at leisure, buy your train ticket (at the counter) and pay for the berth charges.

The train for Colombo should leave around 10.30 pm but it usually departs only when the last passenger has been cleared. It has been known to leave right on time, stranding half the passengers from a late ferry arrival so don't be too confident that it will leave late. If you've got a berth you'll have a comfortable little room all to yourself (with two or four berths), padded fold-down bunks and all the comfort you could ask for. In first class you even get sheets! If you've not got a berth (and most people don't) you'll have a crowded, fairly sleepless night and you're advised to keep a close eye on your gear on this particular train journey.

If you can't face the long trip to Colombo — arrival is usually around 9.30 to 10.30 am the next morning — there are a couple of outs. One is not to take the train at all. There is only a, generally booked-out, rest house in Talaimannar but you can make a 40 minute bus ride to Mannar and stay at the small guest house there. There will usually be somebody touting it around the platform. Next morning you could then take the less crowded day train onwards and be able to see the countryside.

Alternatively you can detrain at Anuradhapura around 1 or 2 am and start your Sri Lankan travels there rather than in Colombo. Or you can push straight through — you'll find Sri Lankan train travel curiously quiet and hassle free after the all-singing-and-dancing Indian variety. No hordes at every station, no raucous cries of "chai, chai" to periodically rouse you. And if you're lucky enough to grab a berth you'll have a very comfortable night.

Fares from Talaimannar are:

1st — Rs 41.20   2nd — Rs 27.50   3rd — Rs 13.80

1st class is only available with sleeping berths (Rs 25 extra), 2nd class is available with or without sleeping berths, 3rd class only as seats.

Coming from Colombo the pre-ferry departures are at 6.50 pm arriving in Talaimannar at 4.30 am for the early departure for India. On other days the train departs at 8.30 pm and arrives at 5.15 am. Asha Agencies, 72 New Bullers Rd, Colombo 4 (tel 87892-4) are the agents in Colombo for the ferry. At certain times of year it may be quite wise to try booking your ticket in advance. Around March the ferry can be very busy as many travellers start heading back up through India before the height of the hot season makes things unbearable.

BANDARANAIKE INTERNATIONAL AIRPORT — KATUNAYAKE

Sri Lanka's international airport is 35 km (22 miles) north of Colombo and only 13 km (eight miles) from Negombo. Actually Jaffna also has been used as an international airport for short flights from the south of India but in practise Katunayaka is "the" airport for Sri Lanka. The domestic airport at Ratmalana, south of Colombo, is little used since with the demise of Air Ceylon there have been no domestic flights.

Katanayake is not rated by international airlines as one of the world's better airports but from the passengers point of view its principal drawback is likely to be in the difficulty and/or expense of getting to it — there is no regular airport bus service and the Sri Lanka taxis tend to be very expensive, by Asian standards, for the admittedly long haul into the city.

At the airport there is a bank with facilities for changing money or re-exchanging your unspent rupees; a post office; a reasonably priced restaurant; a Ceylon Tea Counter (75c for a cup of "best quality" Ceylon tea); a tourist information counters for hotel reservation, rail bookings, rent-a-car reservations and so on.

A peculiarity of the airport is that non-passengers are allowed in only with a permit. Each passenger is allowed two permits free and up to seven more at Rs 5 each. In practise it's not too carefully policed for foreigners. International departures are subject to a Rs 25 airport tax.

Once you've checked in, paid your airport tax, gone through a very cursory customs inspection and handed in your D-form, you'll find yourself in the transit lounge where you are no longer allowed to spend rupees. The restaurant here charges 300 to 400% of prices just the other side of the wall. A cup of tea here is the equivalent of Rs 9 against Rs 2 in the airport restaurant or just 75c from the tea counter. Duty free goods are inclined to be pricey too — film is fairly readily available but at much more than usual western prices.

Getting to the Airport
It's not exactly cheap to get into Colombo from the airport — or, alternatively, not exactly easy. A taxi between the capital and the centre can be expected to cost something around Rs 125. The only airport bus service is operated for Aeroflot's three weekly flights and departs from the Hotel Taprobane at 5 pm on Monday, 9 pm on Tuesday and 7 pm on Thursday — cost is Rs 25 and anyone is free to use it but check with Aeroflot about departure time first.

There is an approximately hourly public bus service and costs less than Rs 2 — but it's every bit as crowded and uncomfortable as every other CTB bus so read more about them before resorting to this option.

There's actually a train station right at the airport but its potential usefulness is rather eroded by the fact that there are only two services a day — departures from the airport are at 8.10 am (8.30 on Saturdays and Sundays) and 4.20 pm. To the airport the train leaves at 6.50 am and 2.40 pm. The service takes just over an hour and costs Rs 1.40. The branch off to the airport is only about three km (two miles) away so you could get to Katunayake and catch one of the regular Colombo-Negombo trains although these are mainly a weekday commuter service and Colombo bound no trains at all leave Negombo between 10 am and 5 pm. Train tickets must be purchased at the ticket counter in the airport building.

Another route which some people use, particularly on departure, is not to go to or from Colombo at all but to Negombo the beach resort/fishing village about 35 km north of the capital and only 13 km from the airport. Buses run between here and the airport approximately hourly and cost 70c or you can get a taxi from around Rs 50. There are frequent train and bus connections to Colombo from Negombo for less than Rs 2 — it takes a bit over an hour. If you can't bother hanging around at the airport for a bus to Colombo or Negombo the airport junction to the Colombo-Negombo road is three km away and buses pass by continuously.

FLYING OUT OF SRI LANKA
Colombo is not like Bangkok or Singapore for hunting out cheap flights but it is definitely worth a little shopping around if you want to fly somewhere. A lot of airlines fly to Colombo so there is bound to be a little fare bending, free stopovers thrown in and so on. Some approximate fares in Rs and US dollars:

Kathmandu, Nepal	Rs 300	US$150
Bangkok, Thailand	Rs 2,900	US$190
Singapore	Rs 3,700	US$240
London, England	Rs 6,000	US$400
Sydney, Australia	Rs 10,000	US$650
USA — west coast	Rs 12,250	US$800

The cheapest fare to London will be with Aeroflot via Moscow (ask about their amazing free stopover offer); with other airlines expect to pay about Rs 700 (US$50) more.

Getting Around

RAIL

Train travel is, in most cases, the best way to get around Sri Lanka. It's generally nowhere near as crowded as in India and the simple act of buying a ticket or making a reservation involves none of the Indian style bureaucratic hassles. Plus, although the trains are really quite slow, the distances are short so there are few overnight or all day ordeals to contend with. Compared to the buses they're sheer luxury.

On many services there is only a choice of 2nd or 3rd class and although 2nd class is twice as expensive as 3rd it's the option to take — not for the extra comfort, which is often minimal, but for the less crowded conditions. Anyway it's only a cost difference between "virtually nothing" and "very little": train fares are cheap.

When 1st class is available the cost is three times the 3rd class fare and seats can be booked. Actually it will be more expensive still because 1st class also means either an observation saloon, an air-conditioned coach or a sleeper berth, any of which involve extra charges.

At night there are additional possiblilites thrown in. There may be 2nd or 3rd class sleeperettes which in 2nd class are very comfortable individual reclining seats. Or there may be sleeping berths which are individual twin bunked rooms and are the absolute last word in Asian train comfort — if you've just come from India anyway. They're only available in 1st or 2nd class versions — main difference is the 1st class berths have a sink and sheets on the bunk.

Supplementary costs over the standard 1st, 2nd and 3rd class rail fares are Rs 7.50 for the 1st class observation saloon (on the hill country services) or Rs 15 for the air-conditioned coach in 1st class. Sleeping berths cost an additional Rs 25 in 1st or Rs 15 in 2nd. There is no such thing as a straightforward 1st class seat — if you travel 1st class it means an observation coach, air-conditioned coach or sleeping berth. In 2nd class you may have the option of a sleeping berth or a sleeperette (reclining seat) which costs Rs 7.50. The only possibility in 3rd class is a sleeperette (Rs 5) on some night services. Note that on any rail journey over 50 miles you can break the trip for up to 24 hours without any extra ticketing. Thus if you were going by rail from

Colombo to Polonnaruwa, for example, you could hop off the train at Auk-ana, go to see the huge Buddha image, then catch another later train.

Life does not revolve around the railway station in Sri Lanka to anything like the same extent it does in India. Railway station restaurants are generally terrible in Sri Lanka whereas they're little havens of safe, reasonable-quality food in India. But there are railway retiring rooms at certain stations and they're worth remembering when all else fails. Rates vary from Rs 10 to Rs 30 for a single, Rs 20 to Rs 50 for a double. You'll find them in Anuradhapura, Galle, Jaffna, Kandy, Polgahawela and Trincomalee.

Ceylon
Daily News [CITY EDITION]

The English Daily with the largest circulation in Sri Lanka

★

● Insolent crews ● Commuters shortchanged ● Overloading ● Officers warm seats

CTB makes bus travel a nightmare

BUSES

The headline above from the *Ceylon Daily News* more or less sums up the CTB — Ceylon Transport Board. Sri Lanka's bus network is comprehensive, fairly frequent, very cheap but impossibly crowded. At times a Sri Lankan bus journey can become sheer torture. Even if you manage to get a seat — which is not difficult if you turn up a little early at the commencement point — you'll still be hopelessly crushed. Buses in Sri Lanka seem incapable of movement until there is at least one and a half people to every seat plus twice as many standing as seems humanly possible. So even if you get a seat you'll be leaning to one side, squashed up against the window, unable to see very much. I worked out a cynical rule-of-thumb that if there is a bus departure every hour it means there are enough passengers to fill a bus every half hour.

The overcrowding leads to further discomforts. With so many passengers, stops are frequent and lengthy as passengers disentangle themselves from the crush or struggle to squeeze themselves on. Don't count on averaging much over 20 or 25 km in an hour (15 miles, 20 at the most). Plus all that tightly packed, bumpy, stop and go motion inevitably leads to at least one person whose stomach is unable to take it. When he or she throws up the results can be rather unpleasant if they don't happen to be by a window! The only difference between Colombo city travel and long distance travel is the journeys are mercifully shorter.

On buses (and trains) there are certain seats generally reserved for ladies. Like the "smoking prohibited" signs this injunction is completely ignored, it's first come first served. On the other hand the first two seats are always reserved for "clergy" (ie Buddhist monks) and this is never ignored — a pregnant lady would have to stand if a strapping teenage monk hopped on.

Bus travel is very cheap — about one rupee for each 20 km is a good approximation. At that rate you could get from Perth to Sydney or New York to Los Angeles on a Sri Lankan bus for less than $20. Of course it would take you about ten days of solid travelling...

The reason for the chaotic state of Sri Lanka's bus system? Well in a bout of inspired socialism Sri Lanka once decided to get rid of every private bus operator and run every service in the country by one giant super-efficient national concern. Not surprisingly the result turned out to be a gigantic, superinefficient, bureaucratic monster. Basically the problem is there are simply not enough buses but, as one newspaper editorial pointed out while I was in Sri Lanka, simply buying more buses would not solve the problem. Lack of maintenance would soon condemn them to joining the hundreds of other buses already clogging up CTB depots all over the country; futilely waiting to be patched up and flung back into the fray.

●

For the independent traveller Sri Lanka's one enormous drawback is the sheer misery of road travel. When you can get from A to B by rail Sri Lanka is just fine. When you must resort to the depressingly crowded, terribly unreliable, horrifically slow buses the hassles set it. It's not only that there are almost always twice as many people as there is space for — all too often scheduled buses simply never show up at all. When a bus finally does depart you then have not twice as many passengers as it could comfortably carry but four times. This problem of insufficient buses, poorly utilised, is compounded by the complete absence of any secondary form of road transport. Sri Lanka is crying out for a faster, if necessary slightly more expensive, second level of public transport — either on the lines of Indonesia's pickuplike "bemos" or the similar, in concept, Philipino "jeepney". Or alternatively cheap, three wheeler taxis as they have in India or Thailand. Don't think that moaning about the state run CTB is a tourist-only occupation; few Sinhalese are very satisfied with it either.

●

CAR RENTAL & CARS IN GENERAL
By Asian standards car rental is reasonably expensive in Sri Lanka and the rental companies actively discourage self-drive rental: rates are generally somewhat lower for chauffeur-driven rentals than for self-drive, excess mileage charges are about the same but the chaffeur-driven excess miles include fuel where the self-drive ones do not! Plus there is an insurance charge for self-drive hire although with a driver you're also up for a "subsistence" cost but this is only Rs 30 (say US$2) per night. If the chauffeur cannot arrange free accommodation with your hotel he'll no doubt sleep on the back seat and ensure a small extra profit. Ostensibly the reason for this slant towards chauffeur-driven hire is the danger of accidents and damage to hard-to-obtain vehicles. The standard of driving in Sri Lanka is decidedly on the hair-raising side.

The major hire companies are:

Quickshaws (Hertz), Kalinga Place, Colombo 5 (tel 83133)
Mercantile Tours (Inter-Rent & American International), 23 York Arcade, Colombo 1 (tel 28706, 28707, 22261)
BOT Travel Service (Europecar, National Car Rental), 77 Dickman's Rd, Colombo 5 (tel 82980)

Small cars are a little cheaper but the most popular rental vehicles are Peugeot 404s which cost around Rs 200 to 250 per day, chauffeur-driven including 50 miles, excess miles are charged at Rs 4 to 5 per mile. Self-drive rates are generally Rs 50 higher with excess miles at the same rate but without fuel. Insurance for self-drive rental costs around Rs 200 per week but does not cover windscreen or tyre damage or loss of hubcaps and windscreen wipers — popular items for thieves. You are not allowed to take rental cars into the wildlife sanctuaries although the rental companies do hire 4 wheel-drive vehicles for the parks.

The rental companies face severe problems in obtaining new cars because of foreign exchange restrictions and many of their cars are a well-preserved 10 years or more old. Cars find their way into Sri Lanka by a rather fascinating process — since there is no local industry as in India, all cars are imported and generally second-hand. Dealers put ads in the papers announcing they will be buying various cars (usually in the UK although Singapore is becoming an increasingly important used-car market for Sri Lanka) and the prices for models and years. Their agents in the UK then buy up so many 1972 Ford Escorts, so many 1968 Renault R16s or whatever and ship them to Sri Lanka. Apart from foreign exchange restrictions there is a sliding scale import duty based on the CIF price of the imported car which often totals more than the actual price of the car — above about US$2500 the value is taxed at 200%! Plus cars above 1500cc are totally banned apart from those for official use. Sri Lanka has many fine condition old cars on the road including an amazing number of pre-war Austin 7s and many British sports cars of the '50s including MG-TCs and MGAs, frog-eye Sprites, TR2s and the like.

MOTOR CYCLE RENTAL
If you can't face the buses and can't afford to rent a car then motorcycles might seem like a reasonable alternative. Distances are relatively small and some of the roads are simply a motorcyclist's delight. Unfortunately motorcycle rental is nowhere as developed as in, for example, Bali or Thailand and the costs, if you can find one, are much, much higher. Your best hope is to contact motorcycle dealers in Colombo, some of whom will hire out second hand bikes which they have waiting for a buyer. One dealer who does this is at 263 Galle Rd, Kollupitiya where they had a Honda 125 for Rs 150 per day or a Honda 250 at Rs 200 per day — plus a Rs 600 deposit. These rates are really much the same as car rental but they do not include any excess

mileage costs and you don't, of course, have to tow along a chauffeur! Nobody we saw on rental machines had the small 100 cc bikes which are the mainstay of bike rental in Indonesia and Thailand.

BICYCLES
Keen round-the-world bicyclists will probably find Sri Lanka a joy, apart from the uphill sections of the hill country, but hiring a bike in Sri Lanka is often far from that. We hired bikes in Anuradhapura, Polonnaruwa, Kalkudah, Hikkaduwa and Negombo and the bikes generally ranged from barely reasonable (the Negombo ones were an honourable exception) to diabolical. Flat tyres come with alarming regularity and if one brake works with 25% efficiency you're doing well (one bike Maureen was handed in Polonnaruwa had absolutely no brakes at all, ever tried stopping a bike with your feet on the ground in an emergency?). Altogether bicycles show the Sinhalese total disdain for maintenance at its worst!

FLYING
Sri Lanka has never had (or needed) much of a domestic air service but with the demise of Air Ceylon even the Colombo-Jaffna and Colombo-Trincomalee air services stopped. It is planned to recommence some domestic services under the new Air Lanka banner but at a considerably higher cost than the old operations. If you really want to fly, the Sri Lanka Air Force operate Helitours. They charter out helicopters at US$300 per hour (up to four passengers) and also light aircraft. For more details contact Helitours, Sir Chittampalam Gardiner Mawatha, Colombo 2 or phone 31584 or 33184, extension 33.

TOURS
Colombo has a great many travel agencies and tour operators with day or longer tours to all the main attractions. The tourist office can advise you on tours to all the main attractions. The railways also operate tours from one to six days using their luxury air-conditioned coaches. They have an information office at the Fort Station in Colombo. Day tours include Hikkaduwa and Galle; Kandy; or Polonnaruwa, Aukana and Sigiriya with costs from around Rs 200 to 350. Longer tours start from around Rs 500 for two days and run all the way to Rs 1500 for the longest tours — these also include several bus trips as well as the rail travel.

Colombo

The easy going capital of Sri Lanka is not a great attraction in itself — there is little of real interest here compared to the rest of the country — but it is a pleasant place to spend a few days in and makes a good base from which to start out into the real Sri Lanka. Colombo is the bustling commercial centre of Sri Lanka as well as the gateway for all arrivals by air yet somehow its size (around three quarters of a million population) is very far from overwhelming. Indeed the centre (known as "Fort" although there is little sign of that today) is distinctly handy and very easy to get around in on foot.

Fort
During the Portuguese and Dutch periods "Fort" was indeed a fort but today it is simply the commercial centre of Sri Lanka. Here you'll find most of the major offices, some of the big hotels, and the majority of the department stores. Not to mention airline offices, the GPO, the immigration office, travel agents, restaurants, and countless street hustlers ready to sell you everything from a padded bra to a carved mask. A good landmark in Fort is the clock tower at the junction of Chatham and Queens Sts, which 140 years ago was a lighthouse. It's almost exactly midway between the big Ceylon Inter-Continental Hotel and the GPO. Other sights in Fort include the busy port area, the President's house (known as "Queen's House"), and the boulder in Gordon Gardens, inscribed with the Portuguese coat-of-arms, which marks the place where they first set foot on the island in 1505. Unfortunately it's not on public view since it's in the Presidential Gardens. But mainly it's the street scenes and street life which attract attention in Fort. Here you'll see everything from briefcase toting city workers to Buddhist monks, apprentice snake charmers to young schoolgirls.

Galle Face Green
Immediately to the south of Fort is the Galle Face Green — a long expanse of open land back from the seafront. Life goes on around the clock on the green whether it's an early morning cricket match or a late evening stroll. Facing each other from opposite ends of the green are the delightful old (1887) Galle Face Hotel and the contemporary Ceylon Inter-Continental while in the middle you'll find the Samudra Hotel, where the tourist office is located.

Pettah
Adjacent to Fort and immediately inland from it is the Pettah, the bustling bazaar area of Colombo. You name it and some shop or street stall will be selling it in the Pettah. You can also find a selection of Hindu temples and Moslem mosques including the decorative Jami-Ul-Alfar Mosque with its

red and white, candy-striped brickwork. There's an old Dutch building (once the post office) in Prince St which is being restored by the government to become a Dutch-era museum. The Fort Railway Station, which marks the southern boundary of the Pettah, has an interesting small museum of old railway equipment. It's open on weekend afternoons or other times by arrangement. The word Pettah is a derivation of the Tamil word "pettai" which literally means "outside the fort".

National Museum
Located on Albert Crescent. a few km out from the central Fort area, the museum is housed in a fine old colonial era building and has a good collection of ancient royal regalia; Sinhalese art work — carvings, sculptures, etc; antique furniture and china; and ola leaf manuscripts. I particularly liked the reproductions of English paintings of Ceylon made between 1848 and 1850 and the excellent collection of antique demon masks. But the high point, leaving culture totally to one side, would have to be the superbly awful collection of the presents that heads of state feel obliged to shower upon other heads of state. In the grounds around the museum there is a particularly fine banyan tree. Admission is Rs 10 for foreigners, only Rs 1 for local residents.

Temples, Mosques & Churches
Colombo is a relatively young city so there are no great religious monuments of any age. The most important Buddhist centre is the Kelaniya Raja Maha Vihara about 11 km from Fort. The Buddha is reputed to have preached here on one of his visits to Ceylon over 2000 years ago. The temple which was later constructed on the spot was destroyed by Indian invaders, restored, destroyed again by the Portuguese and not restored once again until comparatively recently. The dagoba is unusual in being hollow and is the site for a major perahera (procession) in January each year. There is a particularly fine reclining Buddha image here.

Other important Buddhist centres in Colombo include the Isipathanaramaya temple at Havelock Town which has particularly beautiful frescoes. The Vajiraramaya at Bambalapitiya is a centre of Buddhist learning from where monks have taken the Buddha's message to countries in the west. Located six km east of the centre, the modern Gotami Vihara at Borella has impressive murals of the life of the Buddha.

Hindu temples, known as "kovils" in Sri Lanka, are numerous. On Sea St, the goldsmith's street in the Pettah, the Kathiresan and the old Kathiresan Kovils are the starting point for the annual Vel Festival (see "Festivals" in the introduction). The huge Vel chariots are dragged to two corresponding Kathiresan kovils on the Galle Rd in Bambalapitiya. The Sri Ponnambalam-Vaneswaram Kovil is built of imported south Indian granite and is located three km north of Fort. Other kovils are blessed with equally unpronounceable names such as the Sri Bala Selva Vinayagar Moorthy Kovil with shrines to Shiva and Ganesh; the Sri Siva Subramania Swami Kovil on Kew Rd, Slave Island; or the Sri Muthumariamman Kovil on Kotahena St.

Colombo also has many mosques most important of which is the Grand Mosque on New Moor St in the Pettah where you'll also find the already mentioned Jami-Ul-Alfar Mosque. There are many mosques on Slave Island which really was used for keeping slaves on during the Dutch era but in the British days was the site for a Malay regiment's quarters — from which the name Kompanna Veediya, Company Street, derived.

Nor does Colombo neglect churches — Wolvendaal Church in Colombo 13 is the oldest Dutch church, it was erected between 1749 and 1757. Tombstones from an even older Dutch church now pave the floor. Right in Fort, near the Hotel Taprobane, St Peter's Church was once part of the Dutch Governor's residence — it was first used in 1804. The 1842 St Andrew's Scots Kirk stands a long way from the bonny Highlands on the Galle Rd, Kollupitiya, next to the Lanka Oberoi.

Dehiwala Zoo
One of Colombo's big tourist attractions is the zoo at Dehiwala, 10 km from Fort. By Asian standards it's a very fine zoo — in terms of the sort of treatment the animals get — although the big cats and the monkeys are still rather squalidly housed. Major attraction is the 5.15 pm elephant show — they troop on stage in true trunk-to-tail fashion and perform a whole series of feats of elephantine-agility, dance around with bells on their legs, stand delicately on little round platforms, balance momentarily on their front feet, one picks up his keeper in his trunk, and finally they all troop out, their leader tootling merrily on a mouth (trunk?) organ. The zoo also has a fine collection of birds, a cage of siamese cats (!), and a gibbon who had obviously been studying Indians too long. After a virtuoso slow motion performance for us, swinging around his enclosure, the gibbon swooped over to the front and stuck his open palm out through the bars, obviously looking for a little baksheesh! The zoo is open from 8 am to 6 pm and costs Rs 10 for foreigners, Rs 2.50 for residents.

Other
At one time Cinnamon Gardens really was a cinnamon plantation but today it's simply the diplomatic quarter and Colombo's ritziest address — more commonly known as Colombo 7. In Fort the government run Laksala (in the Australia Building on York St) is a complete exhibition of Sinhalese handicrafts expertise; far more than just a shop. Colombo has a number of private and public art galleries including the public gallery on Ananda Coomaraswamy Mawatha (Green Path) in Colombo 7 and the more contemporary Lionel Wendt centre. The Vihara Maha Devi Park actually occupies the site where the cinnamon plantation in Cinnamon Gardens used to be.

ORIENTATION IN COLOMBO
Once you've got a few directions down you'll find Colombo a relatively easy

city to find your way around. If you're going to be spending any time in the capital a copy of the handy little *A to Z Colombo* street directory will come in useful. It only costs Rs 8, is readily available from the map sales office on Lower Chatham St, Fort but unfortunately does not extend as far south as Dehiwala and Mt Lavinia. It does, however, include a very useful foldout map showing all the main bus routes.

From the visitors point of view Colombo is virtually a long coastal strip extending 10 or 12 km south of the central Fort area. The spine of this strip is the Galle Rd — if you kept on along it you'd eventually leave Colombo far behind and it would take you all the way to Galle. South of Fort (Colombo 1) you come first to the Galle Face Green, inland from which is Slave Island which isn't really an island at all since only two of its three sides are surrounded by water. This area and Kollupitiya, into which the Galle Rd runs next, are Colombo 3. Next up along the Galle Rd is Bambalapitiya, Colombo 4; followed by Wellawatta, Colombo 6; Dehiwala and finally Mt Lavinia. Finding places along the Galle Rd is slightly complicated by the numbers starting back at one as you move into each new district. Thus there will be a 100 Galle Rd in Colombo 3, again in Colombo 4 and again in Colombo 6.

Back in the central Fort business area if you headed straight inland you'd quickly find yourself in the Pettah, Colombo 11. If you arrive in Colombo by rail you'll find yourself at the Fort Railway Station which is at the southwest corner of the Pettah, very close indeed to the downtown Fort area. The central bus station is at the south-east corner and requires another bus ride into the centre.

Moving down the Galle Rd again, if you turned directly inland (east) at Dharmapala Mawatha in Kollupitiya you'd soon find yourself in Colombo 7 — home for the art gallery, museum, university and most of the embassies (but not the British and US embassies which are on the Galle Rd in Colombo 3). Continue down the Galle Rd to Bambalapitiya and turn inland at Dickman's Rd and you'd find yourself in Havelock Town, Colombo 5.

ACCOMMODATION IN COLOMBO
Apart from the fancy top end places there is not much accommodation in central Colombo — if you want to stay cheaper you'll have to put up with being further out from the centre. See the "Orientation" information for where is where in Colombo. Basically you'll find the most expensive hotels in the centre or at the city end of Galle Rd — Kollupitya which is Colombo 3. As you move down Galle Rd you'll find cheaper places in Bambalapitya Colombo 4) and especially Dehiwala (Colombo 6 — more or less). Prices generally go down as you get further out, Dehiwala is about eight km (five miles) straight out the Galle Rd from the centre. After Dehiwala they climb again as you move into the beach resort of Mt Lavinia.

Accommodation in Colombo — the bottom end
There are two cheap places to stay right smack in the middle of Colombo

but both tend to be perpetually full so you have to be lucky to find anything. The *Central YMCA* is at 39 Bristol St which is only a short stroll from the Fort Railway Station. There are 58 beds here with singles costing from around Rs 15, doubles Rs 25 to Rs 40, plus a Rs 1 daily or Rs 2.50 weekly, temporary membership charge. The Y also has a cheap self-service restaurant open to outsiders as well as residents.

The *Sri Lanka Ex-servicemen's Institute* is virtually next door at 29 Bristol St and has eight rooms with very similar charges to the Y. Other hostel and Y style places are scattered further out from the centre. There's a ladies only *YWCA* at Union Place in Colombo 2 (tel 24694) with 20 beds costing Rs 25 single, Rs 45 double. Parking space is available here for Kombi driving overlanders. The *Scout Hostel* also has parking and camping facilities plus just eight dorm beds at Rs 10 each. It's at 131 Baladaksha Mawatha, Colombo 3 (tel 33131).

A bit further out at 50 Haig Rd in Bambalapitiya (Colombo 4) there is the *Youth Council Hostel* with 30 beds costing Rs 6.50 a night if you're a YHA member, Rs 1 per night more if you're not. Finally right out at 35/1 Horton Place in Colombo 7 there's the *Horton Youth Hostel* which has 35 beds in singles costing around Rs 15, doubles around Rs 30 — plus there's car parking/camping space. Get there on a bus number 120, 121, 122 or 128 (get off at St Bridget's Convent) or a 177 (get off at the Central Hospital). The hostel is near to the Colombo Museum.

Colombo has a whole series of places on the travellers' halt network, most of which are at Dehiwala. If you take a bus number 100, 101, 102, 105, 106, 112, 132, 134, 139 or 165 you'll soon find yourself trundling down the Galle Rd. Dickman's Rd in Bambalapitiya is the first place to look — get off the bus by St Paul's Church and walk up Dickman's Rd to Bethesda Place, the first turn on your left. At 8A Bethesda Place you'll find the *Perpetual Tourist Lodge* (tel 82419) where there are dorm beds from Rs 5, right on up to double rooms with fan and toilet for Rs 35. It's a friendly place but the gates are shut (firmly) from 11 pm each night. A bit further down Dickman's Rd and you can turn right on to Elibank Rd. *8/1 Elibank Rd* is a step up in standard — Rs 30/50 for singles/doubles.

Or you could continue further down the Galle Rd to Dehiwala, bus fare is still only 50c this far out from the centre. The cheap accommodation here is mainly on the coast side of the Galle Rd. *Seabreeze* at 37 Campbell Place, Dehiwala (tel 071 7996) is one of the travellers' halt places in this area. You could also try *Sea View* which is at 34 Albert Place, the next street to Campbell Place. St Mary's Church in Dehiwala is the place to hop off the bus for these cheapies. Or you could try Big John (kingpin of the travellers' halt set up) himself — *22 Albert Place* (tel 071 321). Vanderwort Place is four streets further from Campbell Place and here you'll find *Beach Spot* at number 55 (right by the railway line which in turn runs right by the beach). You can see the Mount Lavinia Hotel from here so Mt Lavinia itself is no distance away. All these travellers' halt places are very similar in price —

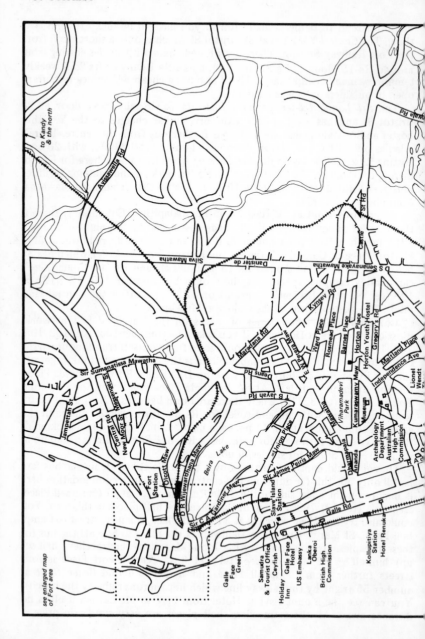

Colombo

0   ¼   ½   ¾   1 km

Bambalapitiya Station

Perpetual Tourist Lodge

Ottery Guest House

Wellawatta Station

Dehiwala cheap accommodation centre

Dehiwala Station

to Mt Lavinia & Galle

Galle Rd

Nawala Rd

Narahenpita Rd

Elvitigala

Kirula Rd

Park Rd

Thimbirigasyaya Rd

...atte Rd

Park Guest House

Havelock Rd

Ispatana Maw

Isipatana Maw

Green Rd

Vajira Rd

Galle Rd

Lumbini Theatre

W A Silva Mawatha

Hotel Sapphire

Galle Rd

R Star Inn

Duplication St

Hospital Rd

Sri Saranankara Rd

Sunethradevi St

Quarry Rd

Allen Ave

Zoo

Dehiwala Rd

dorm beds from under Rs 10, singles from Rs 15 up, cheapest doubles from around Rs 25. Generally Rs 30 for a single, Rs 45 for a double will be more in the price bracket you can expect to pay. Not all the buses that go as far down the Galle Rd as Dickman's Rd in Bambalapitiya continue as far as Dehiwala so you should look for a 100, 101, 102, 105, 106, 134, 154, 155 or 167.

Accommodation in Colombo — in the middle
There are a great number of places in the middle price range in Colombo including many guest houses. The Tourist Office's *Welcome to Sri Lanka* brochure lists quite a few places. One of the best value places in this category is the *Samudra Hotel* (tel 36161) on the Galle Face. The tourist office is actually located in the Samudra which is used as a training school for Sri Lankan hotel industry workers. There are only 10 rooms but they're large, well appointed and airy — not super-deluxe hotel standard but at Rs 100 to 150 for a double they're quite exceptional value. If you want to stay here you'd better book ahead because bargains like this don't go unnoticed.

Not quite so close in as the super-convenient Samudra the *Sea View Hotel* (tel 26516 is, nevertheless, still fairly near to the centre at 15 Sea View Avenue, just off the Galle Rd in Colombo 3. There are 21 rooms with doubles starting from around Rs 150. Or continue a little further along the Galle Rd to Bambalapitiya where the *Ottery Inn* (tel 83727) at 29 Melbourne Avenue has singles/doubles from just Rs 60/80 or an extra Rs 10 for breakfast. Only eight rooms but it's quiet and well kept. Melbourne Avenue is almost directly across the Galle Rd from Dickman's Rd so the same instructions apply for getting there as to the Dickman's Rd cheapies.

If you continued down Dickman's Rd to Havelock Rd, turned right and then left into Park Rd you'd soon find the *Park Rest Guest House* (tel 84416) at 40/18 Park Rd in Havelock Town (Colombo 5). There are 11 fairly spartan and straightforward rooms with doubles in the Rs 50 to 70 bracket. Or continue further again along the Galle Rd and turn off at Canal Bank Rd or Hospital Rd (just after the Dehiwala Canal and a half km or so before the zoo turn-off) to Sri Saranankera Rd. At 73/22 you'll find the comfortable 12 room *Star Inn* (tel 071-7583 & 82359) where doubles are in the Rs 60 to Rs 90 bracket.

Accommodation in Colombo — the top end
Colombo has four top of the "top end" hotels and several others close to that price bracket. One of the top end places is right in Fort, the other three are close to the south end of the Galle Face Green. The *Ceylon Inter-Continental* (tel 21221 & 20836) is in Fort, looking out over the Galle Face Green from the north end. It has 250 rooms with prices ranging from around US$45 for a double — all the usual "international standard" luxuries including air-conditioning throughout, swimming pool, restaurants, night club and quite a good little bookshop.

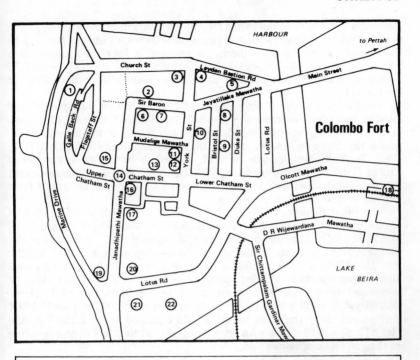

1	Immigration Department	12	Laksala
2	Singapore Airlines	13	Pagoda Tea Room
3	Hotel Taprobane	14	Clock Tower
4	American Express	15	Thai Internationl
5	Indian Airlines	16	Foreign Currency Shop
6	GPO	17	Ceylinco House &
7	Air Lanka		British Airways
8	Ex-Servicemen's Institute	18	Fort Railway Station
9	YMCA	19	Hotel Inter-Continental
10	Aeroflot	20	Tourist Police
11	Nectar Cafe	21	State Assembly
		22	Old Secretariat

Facing it from the south end of the Galle Face Green is a hotel from quite another era — the 1864 *Galle Face Hotel* (tel 28211). The majestic old Galle Face was the superior establishment during the British colonial era and still has plenty of charm today. A major restoration project is nearing completion as this is written. There are 147 rooms with doubles prices at around US$42 to 50.

Just around the corner from the Galle Face Hotel, the *Lanka Oberoi* (tel 20001 & 21171) is on 77-79 Stewart Place — actually on the Galle Rd in

Colombo 3. Externally the Lanka Oberoi is a rather unexciting looking cube but internally it's hollow with gigantic batik banners hanging from top to bottom of this airy lobby. Rooms are arranged in four levels looking into the lobby — a bit like an American prison some cynic said! There are 376 rooms with a 110 room addition on its way, doubles are in the US$40 to 48 bracket.

Finally there is the *Holiday Inn* (tel 22001) at 30 Sir Mohamed Macan Markar Mawatha, Colombo 3 — just off the Galle Rd. There are 110 rooms with prices from around US$33 for a double. Other hotels moving up towards this top end bracket include the *Hotel Taprobane* (tel 20391-4) on York St at the harbour side of Fort. It used to be known as the Grand Orient Hotel and is renowned for its high altitude Harbour Room restaurant with stunning views out over the harbour. The 60 rooms are priced from around Rs 250 a double.

The *Hotel Renuka* (tel 26901) is at 328 Galle Rd, Colombo 3 and has 44 rooms priced from around Rs 300 a double. Or there is the *Ceylinco Hotel* (tel 20431-3), just across from the Inter-Continental at 69 Janadhipathi Mawatha in Fort. There are 20 rooms with doubles priced from around Rs 225. The *Hotel Ranmuthu* (tel 33986-9), 112 Galle Rd, Colombo 3 has 54 rooms priced from around Rs 300 for a double. The *Havelock Tourinn* (tel 85251-3) is a little further out from the centre at 20 Dickman's Rd, Colombo 5 (Bambalapitiya). The 32 rooms are priced from around Rs 300 for a double. Still further out along the Galle Rd (at 371 in Colombo 6) the *Hotel Sapphire* (tel 83306) has 40 rooms with prices from around Rs 175 a double, cheaper in the non air-conditioned part.

Colombo — places to eat

Colombo probably has a better selection of restaurants than anywhere else in Sri Lanka and it is also one of the better places for finding real Sri Lankan food. One of my Colombo favourites is the *Pagoda Tea Room* on Chatham St in Fort. It's a big, old fashioned, crowded place — definitely a lot more genteel than your average run of the mill Asian cheapies. White tablecloths and hovering waiters are all part of the picture. But the food is of excellent quality and remarkably low in price. They certainly had the best selection of short eats anywhere in Ceylon — and the most appetising. Or you can have a fillet steak and vegetables for Rs 10. On hot days their lemon squash is a knockout and so is their ice cream.

So it's hardly surprising that I also liked *Green Cabin* at 453 Galle Rd, Colombo 3 just as much — because it's run by the same people. The Green Cabin is rather smaller than the Pagoda but the food is of equally high quality and it has one big advantage over the Pagoda. The Pagoda is nice for lunch but shuts up at 6 pm while the Green Cabin is equally good for an evening meal. Don't miss their excellent *lamprai*.

If you're looking for something really cheap, or just a quick snack or cool drink then head for the *Nectar Cafe* on the corner of York St and

Mudalige Mawatha in Fort. It's a self service cafeteria with very reasonably priced food and snacks. Ice cream (with nuts) for just Rs 1 is one dish that packs in the travellers. There are a number of very cheap places along Mudalige Mawatha offering vegetarian food (like south Indian talis) for just two to three rupees — as much as you can eat. Still in this same central area the *YMCA* on Bristol St has a cheap self service cafeteria and is a good place for a very early breakfast when most of Colombo is still asleep.

Also in Fort there are quite a few Chinese restaurants near the Pagoda Tea Room. They have the commendable virtue of being open very late at night — well very late at night by early-to-bed Colombo standards anyway. Their menus are the international Chinese standard and the food quite acceptable. *Peiping* at 100-102 Catham St, the *Nanking Hotel* and *Kokos* at 82 Catham St are a few of them. The *Chinese Victory Cafe (Chopsticks)* is on York St as is the *China Hotel* at number 106.

Moving up a price bracket the *Ceyfish Restaurant* is virtually next door to the Samudra Hotel (and the tourist office) on Galle Face. Excellent quality seafood with most dishes in the Rs 10 to 15 bracket. Stick to the fish though, they don't do other things so well. The *Samudra Hotel* has a fixed price lunch which is usually good value at Rs 12.50.

Also a notch up market there's the *Windmill* at 41 Galle Face Court, opposite the Galle Face Hotel, for western and local food. Or continue further along the Galle Rd (beyond the Green Cabin) if you like Indian vegetarian food. There is plenty of that at *Greenlands Hotel*, 3a Shrubbery Gardens, Colombo 4. Shrubbery Gardens is on the sea side of the Galle Rd; just a few roads before Dickman's Rd.

If you want to move really up-market the big hotels all have restaurants. The *Harbour Room* on top of the Taprobane Hotel is renowned for its view — which I think outshines the food. Most meals are in the Rs 25 to 35 bracket, competent but unexciting western food. There's also a fine view from the *Ceylinco Hotel*'s roof top snack bar. The *Galle Face Hotel* is, naturally, a good place to go if you want that old world elegance. Local residents speak very highly of the *Palmyrah* at the Hotel Renuka or *La Langousterie* for seafood, on the beach at Mt Lavinia.

Getting Around Colombo

Colombo is the gateway to Sri Lanka from abroad and also the centre of the rail and bus network. See the introductory section on "Getting to Sri Lanka" for details on airport transportation and the relevant regional sections for getting out of Colombo and around the country. The main railway station, Colombo Fort, is within easy walking distance of the city centre. The bus station is just the other side of the Pettah from the centre.

You can use the railway service for getting to the suburbs dotted along the Galle Rd — Bambalapitiya, Kollupitiya, Dehiwala and Mt Lavinia, but otherwise it's a simple choice between buses and taxis. There is no intermediate transport system — a missing link which the city badly needs to bridge the gap between the cheap, but hopelessly crowded buses, and the expensive, by Asian standards, taxis. A bus route map is a wise investment, they're easily obtainable in Colombo. A timetable is not necessary at all since the buses can hardly be described as running to any sort of timetable although they are quite frequent. The only other advice is to use your elbows and keep a tight grip on your money. In the inevitably crowded conditions pickpockets are rife — embassies in Colombo do a steady turnover in replacement passports.

Taxis are all old British Morris Minors. They're also all metered and, wonders will never cease, the meters work. Rather too well in fact, they clock up the cents and rupees at a stunning rate. Per mile the cost is about Rs 6, count on Rs 40 or so for a trip from Fort to Dehiwala.

ENTERTAINMENT
Colombo is not the place to head for if you're after the excitement of Asia after dark — it's distinctly sleepy. Cinemas showing English language films are mainly along the Galle Rd. The big hotels have night clubs and the Lanka Oberoi has Kandyan or low country devil dances most nights of the week — about Rs 50 admission. There is quite an active Sinhala language theatre, particularly at the Lumbini Theatre in Havelock Town and the Lionel Wendt Theatre at 18 Guildford Crescent, Colombo 7.

West Coast Beaches

The west coast is the major sea-and-sand tourist area of Sri Lanka and with very good reason. There can hardly be a strip of coastline anywhere in the world endowed with so many beautiful beaches. Round every bend you seem to come upon yet another inviting tropical vista — the appropriately beautiful palm trees, bending over the appropriately gold sands, lapped by the appropriately blue waves.

The accessible west coast region extends for about 270 km (170 miles) starting at Negombo (about 35 km north of Colombo) then running south of Colombo through Mount Lavinia, Beruwela, Bentota, Ambalangoda, Hikkaduwa, Galle, Weligama, Matara, Tangalla and Hambantota before finally turning inland towards the hill country. The road skirts around the Yala wildlife reserve before joining the coast again at Pottuvil near Arugam Bay, the southern end of the "East Coast" beach strip. The west coast road also runs north of Negombo but this region is not of such great interest.

At present the bulk of Sri Lanka's beach resort development is concentrated on the west coast but beaches are not all the coast has to offer. You can visit the mask carvers at Ambalangoda, explore Sri Lanka's most historically interesting town (Galle) and find many other attractions. The coast is at its best from around October to April. In May the south-west monsoon means it is time to move across to the east coast.

NEGOMBO

Negombo was our last stop in Sri Lanka and after the magnificent beaches of Hikkaduwa and Tangalla on the west coast or Passekudah and Nilaveli on the east it was frankly a disappointment. Compared to those resorts Negombo's beach is not very attractive — but there's much more to Negombo than just a stretch of sand. It's picturesque and fascinating both historically and in its everyday life. During the Dutch era this was one of their most important sources of cinnamon and there are still a number of reminders of the Dutch days. Close to the seafront you can see the ruins of the old Dutch fort with its fine gateway inscribed with the date 1672. There are several old Dutch buildings still in use including the lagoon rest house (Negombo has two rest houses). Plus the Dutch revealed their love of canals here, like nowhere else in Sri Lanka. The canals that run through Negombo extend south all the way to Colombo and north to Puttalam, a total distance of over 120 km. You can easily hire a bicycle in Negombo and ride along the canal side path for some distance.

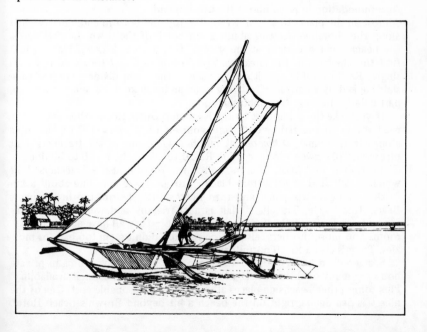

The Dutch did not find it too easy taking Negombo from the Portuguese, they first captured it in 1640, lost it again the same year, then captured it permanently in 1644; but the British took it from the Dutch in 1796 without a struggle. The people of Negombo, the *Karavas*, fisherfolk of south Indian descent, remained totally unaffected by the colonial comings and goings. To this day they take their outrigger canoes, known as *oruvas*, out each day in search of the fish for which Negombo is famous. Fish auctions on the beach and fish sales in the market place are a common Negombo sight. Nor is it all from the open sea, the Negombo lagoon is famous for its rich harvest of lobsters, crabs and (particularly) prawns. The fishing boats, sweeping into the lagoon after a fishing trip, are still a fine sight but Negombo also has a flourishing local boat building business.

The Negombo town centre is a bustling little place and all of Negombo is dotted with churches — so successfully were the Karavas converted to Catholicism that today the town is often known as "little Rome". The island of Duwa, south of the lagoon, is famed for its annual passion play which involves the whole village. Small villages dot the coast to the north and south, you can easily reach them by bicycle. Yet the English side also shows through — down by the lagoon mouth, with its Dutch fort and cemetery and the magnificent Banyan tree on the green, cricket matches are still the big attraction on weekends.

Accommodation in Negombo — the bottom end

Almost all the places to stay in Negombo, top and bottom end, are stretched along the shoreline, starting about a km north of the town. Lewis Place is the beach road and right at the start of this stretch, 2 Lewis Place, you'll find the cheapest of the cheapies. The *Negombo Guest House* costs Rs 20 single, Rs 30 double and it's very plain — the room dividers are just cane slats backed by a curtain — but very clean and well kept. Excellent food too, particularly the fresh Negombo seafood.

If you take the other fork by the Negombo Guest House, then follow the road round to the right you'll find yourself on Anderson Rd which runs alongside the canal. *Dillwood*, at number 47, is one of the travellers' halt places and has seven rooms costing Rs 20 to 25 single, Rs 40 to 50 double. Comfortable, well kept, fans in the rooms. There is also a *Travellers' Halt* which you'll find at 26 Perera Place — to get there continue about a km further along Lewis place and turn right shortly before the big Brown's Beach Hotel. The Travellers' Halt is also friendly and well kept and has rooms from Rs 25 to Rs 40 depending on size — they all have attached bathrooms and mosquito nets, although Negombo didn't seem too bad for mozzies. There's also a Rs 10 dormitory here.

Scattered around Negombo there are also quite a few rooms in private houses — many of them have signs outside to advise you of their availability. Plus some other beachside places at more or less reasonable cost. One of the nicest is *Sea Sands*, right on the beach a bit beyond Brown's Beach Hotel.

Singles here cost Rs 30, doubles Rs 50 to Rs 60 — pleasant rooms with a verandah outside. Also right on the beach and almost next door is the *Beach View* where doubles cost Rs 75. Back in the main hotel section of Lewis Place there are a couple of guest houses on Carron Place opposite 74 Lewis Place. *Sea Drift* at number 2 has singles and doubles at Rs 40 and Rs 80 for bed and breakfast plus 10% service charge.

There is nothing along Lewis Place by the way of places to eat — apart from the guest houses themselves and the rather pricey *Sea Food Restaurant* opposite Brown's Beach Hotel. In town, however, you'll find quite a selection of the standard rice and curry places plus the *Coronation Hotel* which offers various rice dishes, excellent short eats and lots of baked goodies.

Accommodation in Negombo — the top end

In terms of number of hotels Negombo is the biggest beach resort in Sri Lanka. Most of them are scattered along Lewis Place and starting from the bottom end of the road some of the places you'll find include the *Interline Guest House* (tel 013 2350) which is just off Lewis Place on Seneviratna Mawatha — seven rooms from around Rs 80 double, room-only. The *Rainbow Guest House* (tel 031 2082) is also just off Lewis Place on Carron Place — eight rooms with room-only prices also at around Rs 80. Then there's *Don's Beach Hotel* (tel 013 2448 & 2120) at 75 Lewis Place — 61 rooms from around Rs

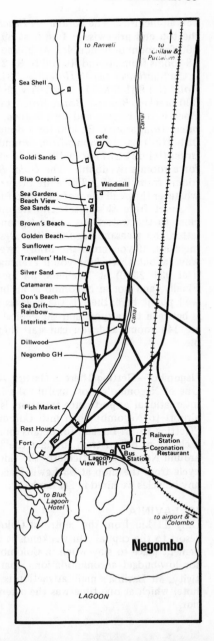

450 all-inclusive. The *Catamaran Beach Hotel* (tel 031 2342) is at the top of the top end pricewise — find it at 89 Lewis Place, 42 rooms at around Rs 500 for room-only doubles. At 95 the *Silver Sands Hotel* (tel 031 2402) has 18 rooms from around Rs 100 to Rs 250 depending on facilities. Then there is the *Sunflower Beach Hotel* (tel 031 2042) followed by the *Golden Beach Hotel* (tel 031 2 & 2113) at 161 with 37 rooms with doubles in the Rs 250-300 bracket. *Brown's Beach Hotel* (tel 031 2031, 2 & 2076) at 175 Lewis Place is the biggest and best known. There are 75 rooms with room-only prices from around Rs 500 for a double. The *Sea Garden Guest House* (tel 031 2150) has 13 rooms from around Rs 150 a double. The *Blue Oceanic Hotel* (tel 031 2377 & 2642) has 55 chalet style rooms from around Rs 400 for a room-only double. The *Goldi Sands* (tel 031 2021 & 2348) has 50 rooms from Rs 350. There are others even further along Lewis Place — or whatever they call the seafront road further down.

Apart from this hotel strip Negombo also has two rest houses — one close to the waterfront and a lagoon and one rather closer to town. The latter, the pleasant *Lagoon View Rest House*, costs Rs 75 per person all-inclusive. If you cross the bridge over the lagoon and continue for a long way (about three km) you'll eventually come to the *Blue Lagoon Hotel* (tel 031 2380) at Talahena: 53 rooms from around Rs 400 room-only. Finally, and not in Negombo at all but nor is it in Colombo so I might as well put it here, there is the *Pegasus Reef Hotel* (tel 070 205 to 9) which is between the airport and the capital, about 13 km from the latter. There are 144 rooms and you can start thinking from around US$36 for a double.

Negombo — Getting There & Getting Around
One of Negombo's most useful roles is as a transit point for getting to the international airport since transport is much simpler and cheaper from the airport to Negombo than into Colombo. See the introductory section on "Getting to Sri Lanka" for details on airport transport. Basically you've got a choice of bus or train to make the 35 km trip. If you want to have a look around Negombo, particularly the ride along the canal bank, then hire a bicycle from the shop at 93 Lewis Place. They were in the best condition of any bicycles we hired in Sri Lanka.

MT LAVINIA
Only 11 km from the centre of Colombo, Mt Lavinia is the closest beach resort to the capital. On weekends it can get very crowded. It can be a convenient place to stay when in Colombo although nearby Dehiwala is better for low-budget accommodation. Apart from the beach and associated activity, Mt Lavinia's main attraction is the magnificent Mount Lavinia Hyatt hotel which at one time was the ostentatious residence of the British governor.

Accommodation in Mt Lavinia — the bottom end

Mt Lavinia is not really a place to look for cheap accommodation although there are quite a few private homes offering accommodation which you will find listed in the *Welcome to Sri Lanka* booklet. There are also several guest houses in the medium price bracket with singles up towards Rs 100, doubles from around Rs 120. They include the *Mount Lavinia Holiday Inn* (tel 071 7187) at 17 de Saram Rd; the *Ocean View Tourinn* (tel 071 7200) at 34/4 de Saram Rd; *Marina Nivasa* (tel 071 7337) at 30 Sri Dharmapala Rd (even has a swimming pool); the *Ran Veli Beach Resort* (tel 071 7374) at 34/1 de Saram Rd; and the *Estorial Tourist Lodge* (tel 071 494) at 5/2 Lilian Ave.

Accommodation in Mt Lavinia — the top end

The magnificently colonial *Mt Lavinia Hotel* (tel 071 221, 223, 7136) is by the waterfront and very close to the Mt Lavinia railway station. It has 180 rooms, all air-conditioned and all the usual "international standard" mod-cons. Double rooms are in the US$26 to 30 bracket. Other places include *Tilly's Beach Hotel* (tel 071 353, 7001, 7031) at 20 de Soysa Ave which has 69 rooms with doubles from around Rs 300. *Saltaire Beach Resort* (tel 071 7786, 7731) has 23 cabana style rooms from around Rs 200. The small *Lavinia Beach Inn* (tel 071 7038) at 22 Barnes Ave is marginally cheaper as is the *Air Inn Guest House* (tel 071 525) at 46 New Airport Rd, Ratmalana which is quite close to Mt Lavinia.

BERUWELA

Close to the coast 58 km (36 miles) south of Colombo the first recorded Moslem settlement on the island took place here in 1024 AD. The Kechimalai Mosque is situated on a headland just after the coastal road forks off from the main road through the town. The mosque is said to be built on the site of the first Moslem landing and is the focus for a major festival at the conclusion of the fast of Ramadan.

Accommodation in Beruwela

There is nothing really to attract the independent traveller at Beruwela, it's mainly for package tourists. There is a *Rest House* situated on the coastal road a short distance after it forks from the main road at the Colombo end of town. It doesn't enjoy the usual Rest House advantages of a beautiful situation nor is it in any way a very special place to stay — it is however the most expensive Rest House I came across in all Sri Lanka (double Rs 350 all inclusive) so it is definitely not recommended. A little further along is the pleasant, but also pricey, *Hotel Berlin Bear* (now I wonder what nationality that is designed to appeal to) where doubles cost Rs 450 all inclusive.

A little further along you come to the complex of new tourist hotels. They are all very much aimed at the package tourists who come to Sri Lanka from chilly Europe for the sun, sea and sand. Smallest, with 40 rooms, and cheapest is the *Barberyn Reef Hotel* where an all inclusive double costs from around Rs 450 per day. It consists of a whole series of individual little cottages/cabanas in a variety of styles. The other hotels are rather more architecturally conventional and range from that price up to the top bracket *Neptune Hotel* where all inclusive doubles cost Rs 750 per night. The other Moragalla beach hotels in Beruwela are the *Confifi Beach Hotel*, the *Hotel Swanee*, the *Pearl Beach Hotel*, the *Palm Garden Hotel* and another new one which was still under construction.

BENTOTA
Beruwela and Bentota are so close they almost run together, between the two you pass through Alutgama which serves as the main rail station for both centres and also has a raucous fish market. The Bentota River divides Alutgama from the Bentota tourist complex and a few km inland, on the south bank of this river, is the old Galpota Temple said to date from the 12th century. Bentota village itself is a little inland from the coast — the Bentota which overseas visitors experience is a totally new construction, built solely as a place to attract tourists. The "Bentota National Holiday Resort" consists of four major hotels plus its own small shopping complex, bank, police station and even its own modern little railway station — where not all the trains bother to stop. Naturally other shops and facilities, including a few cheap places to stay, have also sprung up around the main complex. Bentota enjoys a double attraction for tourists — on the coast line they've got a fine beach while the Bentota River curves inland behind the coast and offers calm water for sailing, windsurfing and water skiing.

Accommodation in Bentota
Although there are some cheaper places to stay here the emphasis is, like Beruwela, very much on the package tour visitors. Independent travellers will generally keep on heading south towards Hikkaduwa. The top hotel here, and one of the biggest in Sri Lanka, is the 135 room *Bentota Beach Hotel* complete with everything from air-conditioning, a swimming pool and discotheque to a full sized elephant for the amusement and edification of guests — and a half size baby one. Room-only rates start from around US$30 for a non air-conditioned single and range upwards. The resort is built on the site of an old Dutch fort and this hotel is modelled after the star fort pattern.

Other hotels include the similarly priced *Serendib Hotel* and the somewhat cheaper (from around Rs 300 for a room-only double) *Lihiniya Surf Hotel* and *Hotel Ceysands* which is to the north of the complex. There is also a small, two room, *Holiday Cottage* which costs Rs 100 per day and will accommodate up to six people.

Outside the resort complex there are some other cheaper places such as the *Palm Beach* to the south. The area south of the resort, close to the beach, is a popular area for campers and there is usually a group of VW

Kombi driving overlanders parked here. Closer to the Bentota railway station there is the *Susanta Guest House*, room-only doubles around Rs 10, while about 100 metres down the main road towards Ambalangoda and Hikkaduwa you'll come across a very fine looking old house called *Thewalauwa*. Although there is nothing to indicate from the outside that this is a guest house you can get rooms here from Rs 50 to Rs 100 — a rather pleasant place with a fine garden. You'll find some guest houses in Alutgama too. The *Tharanga Restaurant* in the Bentota resort shopping centre, close to the main road, offers a variety of snacks at very reasonable prices — considering the sort of resort it's attached to.

Transportation to Beruwela & Bentota

Both centres are on the main road and rail route south from Colombo through Galle but Alutgama, the small town sandwiched between the two resort areas, is the main bus and rail terminus. Alutgama is a rail terminus for trains heading south or north — at certain times of the day if you are coming north from Hikkaduwa towards Colombo you will have to change trains at Alutgama. Bentota's small railway station is not a stopping point for all express trains. It's a one and a half to two hour train trip from Colombo Fort to Bentota, cost is about Rs 5 for 2nd class. From Bentota to Hikkaduwa costs Rs 3 in 2nd class and takes under an hour on the express. This route tends to be quite crowded.

AMBALANGODA

South from Bentota the road and railway run close to the continuously beautiful coast. There are a handful of guest houses and small hotels dotted along this stretch should the urge to stop become overpowering. Ambalangoda is a fair size but sleepy little town, considerably over-shadowed by its more glamorous neighbour Hikkaduwa, 13 km (8 miles) further south. Despite which it is a very pleasant stop as Ambalangoda has a beautiful sweep of sandy beach to the north of the town centre and an interesting looking rocky little islet straight off from the town centre and the (as usual, this is getting boring) beautifully sited Rest House.

Ambalangoda is most famous for its mask carvers and you will find them concentrated on the northern edge of town, around the point where the road doglegs in from the coast. From the bus or railway station you have got a couple of hundred metres walk back up the road. See the "What to Buy" section for more information on masks and mask carving. You will probably be told that the famous mask carver Ariyapala, whose house and shop is right on the corner, does the best masks in Ambalangoda — but I didn't think so. Masks in his son's (also Ariyapala) place 50 metres up the Colombo road looked better to my inexpert eye. And those a hundred metres further in towards town, the place simply signposted "Mask Centre" looked better still — more carefully finished and painted. It's probably a case of making a big name then handing over to younger, less experienced and motivated apprentices.

Accommodation in Ambalangoda

Right by the seashore the *Rest House* has nine rooms and costs Rs 25 per person room only — or an all inclusive double will set you back Rs 190. As usual it has nabbed the best location in town with its own little rock protected bathing pool in front of it and beautiful views to north and south. *Brooklyn* on New Galle Rd, right in amongst the rock carvers and *Shangrela* on the Sea Beach Rd, are two private guest houses with bed & breakfast doubles in the Rs 60 to 80 bracket. Brooklyn in particular is a very pleasant looking house with well kept garden. As usual there are plenty of people waiting to grab you with offers of cheaper places to stay should you want an economical stop in this untouristed little town.

HIKKADUWA

Situated 98 km (61 miles) south of Colombo, Hikkaduwa is the most varied and probably the most popular of the beach centres. It's the variety that attracts people — there are a handful of "international standard" hotels and literally dozens of smaller guest houses and hostels backed up by an equally varied selection of restaurants, snack bars and cafes. Plus there's an equally varied choice of beach and sea. Hikkaduwa is famed for its "coral sanctuary", a large shallow area enclosed by a reef, carpeted with multicoloured corals, populated by countless colourful tropical fish. Yet only a short distance south of the centre the reef fades out, the beach widens and you've got a sandy-bottomed surfing beach with good waves for board surfing (the Aussie surfing freaks are here en masse) or just body surfing.

The Coral sanctuary is just that — a sanctuary for fish where no fishing or spear fishing is allowed. It starts with a very shallow and calm area right in front of the three "Coral" hotels — it's really too shallow for anything but the most lethargic dabbling around. Further over by the Coral Gardens Hotel a deeper reef runs straight out from the shore to the Rocky Islands Sanctuary, a conglomeration of tiny islets surrounded by beautiful coral formations. It's an easy swim out to the islands, a couple of hundred metres from the shore. The water over the reef is never more than three or four metres deep and the fish are as varied as you could ask for. Large turtles also circulate around the reef, I once came across one which must have been three metres long. They lazily glide away from you if you try to pursue them.

If you've not got your own mask, snorkel and fins there are plenty of places which will hire them out to you — try Reefs' End for example where a set for the day will cost you Rs 15, or Rs 10 for the half day. At Underwater Safaris in the Coral Gardens Hotel a snorkelling set costs Rs 25 per day or a complete scuba diving outfit Rs 150 per day — they also hire out boats, experienced diving guides and provide scuba diving lessons. At Poseidon Diving Adventures they'll take you to dive on wrecks in 15 to 20 metres of water for Rs 100 for equipment and the boat. Or you can hire your own outrigger to dive from around the islands, or simply take a half hour cruise in one of the big hotels' glass-bottomed boats for Rs 50.

On the other (southern) side of the Coral Gardens Hotel the reef ends and the long sweep of surfing beach starts. Several of the places along here hire out surf boards (Rs 30) and there's usually a good break off the reef further out. Another couple of hundred metres south there's a sandy area good for body surfing. The beach here is wider, better for sun bathing than in front of the coral sanctuary area.

Of course life at Hikkaduwa isn't only sea and sand — although it may often feel that way. There are countless shops selling everything Sri Lanka has to offer — masks, gems, jewellery, batik, antiques. Plus clothes shops making all the usual travellers' gear — skirts, light cotton trousers, caftans, even the couple of square inches of fabric that is all a large percentage of Hikkaduwa's swimmers have between themselves and the "Nudism Prohibited" signs. Hikkaduwa's really just one long road, hardly a town at all, and there's always something happening along it. Ox-carts rumble by carrying wood, coconuts or tanks of kerosene. Occasionally an elephant even lumbers lazily by — the Coral Gardens Hotel has a pet one. Plus, unfortunately, there's a fair amount of heavy traffic streaming through at far too fast a pace — any western cop with a radar speed trap would have a field day in Hikkaduwa.

Accommodation in Hikkaduwa — the bottom end

Virtually all Hikkaduwa's places to stay are strung out along the main road. It's certainly not the cheapest place to hang out in Sri Lanka, particularly at the height of the season, but there are plenty of places and a wide variety off costs and standards. You're bound to find something to suit although the best way to find it is probably simply to stroll down the road and look at a variety of rooms. You can find rooms for as little as Rs 15 or 20 although, naturally, they're rather basic. When you add on mosquito nets, fans, bathrooms, a bit of extra space, a verandah area outside with some shade, and so on, the prices soon start to climb. Plus the prices seem very dependent on demand — a Rs 40 room when the guest house is half empty will quickly become a Rs 75 room when it's the last one left.

Just a few of the many to look at, starting from the railway station/bus halt/bank/post office end of town: *Poseidon Diving Adventures* has rooms at the very top of the guest house price scale — full board doubles for Rs 200, half board for Rs 160. Across the road and back over the railway tracks rooms in the *Lovely Guest House* are also at the pricey end of the scale — pleasant doubles with fan and bathrooms at Rs 120 including breakfast, Rs 75 without bathroom. Back on the sea side of the road, and still in the most expensive category, the *Dharshana Guest House* is more genteel than the average run of Hikkaduwa guest houses and costs Rs 175 for a double.

Prices rapidly start to drop with the *Pink House* which is also back over the railway tracks. Doubles in this very popular place range from Rs 25 to

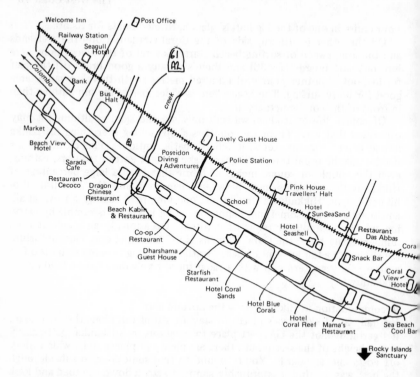

Rs 50 — bathrooms and fans make the price difference. Two more popular cheapies are side by side a little further down — they're the *Hotel Seashells* and the *Sun Sea Sand Hotel*. Both have pleasant verandahs and are at the upper end of the cheap scale, the better rooms are Rs 100 plus. Then the *Coral Front Inn*, still on the railway side of the road has rooms down to Rs 30 but the pleasant rooms opening out onto the verandah and garden are Rs 75, there's also an upstairs part. The *Curio Shop & Guest House* is cheap (Rs 40 a double) and small (just four rooms).

The *Coral View Hotel* has doubles at Rs 40 but they're rather bare. Rooms in the *George Guest House*, back beside the creek, cost Rs 75 for doubles, pleasantly quiet. The *Rising Sun Guest House* is pretty good value for Rs 40 — well away from the noise of the road but right beside the railway track, which do you prefer? The *Udula Guest House* has very comfortable doubles with bathroom and mosquito net, looking out onto a cool, shady verandah, for Rs 65 — more expensive if you want a fan. Across the road and right on the beach the *Lotus Guest House* has nice rooms but again more expensive — Rs 125 a double as you move further along the beach.

Prices go down again as you move further along the beach. At *Reef's End* there are singles down to Rs 10, doubles to Rs 20. They climb again at *Hotel Francis* where bed & breakfast costs Rs 100. Then they drop again at the *Surfers Rest Guest House*, which is a little dreary and has doubles from Rs 25. Back on the beach side of the road the *Surfing Beach Guest House* costs Rs 35 for a double.

The *Homely Guest House* is a fine looking old building run by a very friendly lady with rooms right down to Rs 15. The large gardens are also open to campers and Kombi driving overlanders. Then there's *Wekunagoda Guest House*, rooms from Rs 35, *Lakmal Guest House*, doubles at Rs 80 with their own bathroom, and quite a few others dotted further down the road. The *Seaside Inn*, a pleasantly spacious house with doubles at Rs 105, probably marks the further end of Hikkaduwa. It's between the 63rd and 64th milestone.

Apart from the many guest houses it is also quite easy to get cheaper rooms in village houses. Just wander along looking hopeful and somebody

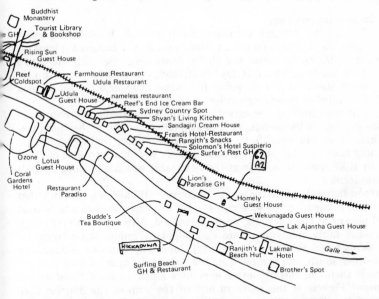

will descend on you! Of course you'll have to do without mod-cons like running water but if the well is OK you can get very cheap accommodation. Down at the southern end of the Hikkaduwa strip or on the many little lanes that run inland from the coast are the places to look.

Accommodation in Hikkaduwa — the top end

There are quite a few guest houses which bridge the gap between the bottom and the top end at Hikkaduwa but basically the top end consists of four hotels. The *Coral Gardens* (tel Hikkaduwa 891) has 48 rooms, all the usual mod cons, doubles around US$30 room-only. It's the most expensive place in Hikkaduwa and also has by far the nicest setting — a large expanse of lawn running down to the waterfront right by where the reef starts and runs out to the coral sanctuary. It's more or less midway between the coral beach and the surfing beach. The hotel also has the elephant which occasionally goes for a morning stroll down the main street.

The other three top end places are side by side on the coral diving beach — just to ensure that you get them nicely confused they all have the word "coral" in their names. Starting from the *Coral Gardens Hotel* end they are the *Hotel Coral Reef* (tel 37) with 30 rooms, the *Hotel Blue Corals* (tel 899) with 30 rooms and the *Hotel Coral Sands* (tel 36) with 28 rooms. Doubles in the *Blue Corals* start from around Rs 200, in the other two they're around Rs 250 or 300. All the Hikkaduwa hotels will arrange glass bottom boat trips for the less energetic, scuba diving for the more energetic.

Hikkaduwa — places to eat

You'll find all the standard travellers' menu items in Hikkaduwa's many eating places. Jaffles, pancakes, fruit salad, milk shakes, banana & pineapple fritters, fruit drinks, ice cream and all the other necessities of life to turn a place into a foodtrip. In a few days at Hikkaduwa an awful lot of money seems to get spent on just dropping into some place or other for a quick curd & fruit salad or something similar.

Many of the travellers' restaurants are remarkably similar, even down to the mis-spellings on the menus. They're also rather variable — they'll fix you something fresh and beautifully prepared for one meal and then serve up something tired and stale for the next. While we were having one of our best meals in Hikkaduwa somebody at the next table was complaining that his food was terrible.

Seafood figures large on the menus of course — Hikkaduwan crab whether it is boiled, roasted, served with chips, salad or ginger sauce is a taste treat (Rs 10 plus or minus a few Rs) not to be missed. All sorts of fish (although it is usually fairly anonymous) are also popular. Popular places to eat include *Udula's* and the *Farm House* next door. The nameless restaurant a little further south, the *Sydney Country Spot* and *Shyan's Living Kitchen* also pack them in. Slightly more expensive are *Restaurant Paradiso* and *Restaurant Francis* at the southern end of the strip or the *Starfish Cafe* towards the northern end where a meal can easily cost Rs 20.

The *Reef Coldspot*, opposite the Coral Gardens Hotel, is a tiny establishment that seems to be packed out at almost any time of the day or night but most particularly at breakfast time. Low prices and friendly service are part of the answer here. Down at the southern end of the strip *Rangith's Snacks* has positively the best ice cream (and milkshakes if milk is available) in Hikkaduwa — the crowds sitting outside at night bear witness to that. Two popular spots for a drink by the beach are *Mama's Beach Restaurant* by the coral beach or *Brother's Spot* directly opposite the popular body surfing part of the main beach. Many Hikkaduwa eateries have slices of excellent cake (I really liked the iced ginger cake) always ready at Rs 1 to Rs 1.50 a slice.

One of those little Asian restaurant exchanges which make you love (or hate) the place — "you've got grilled fish & salad on the menu?" "Yes." "You've got fried fish & chips on the menu?" "Yes." "Then could I have grilled fish & chips?" "No." "Why not?" "It's not on the menu."

Banks Apart from foreign exchange facilities, which are available for residents only, at the big hotels, Hikkaduwa has only one bank. It's small, crowded, stuffy and extremely slow. There always seems to be a queue of at least a half dozen or a dozen tourists and even at 10 minutes each you can work out how long you'll be standing there. Try to change money before you arrive in Hikkaduwa or at some other centre if you make day-trips along the coast. Or arrive early, before the bank opens, and sit and wait.

Hikkaduwa — Getting There & Getting Around
There are six trains daily from Colombo to Hikkaduwa, except on Saturdays and Sundays when there are only five. The trip takes about one hour 45 minutes to two and a half hours and costs Rs 3.90 3rd class, Rs 7.80 2nd and Rs 11.70 1st although generally 1st class isn't available. This is one train route that can be crowded. There are frequent buses from Colombo and also to or from nearby Ambalangoda and Galle. It's very easy to hire bicycles in Hikkaduwa and there's quite a lot of interest in the vicinity.

Transportation further along the Coast
As far as Galle, train schedules are as for Hikkaduwa — six times daily or five times on weekends from Colombo. The cost to Galle, which is only about 20 minutes beyond Hikkaduwa by rail, is Rs 4.70 3rd class, Rs 9.40 2nd class and Rs 14.10 in 1st. Beyond Galle there are only three daily trains and the railway line terminates at Matara. Fares to Matara are Rs 6.50 in 3rd, Rs 13.00 in 2nd and Rs 19.50 in 1st. From Colombo it takes three to four hours to Matara. Beyond here you've got no choice on public transport — bus or nothing.

GALLE
The port of Galle is 115 km (72 miles) south of Colombo and very close to Hikkaduwa. Although Anuradhapura and Polonnaruwa are far older they are effectively dead cities — the modern towns are quite divorced from the ancient ruins. Galle is Sri Lanka's most historically interesting city still functioning today. Until the construction of breakwaters at Colombo harbour was completed, only a hundred years ago, Galle was the major port in Sri Lanka and still handles shipping today.

Historians believe that Galle may be the Tarshish of Biblical times — from where King Solomon obtained gems, spices and peacocks but it assumed real importance only with the arrival of the Europeans. In 1505 a Portuguese fleet, bound for the Maldives, was blown off course and took shelter in the harbour at dusk. Hearing a cock ("gallus" in Portuguese) crowing they gave the town its name but another story relates that it is derived from the Sinhala word "gala" meaning rock, of which the harbour has plenty. At first the Portuguese made little use of the port but in 1589, involved in one of their periodic squabbles with the Kingdom of Kandy, they built a small and primitive fort which they named Santa Cruz. Later they extended this with a series of bastions and walls but the Dutch, after their takeover of the island, destroyed almost all traces of the Portuguese presence and burnt their records. Galle fell to the Dutch in 1640 after a four day siege.

In 1663 the Dutch built the 36 hectare (90 acre) fort which stands in almost perfect repair today and encompasses all the older part of Galle. Later Galle passed into British hands but by this time commercial interest was turning to Colombo and Galle has scarcely altered since the Dutch left. It's a delightful little place, quiet and easy-going within the old fort walls and with a real sense of being steeped in history.

The Fort

One of the most pleasant strolls you can make is the circuit of the fort walls at dusk. As the daytime heat fades away you can, in an easy hour or two, walk almost the complete circuit of Galle along the top of the wall — only once or twice is it necessary to leave the wall. The main gate into Galle is a comparatively recent addition — it was built by the British in 1873 to handle the heavier flow of traffic into the old city. This wall, the most heavily fortified since it faced the land, was originally constructed by the Portuguese with a moat and later substantially enlarged by the Dutch. In 1667 they split this section, originally named the "Sea Bastion" into separate "Star", "Moon" and "Sun" bastions.

Following the fort wall clockwise you soon come to the original gate now known as the "Old Gate". On the outer side the British coat of arms tops the entrance while inside the letters VOC are inscribed in the stone. They stand for the Dutch East India Company and are flanked by two lions, topped by a cock and bear the date 1669. Just beyond the gate is the "Zwart" bastion or "Black Fort" which is thought to be the oldest of the fort bastions and to have been originally constructed by the Portuguese. Today it houses the police station.

The eastern wall ends at the Point Utrecht Bastion close to the powder magazine. The modern lighthouse stands atop this bastion and the lighthouse keeper magically materialises when visitors arrive and, for a few rupees, will show you up to the top of his 18 metre high lighthouse from where you have a fine view over the old town of Galle. The rocky point at the end of the next stretch of wall was once a Portuguese Bastion and from

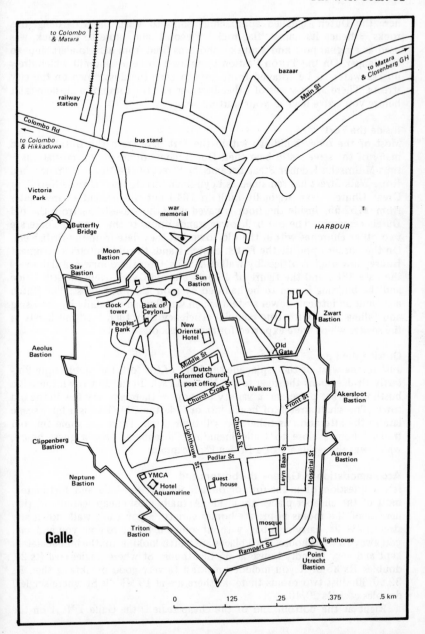

to Colombo
& Matara

railway
station

Colombo Rd

to Colombo
& Hikkaduwa

bazaar

Main St

to Matara
& Closenberg GH

bus stand

Victoria
Park

Butterfly
Bridge

war
memorial

HARBOUR

Moon
Bastion

Star
Bastion

Sun
Bastion

clock
tower

Bank of
Ceylon

Peoples'
Bank

Zwart
Bastion

Aeolus
Bastion

New
Oriental
Hotel

Middle St

Dutch
Reformed Church
post office

Church Cross St

Walkers

Old
Gate

Front St

Akersloot
Bastion

Clippenberg
Bastion

Church St

Lighthouse St

Pedlar St

Leyn Baan St

Hospital St

Aurora
Bastion

Neptune
Bastion

YMCA

Hotel
Aquamarine

guest
house

Galle

Triton
Bastion

mosque

Rampart St

lighthouse

Point
Utrecht
Bastion

0   125   .25   .375   .5 km

here the Dutch signalled approaching ships to warn them of dangerous rocks — hence its name "flag rock". Pigeon Island, close to the rock, was used as a signal post and a musket shot was fired from here to alert ships to the danger. On the Triton Bastion there used to be a windmill which drew up sea water to be sprayed from carts to keep the dust down on the city streets. There are a series of other bastions and the tomb of a Moslem saint before you arrive back at your starting point.

Inside the Fort
Most of the older buildings within the fort date from the Dutch era and many of the streets still bear their Dutch names or are direct translations — thus Mohrische Kramer Staat became the Street of the Moorish Traders and Rope Walk Street has remained as Leyn-Baan Street. The "Groote Kerk", or Great Church, was originally built in 1640 but the present church dates from 1752-55. Inside the floor is paved with the gravestones from the old Dutch cemetery. The old bell tower stands opposite the church. There are two other churches within the old town but they date from the British era. On the corner opposite the Dutch church stands the old Dutch Government House, now used as offices by Walker & Sons. Over the doorway a slab bears the date 1683 and the figure of a cock. The old Dutch ovens are still inside and the building is said to be haunted by more than one ghost! The Dutch also built an intricate sewer system which was flushed out daily by the rising and falling tide. With true colonial efficiency they then bred musk rats in the sewers which were exported for their musk oil.

Outside the Fort
Just to the west of the esplanade, in front of the fort, the picturesque Butterfly Bridge spans the river to the Victoria Park. In the new town there is a bustling market place and a variety of shops — there are very few in the old town. The small stretch of beach just outside the Old Gate is a busy scene late in the afternoon as fishermen sell their catch. There are some fine old traders' homes close to Galle including Closenberg, now a guest house, which was the residence of a British P&O captain.

Accommodation in Galle — the bottom end
It's a question of in-the-fort or outside-the-fort in Galle and fortunately most of the cheaper places are inside. Actually most cheap accommodation here is of the rooms in private homes variety — you can't walk down any street in Galle, carrying a bag, without someone trying to grab you and haul you away to their house. Two places are worth looking up: the immaculately kept and very friendly house at 65 Lighthouse St where singles cost Rs 20, doubles Rs 35 or if you include breakfast (a very good breakfast) then Rs 32.50/60. Just two rooms there, as there are at 19 Middle St where singles/ doubles cost Rs 20/40.

Right at the bottom end of the cheap scale is the Galle *YMCA* on the corner of Pedlar St and Rampart St. Just three beds at less than Rs 10 per person. Or right next door there is the pleasant, though a little overpriced *Aquamarine Hotel* which has rooms at Rs 66, 73 and 88. They are big, airy rooms but only a couple of them have their own bathrooms and at those prices in Sri Lanka you should expect rooms to be at least that well equipped. Excellent food in the restaurant and you can dine outside too. Other than that the only places to eat are the *New Oriental* and a string of grubby places by the railway station.

Accommodation in Galle — the top end

The delightfully olde worlde *New Oriental Hotel* is at 10 Church St in the Fort next to the new Dutch Church. It has got all the old (but very well kept) Victorian flavour you could ask for and costs Rs 80 single, Rs 160 double — room only. It is the only upper notch place actually in the fort at Galle and has 26 rooms.

About three km from the Fort on the Matara side of Galle, the *Closenberg Hotel* once had its own little bay until it was filled in for a land reclamation project; there's still a fine sweep of sand to the south of it. It was originally built by a P&O captain in the heyday of British mercantile supremacy and has eight rooms, priced from around Rs 60 to Rs 125 double, room only — up to Rs 250 with all meals. Or there's the smaller *Harbour Inn* (just four rooms) at Unawatuna, further south of Galle, which costs Rs 100 for a double room only, Rs 250 with meals.

WELIGAMA

About 30 km south of Galle the name means sandy-village and this is indeed what Weligama has — a very fine sandy sweep of bay with a tiny island accessible by foot at low tide just offshore. Along this stretch of coast, and particularly at Ahangama, you're likely to see stilt-fishermen. Each fisherman has a pole firmly embedded in the sea bottom close to the shore. When

the sea and fish are running in the right direction they perch upon their poles and cast their lines out.

The road through Weligama divides just as it enters the town. One road runs along the coast, the other a short distance inland. Take the inland route and just by the railway crossing there is a small park with a large rock carved figure known as the *Kustaraja*. It's been variously described as a king who was mysteriously cured of leprosy or as Avalokitesvara, a disciple of the Buddha. Weligama is also famous for its lacework; some local entrepreneurs are bound to rush out to try and sell you some.

Accommodation in Weligama
There's a cheapie and a more expensive place along the coastal road through Weligama. Behind the place signposted as *Leela Lace Industries* there are three rooms, priced at Rs 15 single, Rs 25 double — you can bargain a little. A couple of hundred metres on the Galle side you will find the attractive *Weligama Bay Inn* where singles/doubles cost Rs 75/90 for room only or Rs 144/288 with all meals — a wide, open balcony, pleasant green gardens and a good view across to the beach.

MATARA
Exactly 100 miles (160 km) from Colombo, this town marks the end of the southern railway. Matara has two excellent Dutch forts, the larger one contains much of old Matara including the excellent rest house which is said to be built on the site where captured elephants were corralled. The other fort, the small 1763 Star Fort, is now used as a library and has a most attractive and unusual gateway. It's about a hundred metres from the main fort gate — on the other side of the road and heading towards Colombo.

Matara is famous for its curd and treacle so you should not fail to try it here. On our south coast treacle tasting expedition we thought the stalls just inland from Hambantato were the number one place though. It's an easy-going town with horse carriages clip-clopping by but for beaches you must head a few km back towards Colombo and turn off to Polhena. Here you'll find a shallow swimming area with a pleasant little beach.

Accommodation in Matara
There's quite a variety of places in the cheaper price category in Matara — a very reasonably priced place for a stay. In the Matara Fort, the entrance is only about a hundred metres from the bus station, you will find the Matara *Rest House* which, as usual is beautifully situated right by the beach with a wonderful view in both directions. Although the original building is quite old there are two recently added new wings with very comfortable rooms, with bathrooms for just Rs 35 a double. That's the room only charge, including meals the cost goes up to Rs 140. The restaurant here has a much more extensive and reasonably priced menu than that usually found in Rest Houses.

About a hundred metres along the shoreline beyond the Rest House still inside the Fort, you will find the *SK Rest House* where plain, but clean and comfortable rooms cost just Rs 10 single, Rs 20 double. The other two good value cheapies are on the way out of Matara towards Galle. If you follow the road from the bus stop it crosses a wide river and bends round to follow the coast. The turnoff to the railway station is about a half km along and a block beyond that you will find the *Chamin Restaurant & Guest House* which has clean, functional doubles for just Rs 30. Like the SK Rest House it would be a real find in almost any other town than Matara.

Virtually across the road from the Chamin you will see a sign to *Jez Look Batik Inn* which is at 12 Yehiya Mawatha, a few steps off the main road Dharmapala Mawatha. It's a batik factory which also has a few rooms — very pleasant atmosphere and you can learn batik making while you stay here, it's included in the price. Per person cost is Rs 35 including all meals or Rs 25 if you're out to lunch, or you can have a double room without meals for just Rs 15. All in all the shoestringers are well catered for in Matara and there's more just a couple of km away at Polhena Beach.

Food is easy to find here too — there are a number of good places along Dharmapala Mawatha including the Chamin which has a long menu of the Chinese regulars plus really excellent fish and chips, and Coca Cola is cheap here. Further back towards the bus station there's the *GOB Restaurant*. Just on the Galle side of the bridge there's a string of fruit stalls selling a wider variety of tropical fruit than I saw anywhere else in Sri Lanka — even mangosteens and custard apples when nowhere else seemed to have them. And right across the road there's a whole bevy of signs calling out to my fellow curd and treacle lovers. What a food trip!

Accommodation in Polhena

As if the plethora of cheap places to stay in Matara wasn't enough there is also Polhena Beach about three km west (the Galle side) of Matara. It is only a 30c bus ride from Matara but there are only a handful of buses right to the beach each day — otherwise you will have to get off at the main road junction and walk the half km down the the beach. There are two places to stay here. One is the excellent *TK Travellers' Halt* which has dorm beds for Rs 5, doubles at Rs 20 or more luxuriously equipped rooms with their own bathrooms for Rs 60. The cheaper rooms have mosquito nets and fans though, so they are no hardship. TK consists of two separate houses about a hundred metres apart, it's got a good menu too.

The other Polhena place is the sole upper bracket hotel at Matara/Polhena — it's the pleasantly sited *Polhena Reef Gardens Hotel*. The 18 rooms cost Rs 140/150 single/double room only, up to Rs 210/290 including all meals. Snorkelling and skin diving equipment is available from the hotel and there is a relaxing garden by the waterside.

MATARA TO TANGALLA

Just as you leave Matara a turn inland will take you to the Weherehena temple where there is an artificial underground cave decorated with comic book-like colour illustrations of scenes from the Buddha's life. Only five or six km out of Matara you come to Dondra the southernmost point of Sri Lanka. A lighthouse marks the actual southern extremity of the island.

WEWURUKANNALA VIHARA — GIANT BUDDHA

If the Weherehena temple in Matara is "Marvel Comics meets Lord Buddha" then here it's Walt Disney who runs into him. At the town of Dikwella, around the 113th milepost, a road turns inland towards Beliatta. About a km and a half along you will come to a huge, 50 metre high, seated Buddha figure. It is the largest Buddha in Sri Lanka. The temple has three parts — the oldest is about 250 years and is of no particular interest.

Larger and newer, a second shrine room has a quite amazing collection of life size and vibrantly coloured figures depicting the Buddha doing everything from taking his first steps, (immediately after birth), through leaving his family to seek enlightenment, finding it, passing on the message and finally achieving nirvana. There are also models of devils, monsters, Veddahs, disciples, 24 of the Buddha's previous incarnations, larger seated, standing and reclining figures and everything else you could ask for. I particularly liked the figure of the Buddha while still a prince, riding away from his family on what looks like a horse from a fair ground merry-go-round.

Finally there is the gigantic seated figure which was constructed only 12 years ago and is still not completed. As if to prove that it really is as high as an eight-storey building, what should be right behind it but (you guessed it) an eight-storey building. You can climb up inside to look over his shoulder at the surrounding rice paddies or on up to his head where you can look through a little glass panel to see what there is inside a 50 metre high Buddha's head. Answer? — all the Buddhist scriptures, a small dagoba and a circle of small Buddha figures. It is all quite a contrast to the supremely tasteful Buddhist art in the ancient cities. There's one other thing to see here, an interesting clock in the adjoining building, — made 65 years ago by a prisoner.

TANGALLA

Situated 195 km (122 miles) from Colombo, Tangalla, (also spelt Tangalle) is one of the nicest places along the coast — particularly if you just want somewhere to laze and soak up the sun. The town itself is an easy going place with several reminders of Dutch days including the old Rest House which was once home for the Dutch administrators. It's Tangalla's series of bays which are the modern attraction however. To the east of the Rest House there is a long stretch of white sand shimmering away into the distance while to the west you've got a choice of a whole series of smaller bays. some of them shelve off very steeply and the resulting waves make them dangerous for poor swimmers if there is any sort of sea running, compounded by the nasty rocks which punctuate the shore line. If the sea is calm they are just fine. The bay just on the town side of the *Tangalla Bay Hotel* is probably the most sheltered although right beside the Rest House there's a tiny bay which is very shallow and generally flat calm. Beyond the *Peace Haven* resort there are two very picturesque and fairly secluded bays which are popular for seekers of an overall suntan.

Accommodation in Tangalla — the bottom end
There are two places on the Travellers' Halt network in Tangalla — both are on the coast road, about a half km out of town but before you get to the big Tangalla Bay Hotel. The nearer one to the town is the *Tangalla Beach Hotel* (a discreetly different name huh?) where there are dorm beds at Rs 6 or rooms at Rs 15 to Rs 35. Prices are a little bit negotiable, depending on demand. The more expensive rooms have proper mattresses and mosquito nets. Good food available too. The *Magic Circle Guest House* is only a hop, step and jump further from town — it's a little simpler and more spartan, dorm beds are only Rs 5, rooms Rs 15. Again there's food available and since the proprietor is a keen magician you can also brush up on your rabbit out of the hat tricks while you're here.

There are quite a few small cafes and restaurants around town — *SK Hotel* is nearest to the two cheapies on the Matara side of town. A good place for a very economical breakfast and the rice and curry is also good here. They have rooms at around Rs 20 a double. Just the other side of the town centre bus station you will find the *Sujatha Restaurant* which also has good, cheap food. Tangalla has a fine little market place right next to the bus station, you'll find stalls around here selling curd and honey should you wish to add to your curd pot collection.

Accommodation in Tangalla — the top end
There are two top end places and a Rest House in Tangalla. You'll find the *Rest House* right in the middle of town, pleasantly situated on the promontory at the start of the beach which seems to stretch endlessly to the east. It's one of the oldest Rest Houses in the country as it dates back to the Dutch days — as a small plate on the front steps indicates. Accommodation here costs Rs 90 per person all inclusive. The seafood here has an excellent reputation — at Rs 42 for the seafood dinner it certainly should.

The other two places are on the Matara side of town, about a km and a half and two km out. Closer of the two is the *Tangalla Bay Hotel*. Situated on a rocky promontory between two small sweeps of sandy bay, it blends in quite well with each room having its own balcony on top of the room below. The central complex has been designed to look like a boat — or at least that is the intention, it doesn't work too well. Room only costs are Rs 280/300 for singles/doubles. All inclusive will come to something over Rs 500 per day for two.

The other upper bracket place is the pleasant *Peace Haven Guest House* situated on the next promontory along. There are 12 rooms in all either in the central building or in a number of separate cabanas scattered around the promontory. Nightly costs range from Rs 35/45 single/double right up to around Rs 100 for the largest room which will sleep four. There's quite a range of room sizes and facilities — the cheapest rooms are very straightforward and simple: just a bare, fanless room with beds and a mosquito net. Peaceful though and the little beach beyond it is ostensibly private. Meals cost Rs 12.50 for breakfast, Rs 22.50 for lunch and Rs 25 for dinner.

HAMBANTOTA

The road turns inland from the coast here, 237 km (148 miles) from Colombo. You can continue inland and rejoin the coast at Arugam Bay (Pottuvil); or head up to the hill country through Haputale or Ella; or double back to Colombo through Ratnapura. Hambantota is not the best place along the coast if you are in search of sand and sea although there are magnificent sweeps of beach both east and west of the small promontory from the town. Eastward there's often a large collection of outriggered fishing boats beached

on the sands. A major industry in Hambantota is the production of salt by the age old method of evaporating sea water from shallow salt pans. You will see these pans alongside the road as you turn inland from the coast. A few km out of Hambantota, or just before you reach it if you are coming down to the coast, is the last (or the first) of the coastal curd specialists. In this small village there are a number of small roadside stalls selling delicious curd and honey — definitely worth a stop if you can manage it.

Accommodation in Hambantota
The Hambantota *Rest House* is nicely situated on top of the promontory overlooking the town and the long sweep of beach. It is a fairly modern (by Rest House standards) place, quite large and moderately priced. Room only costs Rs 27.50 per person, half board is Rs 57.50 and full board is Rs 75 — per person in all cases and there is a 12½% service charge to be added. About a half km from the centre of town and the bus stop, on the Tangalla road, you will find the small *Joy Rest Home* — just a couple of rooms at Rs 15 per person or they'll provide an "out bed" (out on the verandah with the mosquitoes) for Rs 10. If that doesn't satisfy or is full, there are always the private homes — which will soon find you if you don't find them.

INLAND FROM HAMBANTOTA
The road turns inland at Hambantota and runs virtually due north to Wellawaya where you have a choice of turning east towards the east coast or heading into the highlands by turning west or continuing north. Shortly after leaving the coast you come to the Tissamaharama turn-off. The tank here, the Tissawewa, is credited to the brother of Devanampiya Tissa of Anuradhapura and is thought to date from the 3rd century BC. There is also a restored dagoba here which is thought to have been built by the father of Dutugemunu, who liberated Anuradhapura from the Indians in the 2nd century BC. Today the tank is notable for its very active bird life.

Continue another 15 km beyond Tissa and you reach Kataragama, probably the most important place in Sri Lanka when it comes to religion. Kataragama is a holy place to both Hindus and Buddhists — but particularly the former who make great pilgrimages here in July and August each year. Kataragama is also, like Tissa, a jumping off point for the Yala park. See the "Wildlife" section and the introductory "Festivals" section for more details.

The Hill Country

The hill country in the centre of Sri Lanka is totally different to anywhere else in the island. Due to its altitude the often sticky heat of the coastal regions or the dry central and northern plains becomes a cool, perpetual spring. Everything is green and lush and much of the region carpeted with the glowing colour of the tea plantations. This is also the most Sinhalese part of the country for the Kingdom of Kandy resisted European takeover for over 300 years after the coastal regions had succumbed. Kandy remains the cultural and spiritual centre of the island and is one of the top attractions in Sri Lanka. It's a relaxed and easy-going town with a delightful lakeside setting — a place where it's very easy to find the days just drifting by. There are many other hill country towns worth a visit and an abundance of pleasant walks and climbs, refreshing waterfalls and historical sites.

KANDY

Only 115 km (72 miles) inland from Colombo but climatically a world away due to its 500 metre altitude, Kandy is the relaxed, easy-going "capital" of the hill country. It's also the cultural centre of Sri Lanka and in many ways the country's spiritual centre. Kandy was the capital of the last Sinhalese kingdom and after three centuries of defying the Portuguese and the Dutch, finally fell to the British in 1815. In actual fact the Portuguese briefly captured the city on three occasions and the Dutch once but it was not until the arrival of the British that the final spark of Sinhalese independence was extinguished.

Kandy is particularly famed for the great Kandy Esala Perahera held each year over the full moon in the month of Esala (July or August by our calendar) but it has attractions enough to justify a visit at any time of the year. The countryside around Kandy is lush and green and there are many pleasant walks both from the town itself or further afield. The central town itself is a delightful jumble of old shops, antique and gemstone specialists, a bustling two-storey market and a good selection of hotels, guest houses and restaurants.

Kandy Esala Perahera

The big night of the year in Kandy actually comes as the culmination of ten days of increasingly frenetic activity. A perahera is a parade or procession and Kandy's perahera peaks at the time of the full moon in Esala and is held to honour the sacred tooth enshrined in the Dalada Maligawa, the Temple of the Tooth. The procession is actually a combination of five separate processions come from the four Kandy *devales* — shrines to deities that protect the island and are also devotees and servants of the Buddha. There is Natha — a Buddha to be and of special importance to Kandy. Vishnu — the guardian of

Sri Lanka and an indicator of the intermingling of Hindu and Buddhist beliefs. Skanda — the god of war and victory; and Pattini — the goddess of chastity. But the most splendid perahera is that of the Dalada Maligawa, the Temple of the Tooth.

The procession is led by thousands of Kandyan dancers and drummers beating thousands of drums, leaping with unbounded energy, cracking noisy whips and waving colourful banners. Then come long processions of elephants, 50, 60 or more of them. The brilliantly caparisoned Maligawa Tusker is the largest and most splendid of them all — decorated from trunk to toe he carries a huge canopy which shelters, on the final night, a replica of the sacred relic cask. A carpetway of white linen is laid in front of the elephant so that he does not step in the dirt. The Kandy Esala Perahera is the most magnificent annual spectacle to be seen in Sri Lanka and one of the most famous in Asia. It has been an annual event for many centuries and is described by Robert Knox in his 1681 *An Historical Relation of Ceylon*.

Kandyan Dancers

The famed Kandyan dancers are not principally a theatrical performance but you can see them go through their athletic routines every night at one or more locales around Kandy. The performances are widely advertised — either your guest house or the tourist office will be able to tell you where to go. They last one to one and a half hours and cost Rs 30 to 40 for tickets. You can also hear Kandyan drummers every day at the Temple of the Tooth — their drumming signals the start of the daily *poyas*.

The Lake

Kandy's lake, a pleasant centre-piece to the town, is artificial and was only built in 1807 by Sri Wickrama Rajasinha, the last ruler of the Kingdom of Kandy. The island in the centre was used as his personal harem — to which he crossed on a barge. The less romantically inclined British used it as an ammunition store although they did add the fortress style parapet around the perimeter of the lake.

The perimeter road around the lake makes a very pleasant stroll — it's also used by a steady procession of learner drivers, all in old English Morris Minors and all displaying L plates in very proper British fashion. On the far side of the lake, right by the lakeside in front of the monastery, there's a circular enclosure which is the monks' bathhouse. They'll invite males inside to see how a monk takes a fully clothed bath! From the bridge you can make a 20 minute tour of the lake and island by boat for Rs 15 — per boat.

Dalada Maligawa (the Temple of the Tooth)
Located close to the lake the Temple of the Tooth houses Sri Lanka's most important Buddhist relic. The sacred tooth of the Buddha was said to have been snatched from the flames of his funeral pyre in 543 BC and was smuggled into Ceylon during the 4th century AD hidden in the hairdo of a princess. At first it was taken to Anuradhapura but with the ups and downs of Sri Lankan history it moved from place to place before eventually ending at Kandy. For a short period from 1283 it was actually carried back to India by an invading army but was brought back to Ceylon by King Parakrama-bahu III.

Gradually the tooth came to assume more and more importance in Ceylon but the Portuguese, following one of their brief captures of Kandy, and in one of their worst spoilsport moods, assert that they took the tooth away and destroyed it with Catholic fervour in Goa. Not so is the Sinhalese rejoinder, they were fobbed off with a replica and the real incisor remained safely in Kandy.

The present Temple of the Tooth was constructed mainly during the reign of Kandyan kings from 1687-1707 and 1747-1782. It is an imposing pink painted structure, surrounded by a deep moat, but not of any particular architectural significance in itself. The octagonal tower in the moat was built by Sri Wickrama Rajasinha, the last king of Kandy, and houses an important collection of ola-leaf (palm leaf) manuscripts. The temple is open from dawn to dusk and there is morning and evening *poyas* (6 am, 11 am and at 6.30 pm) when the heavily guarded room housing the tooth is open to devotees — and tourists. Of course you do not see the tooth itself — just a gold casket which is said to contain a series of smaller and smaller caskets and eventually the tooth itself. Or perhaps a replica, nobody seems to be too sure. The casket is behind a window and two decidedly mean-looking monks stand heavily on either side so there is no chance of any more sneaky Portuguese carting the sacred relic away.

Also within the temple precincts is the Audience Hall used by the kings of Kandy and the site for the convention of Kandyan chiefs which ceded the kingdom to the British in 1815. It is notable for the tall pillars which support the roof and for a time was used for ceremonial sittings of the Supreme Court.

Kandy Museum

Behind the Temple of the Tooth you'll find Kandy's excellent small museum with much royal regalia and reminders of Sinhalese life prior to the arrival of the Europeans. It was once part of the palace complex and is open from 9 am to 5 pm except on Fridays and Saturdays. There is also an Archaeological Museum within the Temple of the Tooth which is open from 8 am to 4 pm except on Tuesdays.

Monasteries

As the cultural centre of Sri Lanka, the principal Buddhist monasteries have considerable importance — the high priests of the two best known monasteries, the Malwatte and the Asgiriya, are the most important in Sri Lanka. They also play an important role in the administration and operation of the Temple of the Tooth. The Malwatte monastery is directly across the lake from the Temple of the Tooth while the Asgiriya is on the hill off Trincomalee St, to the north-west of the town centre.

Elephant Bath Time

At Katugastota, about four km from the centre of Kandy on the banks of the Mahaweli Ganga, elephants are brought down to the river by their *mahouts* for a midday bathe. There is usually quite a crowd of elephants enjoying a refreshing splash down here during the heat of the day — but note that it is quite a tourist scene these days and the *mahouts* are adept at demanding payment for photographing their noble steeds. You can have a short elephant back ride for as little as Rs 5 but make certain you've specified how far the ride is going to be! Best time to come is between 2 pm and 4 pm.

Scenic Walks

There are many walks almost in the centre of Kandy such as up to the Royal Palace Park overlooking the lake. There is a cannon here captured from the Japanese in Burma and donated by Earl Mountbatten. Further up the hill on Rajapihilla Mawatha there are even better views stretching over the lake, the town and the surrounding hills which disappear in a series of gentle ranges far into the distance.

On the other side of the lake you can take a longer stroll around the cool and pleasant Udawattakele Sanctuary. There is much birdlife and more than a few monkeys in the sanctuary but visitors are advised to be a little careful in this secluded woodland if they're alone. Muggers may be fairly rare in Sri Lanka but they're not unknown.

Arts & Crafts

The Kandyan Arts and Crafts Association has a good display of local lacquerwork, brassware and other craft items (including the delightful, miniature "batik" elephants) at their showroom beside the lake. There is also a government run Laksala arts and crafts shop in Kandy but it has nothing on the big one in Colombo. Kandy is packed with antique shops, particularly along the central lakeside road. Antique (and instant-antique) jewellery, silver belts, and other items are available in abundance. Kandy also has a number of batik manufacturers — I particularly liked those at Fresco Batiks at 901 Peradeniya Rd, towards the Botanical Gardens.

Botanical Gardens

The Peradeniya Botanical Gardens are six km out of Kandy towards Colombo, the Peradeniya railway station is the last stop before Kandy. Prior to the arrival of the British this was a royal park and it is today the largest Botanical Garden in Sri Lanka. The gardens cover 60 hectares (147 acres) and are bounded on four sides by a loop of the Mahaweli River — the longest river in Sri Lanka which has its source close to Adam's Peak. The gardens have some of the original rubber tree plants smuggled out of Brazil, a fine collection of orchids and a stately avenue of royal palms which were planted in 1905. Admission to the gardens costs Rs 5 for foreign visitors, only 50c for Sri Lankans. There is a Royal Gardens Cafeteria about a hundred metres from the entrance, to the left.

Temples around Kandy

There are many temples scattered around Kandy — they are not really terribly interesting unless you're a real temple freak but on the other hand they do make a pleasant trip out into the country. A chance to see a little rural life with some culture thrown in. A particularly pleasant loop will take you from Kandy to three of these temples and back via the Botanical Gardens.

The first stop is the Embekke Devale for which you need a 643 bus from near the railway station (90c). The bus only runs about once an hour and the village of Embekke is about seven twisting and turning km beyond the Botanical Gardens — it seems a lot further. From the village you've got a pleasant countryside stroll of about a km to the temple. The 14th century temple is said to have the best examples of wood carved pillars to be found in Kandy. They are thought to have come from a royal audience hall in the city.

From here to the Lankatilake Temple is a km and a half stroll along a path through the rice paddies until the temple looms up on the left. From Kandy you can go directly to the temple on a 644 bus. Built on a rocky outcrop the temple is reached by a long series of steps cut directly into the rock. The brick structure houses a fine Buddha image and Kandy period wall paintings while outside there are stone elephant figures. It's considered to be

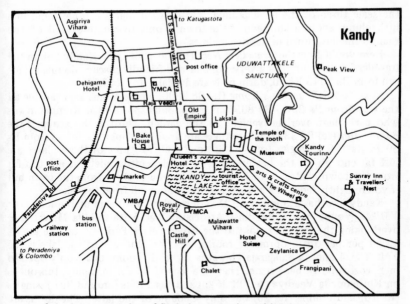

one of the best examples of Sinhalese temple architecture.

It's a further three km walk from here to the Gadaladeniya Temple or you can catch a bus — a 644 amongst others will take you there. This temple too is constructed atop a rocky outcrop and dates from a similar period to the Lankatilake and Embekke Devale. There are definite signs of Hindu influence in the stone construction. A moonstone marks the entrance to the main shrine.

From here the main Colombo-Kandy road is only about a km away, you reach it close to the 65th milestone. A pleasant stroll, from the main road almost any bus will take you to the Botanical Gardens or on into Kandy. The complete loop from Kandy only costs about Rs 2 by bus — 90c out to Embekke, 30c from Lankatilake to Gadaladeniya and 40c from the main road junction to the Botanical Gardens.

Other temples in the vicinity include the Degaldoruwa about 2½ km north-east of the Lewella ferry crossing (also a suspension bridge). It is famous for its recently restored frescoes illustrating scenes from the *Jataka*. The Galmaduwa is architecturally unique and was probably built, during the Kandy period, on the site of a much older dagoba. It is off the Kandy-Kundasale road to the south-east of Kandy. At Medawala to the north-east of Kandy the Medawala Vihara has a frieze illustrating mythical animals composed of parts of a variety of species.

Accommodation in Kandy — the bottom end

Kandy is the guest house capital of Sri Lanka and at the low budget end of the scale three of the most popular and pleasant places can be found in a little clump about a km beyond the town — only five minutes walk off the road to the left, down in the rice paddies.

Here you'll find the *Travellers Nest* (tel 08 2366), the Kandy link in the travellers' halt chain. It's a very popular and friendly place — double rooms run from Rs 20 to Rs 50, dorm beds are available for Rs 7.50.

Next door is *Traveller's Home* (tel 08 2800) where rooms are available all the way from Rs 25 to Rs 80. This is a popular spot for the Kombi crowds who park their overland vehicles in the garden. Third in this group is the *Sunray Inn* (tel 08 3322) where there are double rooms with prices from Rs 50 to Rs 130 — singles from Rs 30 to Rs 80. All three of these places are just far enough off the beaten track to be pleasantly quiet yet not too far from the town centre. A 654 bus will take you to them from the town but if you're lightly laden it's just a pleasant stroll uphill from the lakeside.

Kandy also has a number of "Ys". Probably best value of the lot is the *YMBA* (Young Men's Buddhist Association) at 5 Rajapihilla Mawatha — overlooking the lake and close to the Royal Palace Park. Costs here are Rs 13.50 per person in dorms or rooms. Also on this side of the lake is the *YMCA* at 4 and 4a Sangaraja Mawatha. It has 10 rooms but is only open to men, cost is Rs 14 per person. There is a second *YMCA* in Kandy, this one is on Kotugodella Veediya (tel 08 3529) and has dorms (around Rs 6), singles (Rs 10) and double (Rs 20) but only a couple of the latter. The dorms are

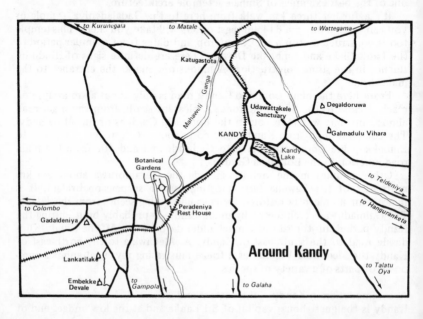

Around Kandy

for men only. It's very close to the town centre. Finally there's a small *Boy Scout Youth Hostel* at the Boy Scout Headquarters, back across the lake again and further up the hill on Keppitipola Rd. Here you'll find seven beds at around Rs 10 per night.

Kandy has a great number of other guest houses and plenty of touts waiting for you at the station. You may not always be too popular if you arrive in the tow of one of these guys (although they do have their uses!). The tourist office by the lakeside will provide you with a comprehensive list of Kandy guest houses and there is also quite a number of them in the *Welcome to Sri Lanka* brochure. Note that the tourist office is closed on Saturdays and Sundays.

With so many other guest houses around I hesitate to make any recommendations. However 15 Malabar St (sometimes known as "Doctor's House") is pleasant and friendly with doubles at Rs 75. *Woodstock*, just up the hill behind the Temple of the Tooth, is also said to be pleasant. There are many, many others scattered around town, particularly along Lady McCallum's Drive, out at Katugastota or along the Peradeniya road towards the Botanical Gardens. *Windy Cot*, 66 Riverdale Rd, Anniewatte (overlooking the Mahaweli River) is a very slightly more flashy guest house although still low priced. Amongst the cheapest of the hotels is the *Olde Empire* at 21 Temple Rd, close to the Temple of the Tooth. Singles/doubles from around Rs 35/70.

Accommodation in Kandy — the top end
Kandy has two well kept top end places in the inimitable Sri Lankan, colonial-era-English style. *Queens Hotel* (tel 08 2121-2) is right in the centre of town and right beside the lake. There are 85 rooms with singles/doubles from Rs 150/250 room only. The Queens also has an excellent restaurant (recommended for a splash out even if you're travelling on a shoestring) and a swimming pool. Across the lake at 30 Sangaraja Mawatha the *Hotel Suisse* (tel 08 2637, 2671-2) also has a swimming pool, a similar number of rooms to the Queens and marginally higher prices. It's rather more secluded and quiet than the centrally located Queens.

The *Mahaweli Reach Hotel* (tel 80 2611) is at 35 Siyambalagastenne Rd close to the Katugastota bridge. It has 23 rooms with singles/doubles from around Rs 175/200, is also equipped with a swimming pool and notes that it is handy for elephant rides! The *Ladyhill Tourist Hotel* (tel 08 2659) is just off the Peradeniya road almost out at the Botanical Gardens. There are 39 rooms, it too has a swimming pool (they're very popular up at Kandy) and nightly costs are also around Rs 175/200 for singles/doubles. *Castle Hill Guest House* (tel 08 4376) at 25 Gregory's Rd and the *Chalet Hotel* (tel 08 4353) at 32 Gregory's Rd both overlook the lake across from the town centre. Rooms in both are in the Rs 150 to 200 bracket. Back in the centre the *Hotel Dehigama* (tel 08 2709) is a modern building with 20 rooms at around Rs 150 a double — pleasant, friendly and with a "charming little beer garden"

A little out from the centre on Anniewatta Rd, the *Hotel Topaz* (tel 08 4150, 3061-2) has 47 rooms with doubles at around Rs 250 room-only. Or there is the small *Frangipani Guest House* just off the end of the lake, the *Riverdale Tourist Guest House* (tel 08 3080) very close to that — both with rooms in the Rs 150 to 200 range. The *Kandy Tourinn* (tel 08 2790) is rather cheaper with rooms in the Rs 75 to 100 range. It's on 17 Sanhamitta Rd uphill towards the Udawattekele Sanctuary. The *Peak View Motel* (tel 084241) is even further up the hill at 102 Dharmasoka Mawatha. There are many other better quality guest houses which the Kandy tourist office can advise you about.

Kandy also has a *Rest House* situated directly across from the main entrance to the Botanical Gardens at Peradeniya — get off the train at Peradeniya station if you're going there, don't continue in to Kandy. There are also railway retiring rooms at the Kandy station but these belong in the bottom end price category.

Finally Kandy's most modern and expensive hotel is 27 km out of Kandy. higher up in a tea estate. The *Hunas Falls Hotel* (tel 802-4 Elkaduwa) has 23 very modern rooms with air-conditioning and all other mod-cons including swimming pool, tennis court, a well stocked fish pool above the Hunas waterfalls, and plenty of walks in the surrounding hills. For the luxury count on around Rs 500 for an all-inclusive double.

Kandy Accommodation Warning At the time of the Esala Perahera prices in Kandy go nuts — if you can find a room. If you're intent on coming be prepared for what it will cost you.

Kandy — Places to Eat

There are a number of popular cheaper places — two of which are on the main road, virtually opposite each other. The *Bake House* is a big, two level place with good short eats and a comprehensive menu. The *Ceylon Cold Store* across the road is not open in the evenings but is good for lunch and popular for quick snacks, drinks or ice cream. Good take-away ice creams from out front too. In both places few meals top Rs 10.

Other cheaper restaurants include the *East China* (painfully slow service) and the *Impala* (buriyana a speciality) on the Bake House side; the *Devon* on the Cold Store side and the *Silver Dale* round the corner (where I had a terrible meal and some other people I met had several excellent meals!). Popular for rice and curry, the *Old Empire* is otherwise a little grey and dreary — it's down beyond the Queen's Hotel.

Good food, pleasant surroundings, but rather higher prices can be found at the *Royal Park Cafeteria* in the Botanic Gardens — lunch times only of course. If you wanted to flash out in the evening the dining room of the *Queen's Hotel* is an excellent place to do it. For Rs 35 (plus 10% service) you can dine in delightfully "olde English" surroundings on far better food than the real "olde English" places in England would serve up. The set meal includes soup, fish course, meat course, dessert and tea or coffee. Plus speedy but impeccable service. Another splash out place is the restaurant at the *Hotel Thilanka*, 3 Sangamitta Mawatha, only five minutes from the Tooth Temple on foot. Excellent Moghul, Chinese and Sri Lankan specialities.

Kandy — Getting There & Getting Around
There are five trains daily to Kandy — two early morning, one a little later on in the afternoon and a night departure involving a change at Peradeniya. The trip takes about three hours and 3rd class (Rs 5.10) can sometimes be a bit crowded particularly on the early morning departures. The fare is Rs 10.10 in 2nd class, no 1st class on this route although the 1st class observation coach does run to Nuwara Eliya and Badulla in the hill country. Some people say the right hand side has the best views, others the left, either way it's a nice view. You can also go by bus — for a similar cost to 3rd class rail but neither the views nor the comfort are so special.

Around Kandy most of the buses depart from close to the market or on the road down to the railway station. For the Botanical Gardens take a Peradeniya bus beside the central market. A Kiribathkumbara or Pilimatalawa bus from the same location will take you to the Lankatilake Temple. For Katugastota and the elephant bath time take a Katugastota bus from in front of the police station. Buses to Hatton go from close to the Temple of the Tooth — Rs 4 to Hatton, Rs 5.40 on to Nuwara Eliya. Rail fare on to Nuwara Eliya (or rather to Nanu Oya from where you have to take a bus into Nuwara Eliya) is Rs 5.60 in 2nd class.

ADAM'S PEAK
Whether it is Adam's Peak the place where Adam first set foot on the earth after being cast out of heaven; or Sri Pada the "sacred footprint", or simply Samanalakande the "butterfly mountain" where butterflies go to die; Adam's Peak is a beautiful and fascinating place. Not all faiths believe the huge "footprint" on the top of the 2224 metre (7300 feet) high peak to be that of Adam -- it is also claimed to be Buddha's, St Thomas the early apostle of India, and even Lord Shiva's. Whichever legend you care to believe, if any, the fact remains that it has been a pilgrimage centre for over a thousand years. King Parakramabahu and King Nissankamalla of Polonnaruwa provided *ambalamas* or "resting places" up the mountain to shelter the weary pilgrims.

Today the pilgrimage season commences in December and runs until the start of the south-west monsoon in April. During that time a steady stream of pilgrims (and the odd tourist) make the weary climb up the countless steps to the top. Many pilgrims prefer to make the longer, and much more tiring climb from Ratnapura via the Carney Estate because of the greater merit thus gained. It is not only the sacred footprint that pilgrims climb to see. As the first rays of dawn light up the holy mountain you're treated to an extremely fine view — the hill country rises to the east while to the west the land slopes away to the sea. Colombo is only 65 km distance and is easily visible on a clear day. It's little wonder that English author John Stills described the peak as "one of the vastest and most reverenced cathedrals of the human race".

Interesting as the ascent is and beautiful as the dawn, Adam's Peak saves its piece de resistance for a few minutes after the dawn. The sun casts a perfect shadow of the peak onto the misty clouds down towards the coast. As the sun rises higher this eerie triangular shadow races back towards the peak, eventually disappearing into its base. As you scramble back down the countless stairs to the bottom you can reflect on how much easier the ascent is today than it was a hundred years ago — as described in a Victorian guidebook to Ceylon:

●

.... others struggle upwards unaided, until, fainting by the way, they are considerably carried with all haste in their swooning condition to the summit and forced into an attitude of worship at the shrine to secure the full benefits of their pilgrimage before death should supervene; others never reach the top at all, but perish from cold and fatigue; and there have been many instances of pilgrims losing their lives by being blown over precipes or falling from giddiness induced by a thoughtless retrospect when surmounting especially dangerous cliffs.

●

Climbing Adam's Peak

Getting to the base of Adam's Peak is quite simple — there's no need to be there until late afternoon so you've got all day to arrive. Starting point is Hatton which is on the Colombo-Kandy-Nuwara Eliya railway line. It's also on the Colombo-Nuwara Eliya and Kandy-Nuwara Eliya road and special buses run to Hatton from Colombo during the pilgrimage season.

From here you have to get to Dalhousie — the trail starts from the tea factory here. During the pilgrimage season there will be buses direct from Hatton to Dalhousie for Rs 3. It's about 33 km and takes nearly two hours. Otherwise you will have to take a bus to Maskeliya, about 20 km from Hatton, and another the rest of the way — fairly frequent. It's a rather hair raising ride; plenty of unguarded sheer drops on tight corners.

Dalhousie has a whole collection of tea shops where you can get something to eat or buy provisions for the expedition ahead. You can get a place to sleep (part of the night) in one of the tea shops; or try the rather rip-off *Wijitha Hotel*. The bus stops right outside this establishment which has rooms ranging from Rs 10 or 15 on to Rs 50 "tourist rooms" — into which you can pack as many people as you wish. Or you can just leave your gear with the police station by the car park.

Apart from the "usual" route from Dalhousie there are two less used routes from the western side. They are rather longer, much less used and much more difficult — for the last few km they join together. The Dalhousie route involves a climb of about seven km — up steps virtually all the way, it's even lit at night by a string of lights which from below look very pretty as they snake up the mountainside.

With plenty of rest stops you'll still get to the top in around three hours. A 2 am start will easily get you there before dawn which is usually around 6 to 6.30 am. From the car park the slope is gradual for the first half hour or so. You pass under an entrance archway, then by the Japan-Sri Lanka Friendship Dagoba, construction of which started in 1976. From here the path gets steeper and steeper until it is simply a continuous flight of stairs. There are plenty of teahouses for rest and refreshment all the way to the top.

Since it can get pretty cold and windy on top, and you'll work up quite a sweat on the climb, there's no sense in getting to the top too long before the dawn and have to sit around shivering. Bring plenty of warm clothes including something additional to put on when you get to the summit.

NUWARA ELIYA

Situated at 1889 metres (6199 feet) Nuwara Eliya was the favourite hill station of the British who kitted it up like some misplaced British village. The charming old pinkbrick post office, the English country house-like Hill Club with its hunting pictures, mounted hunting trophies and fish, the 18 hole golf course (said to be one of the finest in Asia) and even the well stocked trout streams, all cry out "England".

Nuwara Eliya also has a fair assortment of "olde English" style houses, a well maintained central park which comes alive with flowers around March to May and August to September, and the pleasant Gregory's Lake, encircled by a variety of walking paths. The trout hatcheries are still maintained and all-in-all a retired tea planter would feel absolutely at home. Come prepared for the evening cool — Nuwara Eliya is much higher than Kandy.

Pidurutalagala

Mt Pedro, as it is also known, is the highest mountain in Sri Lanka at 2524 metres (8281 feet). It rises immediately to the north of the town and since Nuwara Eliya is already at a considerable height getting to the top is not so much a climb as a gentle stroll along well-marked paths. It takes less than two hours to walk to the top. The path starts from Keen Rd close to the Roman Catholic Church and there are marker stones at 7500 and 8000 feet.

Hakgala Gardens

The second hill country botanical gardens (after the Peradeniya gardens near Kandy) were originally a cinchona plantation — from which is derived the anti-malarial drug quinine. Later they were used for experiments in acclimatizing temperate zone plants to life in the tropics and were run by the same family for three generations right up to 1940s. Today they're a delightful small garden, famed for its roses and ferns. The gardens are about 10 km out out of Nuwara Eliya (and about 200 metres lower) on the road to Welimada and Bandarawela. The name means "jaw-rock" and derives from the legend that the Hakgala rock, to the side of which the gardens cling, was carried back from the Himalayas by Hanuman, the monkey god, in his jaw. He's been sent there by Rama to bring back a medicinal herb but forgetting which one it was decided to simply carry back a representative chunk hoping that the particular herb would be growing on it!

About a km before the gardens you pass the Sita Eliya temple on the left hand side of the road. The temple is said to mark the spot where Sita was held captive by the demon king Rawana and daily prayed for Rama to come and rescue her. On the rock face across the stream you can see a number of circular depressions which are said to be the footprints of Rawana's elephant. The Hakgala Gardens are an 80c bus ride from Nuwara Eliya and there is a Rs 5 admission charge.

Accommodation in Nuwara Eliya — the bottom end

It may be a passing phenomenom but before you opt for anything else at the cheap end of the price scale check if the *Hill Side Guest House* is still operating. It's on Church Rd, behind the town park, and was run by an English couple rather like a friendly communal household. Prices ranged from singles at Rs 20 to the best rooms at about Rs 50 to 60. In between doubles were Rs 35. Very friendly, meal times are everybody together and help yourself functions. Plus music in the living room, excellent vegetarian evening meals, even hot water.

Otherwise — well there's *Molesworth*, part of the travellers' halt circuit and close to the Grand Hotel. Dorm beds here cost Rs 7.50, plus Rs 2 for blankets if you have no sleeping bag. Nice lounge and garden. Close by is the *Nuwara Eliya Inn* (not to be confused with the expensive Nuwara Eliya Tourinn) where doubles cost Rs 35, 50 or 75 — no singles. The *Municipal Rest House* has rooms at Rs 36 but you must pay Rs 5 extra if you don't take breakfast (Rs 15) and a main meal (Rs 25) here. Finally in the main part of town there is *Pedros* — Nuwara Eliya's rock bottom hotel with singles at Rs 15, doubles at Rs 25.

Accommodation in Nuwara Eliya — the top end

Nuwara Eliya's big hotels are both very much in the old English style and located almost side by side. The 104 room *Grand Hotel* (tel 0522 261) is right by the golf course and costs from around Rs 150 for a room-only single up to Rs 400 for an all-inclusive double. It's hard to imagine anything more redolent of the English colonial era than the *Grand* — until you see the *Hill Club*. It's also hard to imagine that the *Hill Club* could have been any better kept in its British heyday than it is today. Even the old magazines look original! The billiard room, dating from 1876, is the oldest part of the building. There are 22 rooms starting from around Rs 175 for a bathless single, room-only, and running all the way to Rs 400 for an all-inclusive suite.

After those two places everything else tends to seem a little dull but there is the *Grosvenor Hotel* (tel 0522 307) with nine rooms from Rs 100 single;

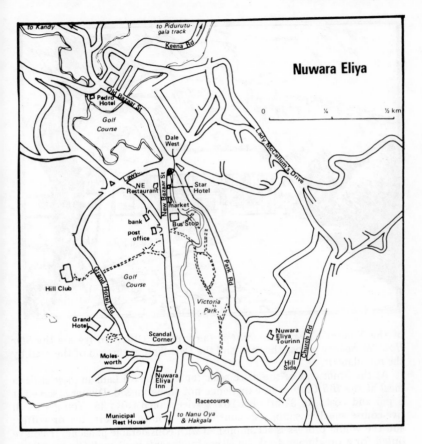

the *Nuwara Eliya Tourinn* (tel 0522 410) at 25 Park Rd with seven rooms from around Rs 300 for a single (room-only). The *Princess Guest House* (tel 0522 462) at 12 Wedderburn Rd also has seven rooms, from Rs 150 for a single. There are a number of other guest houses such as *Princess Guest House* (Rs 150 bed and breakfast double) or *Ferncliff Guest House* (Rs 125). Finally on Upper Lake Drive there are three *Holiday Cottages* (tel 0522 675) costing Rs 100 each, they can accommodate up to six people each.

Nuwara Eliya — places to eat

If you're not eating in your hotel or guest house, Nuwara Eliya has a rather disreputable looking collection of restaurants along the main bazaar street. None of them are terribly appetising looking although the upstairs section

of the *Nuwara Eliya Restaurant* is fairly good. Others to try are the *Star Hotel & Bakery* across the road and the *Dale West* at the end of the road by the roundabout.

At the other end of the price scale (at least the Sri Lankan price scale) a meal at the *Hill Club* is an experience not to be missed. Dinner is served at 8 pm and costs Rs 37.50 plus 10% service; lunch is Rs 35. You get a full five-course meal — soup, fish course, main course, dessert, tea or coffee; and the whole process is accomplished with considerable panache. If you've opted for a pre-dinner drink (in either the "men's bar" or the "mixed bar") you'll be summoned to the dining room when the meal is ready. At your candlelit table you'll be served by white uniformed (and white gloved) waiters. You can retire to the lounge, with its open fire, for your after dinner tea or coffee. All this for less than US$2.50 — although you can soon bump that up if you decide to sample the wine cellar where bottles of European wine run from Rs 180 to Rs 250!

The *Grand Hotel* also has a high class dining area or you can eat rather cheaper at the *Municipal Rest House* and experience their amazing collection of waiters.

Nuwara Eliya — Getting There
From Colombo there are three trains daily to Nuwara Eliya, two of which continue on to Badulla. The break-of-dawn 6.35 am departure stops in

Kandy for half an hour before continuing while the later morning and night departures go straight through. The second morning departure (9.30 am) has an observation saloon as well as 2nd and 3rd class seats; the night departure (8.15 pm) has 1st and 2nd class berths and 3rd class sleeperettes as well as 2nd and 3rd class seats. Fares are Rs 8.60 3rd class, Rs 17.10 2nd class and Rs 25.60 1st class — plus Rs 7.50 for the observation saloon, Rs 25 for a 1st class berth, Rs 15 for a 2nd class berth. The trip takes about five to six hours and offers some truly fantastic scenery on the way through the mountains. Nuwara Eliya does not have a railway station — you have to take a bus (60c) or taxi from Nanu Oya a few km away. If you break the Kandy-Nuwara Kandy-Hatton are Rs 2.60 3rd, Rs 5.20 2nd and Rs 7.80 1st. Hatton-Nuwara Eliya costs Rs 1.40 3rd, Rs 2.70 2nd and Rs 4.00 1st.

●

Tea

Sri Lanka is the world's largest exporter of tea and it is tea which is the cornerstone of the Sri Lankan economy. Yet tea only came to Sri Lanka as an emergency substitute for coffee when the extensive coffee plantations were all but destroyed by a devastating disease. The first Sri Lankan tea was grown at the *Loolecondera* estate a little south-east of Kandy by one James Taylor in 1867. Today the hill country is virtually one big tea plantation for tea needs a warm climate, altitude and sloping terrain. A perfect description of the Sri Lankan hill country.

Tea grows on a bush, if not cut back it would grow up to 10 metres high and would require some very tall ladies to pick the leaves! As it is tea bushes are pruned back to about a metre tall and squads of Tamil tea pluckers move through the rows of tea bushes picking the leaves and buds. These are then "withered" — de-moisturised by blowing temperature controlled air through the leaves either in the old fashioned multi-storey tea factories where the leaves are spread out on hessian mats or in modern mechanised troughs. The partially dried leaves are then crushed which starts a fermentation process. The art in tea production comes in knowing when to stop the fermentation by "firing" the tea to produce the final, brown/black leaf. Tea plantation and factory tours are readily available all over Sri Lanka.

There are a very large number of types and varieties of teas which are graded both by size (from cheap "dust" through fannings and broken grades to "leaf" tea) and by quality (with names like flowery, pekoe or souchong). Tea is further categorised into low-grown, mid-grown or high-grown. The low-grown teas (under 600 metres) grow strongly and are high in "body" but low in "flavour". The high-grown teas (over 1200 metres) grow more slowly and are renowned for their subtle flavour. Mid-grown tea is something between the two. Regular commercial teas are usually made by blending various types — a bit of this for flavour, a bit of that for body. Unfortunately, as in India, the Sri Lankans may grow some very fine tea but they're not always very adept at making a good pot of it. If you've got a taste for fine teas you're best advised to take some home with you.

●

WORLD'S END

The Horton Plains are situated south of Nuwara Eliya, west of Haputale and Bandarawela. They are on a high, windy plateau standing at around 2000

metres (7000 feet). A number of rivers cross this sparsely populated grass-
land and there are many excellent walks — the few roads there are will generally be suitable for jeeps only. Farr's Inn, which used to be a rest house, is
a delightfully old English-style guest house and a convenient landmark on
the plains. From here it is about a five km walk (only the first part of it is
passable by jeep) to World's End. Here the Horton Plains come suddenly to
an end and drop 1500 metres to the coastal plain below. It's one of the
most stunning sights in Sri Lanka but, unfortunately, the view is often ob-
scured by mist. Dawn or the very early morning is usually your best chance
of catching a glimpse of this scenic wonder.

From Haputale you can reach the Horton Plains by taking a train two
stations back to Ohiya. From there you walk along the tracks to the tunnel
then branch off. Farr's Inn can also be reached via the Diyagama Estate in
Agrapatna. Two of Sri Lanka's highest mountains, Kirigalpotta at 2387
metres (7832 feet) and Totapolakanda at 2361 metres (7746 feet) rise on
the western edge of the plains.

Accommodation on the Horton Plains
There are two places you can stay on the Horton Plains. *Anderson Lodge*.
(contact phone 94653) costs Rs 40 and will accommodate up to five people —
you can have the use of the cook but must provide your own food. *Farr Inn*
(contact phone 23501) is close to Ohiya and has seven rooms with room
only prices of around Rs 100/125 for singles/doubles.

BANDARAWELA
Coming from Nuwara Eliya it's a steady descent through Welimada (where
you may have to change buses) to Bandarawela at 1230 metres (4036 feet).
From here you can either head south and leave the hill country from Haputale to the south coast or head north and leave the hills from Badulla to the
east coast. Bandarawela is not of great interest in itself but it does make an
excellent base for exploring other places in the area or for making walks.
About five km out of Bandarawela on the road to Badulla, pause to see the
interesting Dowa Temple on the right hand side of the road. The little
temple is delightfully situated close to a stream and on the rock face below
the road there is a beautiful four metre high standing Buddha image cut in
low relief into the rock. The temple is very easy to miss so ask the bus con-
ductor to tell you when to get off. The turnoff for Ella is eight km out from
Bandarawela.

Accommodation in Bandarawela — the bottom end
Close to the centre of town, but up a rise overlooking it, the *Rest House* is
well signposted and just a few paces beyond the big Orient Hotel. This is an
economy priced Rest House, the four rooms cost only Rs 15 per person or
two people can have room, breakfast and dinner for just Rs 82.50. If it's
full there are a few other possibilities. Right next to the Orient is the *Chi-*

nese Union Hotel — six rooms at Rs 30 double, plus a restaurant. Closer to the town another road branches off and runs up by the very clean and pleasant *YWCA Holiday Home* where there are three rooms plus an annexe available for visitors — couples only. Cost is Rs 15 per person or Rs 30 with meals. Smack in the middle of town you could try *Justin Fernando's*, next door to the post office and across the road from the bus station. It costs Rs 20 a double and has a reasonable looking restaurant downstairs. Or there's the *Himalie Guest House*, a fair distance out of town on the Badulla road.

Accommodation in Bandarawella — the top end
The two top of the top end hotels here are very close to the centre. The *Bandarawela Hotel* is on Welimada Rd, the entrance runs up to it from beside the post office. There are 33 rooms and nightly costs range from Rs 100/115 for room only singles/doubles to Rs 195/305 including all meals. The similarly sized but a little more modern *Orient Hotel* is on Dharmapala Mawatha, the road that runs up to the Rest House but still close to the town centre. Room only charges here run from Rs 150/175 for singles/doubles.

Other places in the upper price category are not so central. The *Ideal Resort* is about a km and a bit beyond the town on the Welimada road. It's an old tea plantation bungalow — a pleasantly spacious and old fashioned place. All-inclusive (it's a long way into town for a meal) costs Rs 150 single, Rs 250 double. The *Alpine Inn* is on the Haputale side of town, also small (just five rooms) and similarly priced. Or there is the *Rovim Tourist Hotel* at Bindunuwewa, again similarly priced, and the *Holiday Cottages* on Golf Links Rd which cost Rs 75 per day.

ELLA
Sri Lanka is liberally endowed with beautiful views but Ella has one of the best. To fully appreciate it walk up through the town to the rest house, up their path and into the garden in front of it. Suddenly the world simply drops away at your feet. In front of you there is a narrow gap in the mountains and you look down from Ella's 1100 metre altitude to the coastal plain nearly a thousand metres below. The road down through the spectacular Ella Gap to Wellawaya, 27 km to the south, was only completed in 1969. Coming uphill from Wellawaya can be quite a struggle for a rickety CTB bus. The railway line from Haputale passes through Ella on the way to its terminus at Badulla. About 10 km out of Ella at Demodara it performs a complete loop around a hillside and tunnels under itself at a level 30 metres lower. There's a model of this spectacular piece of colonial-era railway engineering in the National Museum in Colombo.

Rawana Ella Falls
These spectacular falls are situated about five km down the gap from Ella towards Wellawaya. The water comes leaping down the mountainside in what is claimed to be the wildest looking fall in Sri Lanka. Naturally they

are connected with the Ramayana saga, the demon king Rawana was said to have held Sita captive in a cave, which you can visit, in the cliff facing the rest house.

Accommodation in Ella

A great many of Sri Lanka's Rest Houses are blessed with attractive settings but the *Ella Rest House* tops the lot. If you come from the Badulla or Bandarawela side and walk up the path and across the front lawn, the view of Ella Gap that unfolds before you is simply stunning. The small (just six rooms) Rest House costs Rs 60/80 for singles/doubles room-only or add Rs 14 per head for breakfast, Rs 25 for lunch, Rs 30 for dinner. By contrast the *Ella Gap Tourist Inn* looks rather tame and is no great bargain. Singles/doubles cost Rs 90/150 bed and breakfast. They've got a cheaper room for Rs 25 per person — which is about twice what it should be. You may also find rooms (around Rs 50) at *Sunnylands* about a km before you come into Ella, near the station.

BADULLA

Standing at about 680 metres (2200 feet) Badulla marks the south-eastern extremity of the hill country and is the gateway to the east coast of Sri Lanka. The railway line from Colombo, Kandy and Nuwara Eliya terminates here and if you come by bus you will have to change buses here so either way those heading down to the coast will have to pause in Badulla. It's a pleasant little town, capital of the Uva Province and neatly ringed by mountains. The Church of St Mark in Badulla was built in memory of the British administrator Major T W Rogers who has been described as a "sportsman". Whether that is a correct label to apply to a man whose chief purpose in life seemed to be to wipe out the elephant population of Sri Lanka single-handed, I'm not sure. What is more certain is that some protector of elephants finally decided that enough was enough and Rogers was struck dead by a bolt of lightning while sitting on the verandah of the Haputale rest house!

About six km out of Badulla are the Dunhinda waterfalls — said to be the most "awe inspiring" in Sri Lanka, getting to them involves a 2½ km walk but when you arrive they're a fine spot for a picnic.

Accommodation in Badulla

There is a small, five bed, *YMCA* on Bandarawela Rd with costs under Rs 10 per person. Or try the travellers' halt associated *Uva Hotel* at Rs 20 a double.

Badulla — Getting There & on to the East Coast

Buses run every half hour or so from Nuwara Eliya to Badulla (Rs 4.20), change at Welimada for Bandarawela (Rs 3.60). It's about two (perhaps more) hours in either case and this trip has to go down as one of the most uncomfortable we made anywhere in Sri Lanka. From Badulla to the east coast there are just a few buses each day — sometimes direct but more often the trip involves a change at Monaragala, Rs 3.60 to there from Badulla, another Rs 3.20 to Pottuvil which is only a km or so from Arugam Bay. Badulla is the end of the railway line from Colombo — about Rs 11 3rd class and on up, for the nine hour trip.

HAPUTALE

The little village of Haputale is perched right at the southern edge of the hill country. One of its most spectacular views, which makes its position very clear, is seen coming in from Bandarawella. The road rises up to the ridge which Haputale is built along, crosses the railway line, dips down the main street — then suddenly and unexpectedly simply sails off into space! Actually what happens is that the road makes a sharp right turn at the edge of town and runs along the ridge before dropping down out of the hills, but at first glance it looks like the main street simply disappears into thin air. On a clear day you can see from this ridge right the way to the south coast and at night the Hambantota lighthouse may be visible.

Haputale is a pleasant little town with some good accommodation including one of the best cheapies in Sri Lanka. It also has an excellent market but most important it makes a very good base for exploring other places around the area or simply taking pleasant walks in the cool mountain air. Idalgashinna (only eight km from Haputale and also on the railway line), the Tangamalai nature reserve and the scattered traces of the Portuguese Katugodella Fort (a reminder of one of their attempts to capture the hill country) are all within easy reach of Haputale. It also makes a good base for visits to World's End. If you're staying at Highcliffe there's a book here with a number of interesting walks described. A couple of places to try:

Diyaluma Falls

Heading down from Haputale towards Wellawaya you pass one of Sri Lanka's highest waterfalls just five km beyond the town of Koslanda. If you're heading towards Colombo from Haputale it's only a short sidetrip back from the Beragalla road junction to reach the 170 metre high Diyaluma Falls. The falls leap over a cliff face and fall in one clear drop to a pool below — very picturesque and clearly visible from the road. If you're feeling energetic you can climb up to the beautiful rock pools and a series of mini-falls at the top of the main fall. You can either go more or less straight up the cliff face or go back to the nearby village and follow the ridge line. Either way it's a pretty hard climb but once you're there it's a delightful and secluded spot for a swim.

Adisham

This is a Benedictine monastery about an hour's walk from Haputale, you can bus part way. It's in an old British planter's house, a replica of the planter's Yorkshire home. They take guests here at reasonable prices — a beautiful place and the monks make unbelievably good jam!

Accommodation in Haputale

Haputale's bottom end place is both very pleasant and very popular. *High-cliffe* is in the centre of town, close to where the railway line crosses the main road, it looks directly across the railway line to the Rest House. There are six dorm beds at Rs 7 per person and a number of double rooms at Rs 10 per person. It's an old fashioned and easy going place — food available.

On the other side of the tracks the *Rest House* is definitely not one of Sri Lanka's best. A bit grubby and tired looking and accommodation is only available as full-board, at Rs 143 for two people. The *Monamaya Holiday Guest House* is about a km out of Haputale along the ridge and overlooking the town. A nicely "olde English" looking house and garden with just four rooms and a nightly all-inclusive charges of around Rs 200 for a double *Roehampton Guest House* is on a tea plantation a couple of km out of town towards Bandarawela, again there are just four rooms and charges are similar to Monamaya.

RATNAPURA

The gem centre of Sri Lanka, Ratnapura (the name means "City of Gems") is situated 100 km (63 miles) from Colombo. It's on an alternate route to the hill country, you skirt round the southern edge of the hill country and then ascend into the hills through Haputale. The scenery around Ratnapura is really magnificent and this is reputed to be the best place for views of Adam's Peak. Here you view it from below while from the other side you're looking at it from more or less the same level. Ratnapura is also the starting point for the "classical" (read "hard") route up Adam's Peak via Gilimale and Carney Estate. Less arduous walks can be found much closer to town, even right from the rest house.

A not-to-be-missed excursion in Ratnapura is a trip to the Gem Museum — take a bus (40c) from the railway station to Getangama, it's only two stops. Here you can see the whole process of grading, cutting and polishing stones; inspect a wide range of gems for sale and also see their fascinating collection of gemstones not only from Sri Lanka but all over the world. It's free.

Ratnapura also has a small museum — open from 9 am to 5 pm except on Fridays.

Getting to Ratnapura

Although Ratnapura has a railway station the railway line from Colombo no longer runs all the way there. So it's back to the buses, which cost about Rs 5 for this approximately two to three hour trip.

Accommodation in Ratnapura

The Ratnapura bus station is just off the centre of town, on the rise that culminates in the Rest House. Half way up to the Rest House you will find a sign crying out to the *Economy Travellers* at 28/1 Inner Circular Rd. It's simple and straightforward, a double costs Rs 25 — with a mosquito net.

The *Traveller's Halt* is at 30 Outer Circular Rd, walk towards Ratnapura convent from the railway station — dorm beds from Rs 7.50, doubles at Rs 30 and 35.

Right at the top of the hill road, beautifully situated overlooking the town, the *Rest House* costs Rs 50/100 for bed and breakfast singles/doubles or Rs 100/200 with all meals. There are 11 rooms as well as accommodation for a whole flock of swallows who nest under the porch — a sign warns you not to park your car there. A little distance out of town on the Colombo side, the *Ratnaloka Tour Inns* has 60 rooms, centrally air conditioned, swimming pool and all mod cons. Nightly charges from around Rs 200 for a double, bed & breakfast.

In the town the *Ratnaloka Hotel* (no relation at all) is a good place for a tasty curry and rice for just Rs 3 — go upstairs. Or around the corner from the central square there is the more expensive *Nilani Tourist Restaurant* — it's well signposted. The Gem Museum, out of town, has a pleasant, but rather pricey, restaurant.

●

Gems

Ratnapura is the gem centre of Sri Lanka, every second person you meet on the street is likely to whisper that he has the bargain of all time wrapped up in his pocket. If you're no expert on gemstones the bargain is 100% likely to be on his side of the line, not yours. Gems are still found by an ancient and traditional mining method. Gem miners look for seams of *illama*, a gravel bearing strata likely to hold gemstones. *Illama* is usually found in lowland areas — along valley bottoms, riverbeds, and other, usually very damp, places. On the Colombo-Ratnapura road you'll see countless gem mining operations going on in paddy fields beside the road — but there are far, far more off in the hills and fields all around. Gem mining is a co-operative effort, you can't just set out to dig them all by yourself. You need someone to dig out the *illama*, someone to work the pump to keep water out of the pit or tunnel, someone to wash the muddy gravel and an expert to search through the pebbles for the stone that may make all their fortunes. If a stone is found the profit is divided up between all the members of the co-op from the man who supplies the finance to the one up to his neck in mud and water, clad only in a tiny loin cloth known as an *amudes*. The mines are rarely very deep but they can be vertical or horizontal depending on which way the *illama* runs.

It's a peculiarity of Sri Lankan gemming that a variety of different stones are almost always found in the same pit. There are many different types and varieties of gems and their value depends on a number of factors including the gem's rarity, hardness and beauty. Gems are still cut and polished by hand although modern methods are also coming into use. Some stones are cut and faceted (*en cabochon*) while others are simply polished. The division between precious and semi-precious stones is a purely arbitrary one — there is no clear definition of what makes one stone a precious stone and another only semi-precious. Popular stones include:

Corundrums This group includes sapphires and rubies, both precious stones and second only to the diamond in hardness. Rubies range from pink to red, the latter being most valuable. Sapphires can be yellow, orange, pink, white and, most valuable, blue. You can often find corundrums which contain "silk", minute inclusions which give the stone a star effect particularly with a single light source.

Chrysoberyl Cat's-eye and Alexandrite are the best known in this group. Cat's-eyes with their cat like ray known as *chatoyancy*, vary from green through a honey colour to brown; look for translucence and the clarity and glow of the single ray. Alexandrite is valued for its colour change under natural and artificial light.

Beryl The best known stone in this group, the emerald, is not found in Sri Lanka. The aquamarine, which is found here, is quite reasonably priced since it is not so hard or lustrous as other stones.

Zircon The appearance of a zircon can approach that of a diamond although it is a comparatively soft stone. They come in a variety of colours from yellow through orange to brown and green.

Quartz This stone can vary all the way from transparent to opaque and is usually quite low priced. Quartz can also vary widely in colour from purple amethyst to smoky quartz right through to brown stones so dark they look almost black.

Feldspar The moonstone is almost Sri Lanka's special gem — usually a smooth, grey colour they can also be found with a slight shade of blue although this colouring is rather more rare.

Other Spinels are fairly common but they are also quite hard and rather attractive. They come in a variety of colours and can be transparent or opaque. Topaz is a hard, precious stone and can be very highly polished when it develops a characteristic "slippery" feel. Garnets are a sort of poor man's ruby; light brown garnets are often used in rings in Sri Lanka.

●

RATNAPURA TO HAPUTALE

There is beautiful scenery in abundance from Ratnapura to Haputale, the southern "gateway" to the hill country. Along this route you'll soon realise just how abruptly the hills rise from the surrounding plain. At Belihul Oya there's another of those exquisitely situated rest houses. Here it perches beside the stream that rushes down from the Horton Plains. There's a natural bathing pool in the stream, behind the rest house while out front you can sit on the verandah, sipping afternoon tea, admiring the huge tree and watching the occasional bus cross the stone bridge. You can reach World's End,

A Dutch coat of arms at the "old gate" in Galle
B Dutch built canal in Negombo
C lighthouse/clock tower in Colombo Fort

Farr Inn and the Bambara Kanda Falls, at 240 metres (790 feet) the highest in Sri Lanka, from here but since most roads are only barely passable you'll have to plan on quite a bit of strenuous hiking.

Accommodation in Belihu Oya and Haldummulla
Accommodation in the rest house at Belihul Oya costs Rs 80 for a double, room-only or Rs 220 with all meals. Further on at Haldummulla, only about 10 km before Haputale, shoestring travellers may like to investigate the *Dew Drop Inn*, picturesquely situated and with dorm beds for under Rs 10, also singles and doubles. It's a good base for tea plantation visits.

BUDURUVAGALA — STANDING BUDDHA FIGURE
About 5 km south of Wellawaya, on the road to the coast at Hambantota, a small track branches off the road westward to the huge rock cut Buddha figure of Buduruvagala. A small signpost points the way but although the unsurfaced road is fairly good almost all the four km to the site there are a number of badly deteriorated stretches so unless you have a jeep or a motorcycle you will have to walk it. The half hour stroll is well worthwhile — it's one of the quietest, most peaceful and secluded historic sites in the country. At the end of the track you cross a small footbridge and suddenly a sheer rock face rises before you with a 15 metres (51 foot) standing Buddha figure flanked by six smaller figures.

The figures are thought to date from around the 10th century AD and are of the Mahayana Buddhist school which enjoyed a brief heyday in Sri Lanka. The gigantic standing Buddha still bears traces of its original stuccoed robe and a long streak of orange paint suggests it was once brightly painted. The central of the three to the Buddha's right is thought to be his Bodhisatva (disciple) *Avalokitesvera*. To the left of this white painted figure is a female figure in the "thrice bent" posture which is thought to be his consort *Tara*. The three figures on the Buddha's left appear, to my inexpert eye, to be of a rather different style. One of them is holding up the hourglass shaped Tibetan thunderbolt symbol known as a *dorje* — an unusual example of the Tantric side of Buddhism in Sri Lanka. Several of the figures are holding up their right hands with two fingers bent down to the palm — a beckoning gesture. It is worth obeying for the effort of getting to this uncommercial and unfrequented spot is amply repaid.

A   tea picking near Nuwara Eliya
B   bathtime in the river
C   market stall in Kandy

MP 465 c/o P. O. Box 1135, Colombo.

Govi Buddhist Lawyer father seeks for 24 year old fair good looking Accountant daughter drawing four figure salary a Doctor, Engineer, Accountant or person of similar status. MP 494 C/o P. O. Box 1135, Colombo.

Aunt seeks respectable Goigama Christian partner, 30—36, holding responsible appointment, for attractive English educated niece, accomplished and well-connected, earning over Rs. 450/- in Government establishment and inheriting house worth over one lakh in Kandy. MP 496 c/o P. O. Box 1135 Colombo.

Respectable Karawa parent seeks for pretty graduate (Sri Lanka Administrative Service) daughter (only child) suitable bachelor 45—50 years. Religion, caste immaterial. Correspondence confidential. MP 495 c/o P. O. Box 1135, Colombo.

Doctor come on holiday from abroad seeks partner for pretty educated niece 28 years Govi Buddhist. Dowry Rs. 20,000. MP 501 C/o P. O. Box 1135, Colombo.

Govigama, Catholic parents seek a suitable partner for their only daughter 24 years 5 Feet educated in a Colombo Convent right throughout presently preparing for a Accountancy examination while in a leading Mercantile Organisation qualified in western music, cookery and sewing. Dowry one lakh. MP 502 c/o P. O. Box 1135, Colombo.

Sister seeks for pleasant professionally qualifying Govi Buddhist girl a sober partner age 38—45 well employed. Dowry valuable, well equipped house, property, Colombo suburb. MP 503 c/o P. O. Box 1135, Colombo.

Govi Buddhist father seeks for well accomplished only daughter, slim, tall, 23 years old, third in family, a professionally qualified partner. Assets worth over 3 lakhs. Malifics eighth house. Write with Horoscope & family details. MP 504 c/o P. O. Box 1135, Colombo.

House property, cash, jewellery worth 2 lakhs. MP 448 c/o P. O. Box 1135, Colombo.

Salagama Buddhist parents seek suitable partner age 32—38 for daughter Dental Surgeon Government service drawing over 1200/- monthly. Copy Horoscope necessary. Govigama, Karawa considered. MP 447 c/o P. O. Box 1135, Colombo.

Salagama Catholic mother seeks kind hearted tall smart partner executive status, below 35, for slim attractive well accomplished self employed daughter educated in leading Colombo convent. Reasonable dowry and jewellery. Karawe, Govigama considered. MP 446 c/o P. O. Box 1135, Colombo.

Respectable Govigama Buddhist parents seek a Doctor below 35 for good looking lady Doctor 29 height 62" apply with Horoscope copy and full details. MP 445 c/o P. O. Box 1135, Colombo.

BRIDEGROOMS

Brother seeks partner for handsome divorced brother 37 years with 10 year old child. Highly connected Karawe Christian professionally qualified abroad and holding high position in Government. MP 479 C/o P. O. Box 1135, Colombo.

Karawe, Catholic parents seek partner for son 28 years, Graduate Lecturer permanent with reasonable dowry. MP 481 C/o P. O. Box 1135, Colombo.

Sinhala Govi Buddhist Industrialist non smoker teetotaller with assets worth over Rs 1 million seek educated attractive partner of same caste and religion below 32 years. Reasonable dowry and height over 5 ft preferred. Horoscope and all details required in first letter. Correspondence treated strictly confidentially. MP 484 C/o P. O. Box 1135, Colombo.

Catholic Govigama mother seeks pretty partner with substantial dowry for son 28 handsome medium built presently in Canada,

partner fo
establishe
Engineer
tal assets
in Ceylon
lakhs anc
Rs. 20,000
ligion not
details. M
Colombo.

Indian
nior ret
house in
years, qua
U.K., pres
German :
immediat
as Chief,
22/25 yea
portunity
U.K.).
married a
own Hou
on Holida
religions
ed. MP 34
ombo.

Ceylon
character
back grou
employee
no encum
Character
important
absolute
P. O. Box

Jaffna
Hindu fa
profession
Doctor gi
son an El
in Englan
teetotaller
to Sri Lai
tails with
469 c/o P

Karawa
for 28 yea
cutive a
Ravi, Keti
c/o P. O.

Enginee
ployed in
wants a n
yrs, with
c/o P. O.

Rev. Si
Sinhalese,
LL.B. stu

The Ancient Cities

The ancient city region of Sri Lanka lies to the north of the hill country, in one of the driest parts of the island. The golden age of Sinhalese civilisation reached its peak over a thousand years ago but suffered continual harassment from invading south Indian forces. Despite these problems the Sinhalese contrived to build two great cities and leave many other magnificent reminders of the strength of their Buddhist culture — only to abandon them all. For a thousand years the jungle did its best to reclaim them but major archaeological excavations over the past century have restored them to some of their past glory.

Architecture & Ruins

Sri Lanka's ancient cities have a real lost city story line. After the abandonment of first Anuradhapura and then Polonnaruwa, in the face of repeated invasions from south India, they gradually reverted to the jungle. At times efforts were made to restore them or at least slow the decline but generally it was a downhill slide. Parakramabahu I, the great king of Polonnaruwa, still tried to maintain a foothold in Anuradhapura, even building the Brazen Palace from bits and pieces purloined from other buildings. A king of Kotte and one from Kandy made feeble attempts at minor restoration as late as the 18th century, but overall the ancient cities were little more than a legend when the British arrived. At this time the great archaeological awakening was taking place in Europe but it was not until the late 1800s that the Sri Lankan ruins were effectively excavated. The systematic study of ancient cities began in 1890 with the first Government Archaeologist, H C P Bell, whose truly inexhaustible energy even lives on today. The discovery of some new ruin will still be initially labelled a *bal kalla* or "Bell Fragment".

The ruins display a number of set forms. First there are dagobas — in other countries these might be stupas, pagodas or chedis but everywhere the basic form is the same; a solid hemisphere rising to a point or spire. The Sinhalese variation on this simple pattern is that the "relic chamber" is sometimes raised up above the hemisphere, rather than being buried in its centre. This chamber contains more than just a relic of the Buddha, it is also supposed to represent a model of the Buddhist cosmos. You can see the contents of an excavated relic chamber in the Anuradhapura Museum. The solidity of a dagoba sometimes comes as a shock to westerners accustomed to our hollow churches, designed to hold a congregation. A dagoba is a focus

 Sri Lanka's quality Sunday papers always make fascinating reading for the marriage ads — please supply horoscope and state size of dowry in first reply.

not an enclosure — meditation and worship take place out in the open. You should always walk around a dagoba in a clockwise direction.

Other, more uniquely Sinhalese architectural concepts include the *vatadage* or "circular relic house". Today you can see *vatadages* in Anuradhapura, Polonnaruwa and, perhaps the finest, at Medirigiriya. They consist of a small central dagoba, flanked by Buddha images and encircled by rows of columns. Long ago these columns held up a wooden roof but in all the ancient cities all traces of the wooden architecture have long disappeared and you must get your imagination into top gear to picture how things really were. Only important religious buildings were built of stone — everything else from the king's palace to the monk's monastery was made, at least partially, of wood so the picture we get today from the ancient cities is a very incomplete one. You can see a complete model of the Thuparama *vatadage* in the Anuradhapura Museum.

Another peculiarly Sinhalese style is the *gedige* — a hollow temple with extremely thick walls topped by a "corbelled" roof. Often the walls are so thick that a stairway to an upper level can be built right into the wall. There are a number of *gediges* in Anuradhapura and Polonnaruwa but in almost all cases the roof has long ago collapsed.

The most interesting Sinhalese designs are found not in entire buildings but in the little artistic touches that embellish them. Moonstones, no relation to the semi-precious stone, are one of the recurring elements that you can study at both cities. They're essentially semi-circular stones at the base of stairways or the entrance doors to buildings — like a rock doormat. The design of moonstones follows a set pattern representing the Buddhist view of life with its pain of birth, disease, death and old age. The outermost band is a ring of fire symbolising the state of the world. The next band of animals — elephants, horses, lions or bulls — symbolises the vitality of the world despite its problems and pains. The band of geese symbolise those who leave home in search of the meaning of life and finally in the central half-Lotus those who continue the search find enlightenment.

Guardstones are another design element one sees frequently — they generally flank entrances or doorways with sculptures of cobra kings holding auspicious objects or similar themes. Other interesting figures may also be included in the guardstones including the ever-present dwarves who add a touch of humour to so many ancient buildings. Another element of Sinhalese art and architecture which it is impossible to miss is the extraordinary quality of rock cut figures. It has been said in Burma that the Burmese are unable to see a hill without plonking a pagoda on top of it. Well the Sinhalese seemed, at one time, to be unable to see a rock without cutting a Buddha into it. Some of the best figures include the Gal Vihara in Polonnaruwa, the gigantic Aukana image and the impressive Buduruvagala group in the south of the island.

●

ANURADHAPURA

For over a thousand years Sinhalese kings, with occasional south Indian interlopers, ruled from the great city of Anuradhapura. Today it is the most extensive and important of the Sri Lankan ancient cities but the very length of its history, and equally the length of time since its downfall, make it a more difficult experience to assimilate and appreciate than younger, shorter lived Polonnaruwa. Which is not to say the effort is not amply repaid!

Anuradhapura first became a capital in 380 BC under Pandukabhaya but it was under Devanampiya Tissa (260-210 BC) that it first rose to great importance for it was during his reign that Buddhism reached Sri Lanka and rapidly spread across the country. Soon Anuradhapura became a great and glittering city only for it to fall before a south Indian invasion — a fate that was repeatedly to befall Sri Lanka for over a thousand years. Elara, the last Chola king of this invasion, was a responsible and just man, or so the legends insist, but his reign was a brief one. From a refuge on the south coast Dutugemunu led his army to recapture Anuradhapura for the Sinhalese. The "Dutu" part of his name, incidentally, is from "Duttha" meaning "undutiful" for his father, fearing for his son's safety, forbade him to attempt to recapture Anuradhapura but his son disobeyed him — sending his father a woman' ornament to indicate what he thought of his courage.

Dutugemunu, who ruled from 161-137 BC, immediately set a vast building programme into operation which includes some of the most impressive monuments in Anuradhapura today. Other important kings who followed him included Valagambahu, who lost his throne to another Tamil invasion but later regained it, and Mahasena (276-303 AD) who built the collosal Jetavanarama dagoba and is thought of as the last of the "great" kings of Anuradhapura. He also held the record for tank construction, building 16 of them in all and a major canal. Although Anuradhapura was to survive for more than another 500 years before finally being replaced by Polonnaruwa, this was its acme. In the centuries that followed it was again and again harassed by invasions from south India and the very importance of the city — with cleared land and great roads — make these invasions much easier.

Anuradhapura is spread out and does not have concentrations of related structures like its younger sister Polonnaruwa. Nevertheless there is one important starting point for exploring the ancient city and that is the sacred Bo tree and the cluster of buildings around it.

Around the Sacred Bo-Tree

The sacred Bo-tree makes a convenient centre for Anuradhapura in both a spiritual and physical sense. The huge tree is grown from a sapling brought from Bodh Gaya in India by the Princess Sangamitta, brother of Mahinda, who introduced the Buddha's teachings to Sri Lanka, so it has a spiritual connection to the very basis of the religion of Sri Lanka. It also serves as a reminder of the force that inspired the great building programme at Anuradhapura and it is within easy walking distance of many of the most interesting monuments.

Sri Maha Bodhi The sacred Bo-tree is the oldest historically authenticated tree in the world for it has been tended by an uninterrupted succession of guardians for over 2000 years, even during the periods of Indian occupation.

The steps leading up to the tree platform are very old but the golden railing around it is quite modern.

Brazen Palace So called because it once had a bronze (brazen) roof the ruins of the Brazen Palace stand close to the Bo-tree. The remains of 1600 columns are all that is left of this huge palace — said to have nine storeys and accommodation for 1000 monks and attendants. It was originally built by Dutugemunu over 2000 years ago but down through the ages was rebuilt and restored many times, each time a little less grandiosely. The current rather nondescript jumble of pillars is all that remains from the last rebuild — that of Parakramabahu around the 12th century AD.

Anuradhapura Museum Follow the road which runs between the Bo-tree and the Brazen Palace and you'll soon find yourself at Anuradhapura's excellent museum. Amongst the many interesting exhibits is a restored relic chamber, as found during the excavation of the Kantaka Cetiya Dagoba in nearby Mihintale. There is also a large scale model of the Thuparama Vatadage, as it would have been with its wooden roof. Many fine carvings and sculptures can also be seen plus a few amusing little items like the carved squatting plates from the Western Monasteries. The monks here had not only forsaken the world but also the luxurious monasteries favoured by their more worldly brothers. To show their contempt for these luxury loving effetes they produced beautifully carved stone, squat-style toilets — with their brother monks' monasteries represented on the bottom! Their urinals illustrated the god of wealth, showering handfuls of coins down the hole. The museum is open from 9 am to 5 pm except on Tuesdays.

Ruvanvelisaya Dagoba Continuing north of the museum or the Brazen Palace you soon come to this fine dagoba, guarded by a wall of hundreds of elephants standing shoulder to shoulder. Beside the western entrance to the dagoba platform there are still a few of the original stone elephants left standing, the others are a modern replacement. Dutugemunu was responsible for the Ruvanelisaya and it is said to be the best of his constructions but he did not live to see its completion. As he lay on his death bed, his brother organised a false bamboo and cloth finish to the dagoba so that Dutugemunu's final sight could be of his "completed" masterpiece. Today, after suffering much damage from invading Indian forces, the white dagoba rises to a height of 55 metres (180 feet), considerably less than in its original state, nor is its form the same as the earlier "bubble" shape. A limestone statue standing to the south of the great dagoba is popularly thought to be of its constructor Dutugemunu. On the eastern stairway you can see a stone inscription left by the Polonnaruwa king Nissanka Malla — who also spent so much energy erecting stone slabs in his own city to inform the world of his greatness. This one merely announces that he visited Anuradhapura and restored a few dagobas. Close to the northern porch there is a huge octagonal limestone pillar rising to a height of over six metres.

The land around the dagoba is rather like a pleasant green park, dotted with patches of ruins, the remains of ponds and pools, or collections of columns and pillars all picturesquely leaning in different directions. If you continued walking north you would soon come to the oldest dagoba in Anuradhapura.

Thuparama Dagoba Constructed by Devanampiya Tissa this is the oldest dagoba in Anuradhapura, if not Sri Lanka, and is said to contain the right collar-bone of the Buddha. The dagoba was originally in the classical "heap of paddy" shape (shaped like a heap of paddy rice) but was restored in 1840 to a more conventional bell-shape. It is only a small dagoba, standing just 19 metres (63 feet) high and at some later point in its life was converted into a vatadage or circular relic house. The circles of pillars of diminishing height around the dagoba would have supported the conical roof. Although the Thuparama is an attractive ruin, with a beautiful woodland setting, it suffers from a bad case of the honky-tonks — festooned with coloured lights, banners and flags, all of which detract from its natural simplicity.

Northern Ruins
There is quite a long stretch of road running north from the Thuparama to the next clump of ruins. Coming back you can take an alternate route to visit the Jetavanarama Dagoba.

Royal Palace The Sangamitta Mawatha, the road running north from the Thuparama to the Abhayagiri, runs through the old Royal Palace site. This palace actually dates from after the fall of Anuradhapura as the Sinhalese capital. It was built by Vijayabahu I around the 11th century AD and is indicative of the attempts made to retain at least a foothold in the old capital. Close to it is a deep ancient well and the Mahapali, a monk's refectory notable for its immense trough, nearly three metres long and two wide, for the lay followers to fill with rice for the monks. You can also find a tooth relic temple and a gedige in the Royal Palace area; the gedige is in very poor repair particularly compared to some of the Polonnaruwa gediges.

Abhayagiri Dagoba During the renovation of Anuradhapura this huge dagoba somehow became confused with the equally huge Jetavanarama dagoba — which still causes confusion today because some books and maps say this is the Abhayagiri, others that it is the Jetavanarama. The name means "fearless Giri" and refers to a Jain monk whose hermitage was once at this spot. When Valagambahu fled from the city, before a Tamil invasion, he was taunted by the monk and so, when he regained the throne, 14 years later, foolish Giri was promptly executed and this great dagoba built over his hermitage in the 1st century BC. After a later restoration by Parakramabahu the dagoba may have stood over 100 metres high but today it is only 75

Anuradhapura

metres (245 feet). The dagoba has some interesting bas-reliefs including an energetic elephant pulling up a tree near the western stairway. A large slab with a Buddha footprint can be seen on the northern side of the dagoba and the eastern and western steps have unusual moonstones made of concentric stone slabs.

Mahasen's Palace If you wander off to the north-west of the Abhayagiri you soon come to the ruins of this palace which is notable for having the finest carved moonstone in Sri Lanka — photographers will be disappointed that the railing around it makes an unshadowed picture almost impossible.

Ratnaprasada Follow the loop road a little further and you will find the finest guardstones in Anuradhapura. The design of guardstones went through a number of phases and these, of the 8th century AD, were the final refinement of guardstone design, illustrating a cobra-king. You can see examples of much earlier guardstone design at the Mirisavatiya dagoba. Towards the end of Anuradhapura the Ratnaprasada was the scene of a major conflict between the forces of the current king and the Buddhist monks who lived here. Court officials at odds with the king took refuge here but the king, ignoring the principle of sanctuary, sent his supporters in to capture and execute them. The monks, disgusted at this invasion of a sacred place, immediately departed en masse. The general population, equally disgusted, then beseiged the Ratnaprasada, captured and executed the king's supporters and the king was then forced to apologise to the departed monks in order to get them back to the city and restore peace.

Samadhi Buddha Statue Returning from your guardstone and moonstone investigations you can continue east from Abhayagiri to this 4th century AD seated statue. It is said to be one of the finest Buddha statues in Sri Lanka and this is a site visiting dignitaries and heads of state are inevitably brought to admire. There may originally have been four statues here, flanking the enclosure which at one time surrounded a Bo-tree.

Kuttam Pokuna The "twin ponds" are a little further along this road on the other side. These huge, swimming pool like ponds were probably used by monks from the monastery attached to the Abhayagiri. They are the finest ponds in Anuradhapura and although referred to as "twins" the northern pond, 28 metres in length, is much smaller than the 40 metre long southern pond. Water entered the smaller pond through a *makara's* (dragon-demon's) mouth and then flowed to the larger pond through an underground pipe. Notice the five headed cobra figure close to the *makara*.

Dalada Maligawa Just beyond the twin ponds the road reaches a junction and a right turn will take you back towards the Bo-tree and Brazen Palace area. On your right you soon reach this building that may have been the

original Temple of the Tooth — now located in Kandy. The tooth originally came to Sri Lanka in 313 AD.

Jetavanarama The huge, grass covered dome of the Jetavanarama rises to the right a little further along. Built in the 3rd century AD by Mahasena the original height of this huge dagoba may have been over 100 metres but today it is only about 70 metres — very similar to the height of the Abhayagiri with which it has been confused. An early British guidebook to Ceylon calculated that there were sufficient bricks in the dagoba (it is constructed solidly of bricks) to make a three metre high wall stretching all the way from London to Edinburgh. The dagoba stands on a platform of remarkably uneven flagstones which were a much later addition. Behind the dagoba stand the ruins of its associated monastery — one building has door jambs still standing over eight metres high with another three metres underground. At one time massive doors opened to reveal a large Buddha image.

Buddhist Railing A little south of the Jetavanarama, and on the other side of the road, there is a stone railing built in imitation of a log wall. It encloses a site 42 metres by 34 metres but the building within has long disappeared.

Along the Banks of the Tissawewa

Three very interesting sites can be visited in a stroll along the banks of the Tissawewa tank. This is a pleasant visit to make on foot and brings you back to the Brazen Palace and Bo-tree area.

Isurumuniya This rock temple dates from the reign of Devanampiya Tissa and is one of the most interesting in the city — not for the temple itself, which is now rather smaller than it was originally and has also had some rather less tasteful later additions, but for its very fine carvings. The rock face is fronted by a square pool, fed from the Tissawewa, and it is around this pool that you can see the sculptures. The best known is the "lovers" which is of the Gupta school and was probably brought here from elsewhere at a later date — since it is carved into a separate slab. It dates from around the 5th century AD and a popular legend relates that it is of Prince Saliya, son of Dutugemunu, who forsook his right to the throne by marrying a commoner.

A bas relief to the south of the image house shows a palace scene — said to be of Dutugemunu with Saliya and Asokamala, the two lovers, flanking him and a third figure, possibly a servant, behind them. Another sculpture shows elephants playfully splashing water from the pool and above them is the fine "man and horse" sculpture showing a man and the head of a horse. South of the pond the image house has a reclining Buddha cut from the rock.

Pleasure Garden If you walk behind the Isurumuniya and follow the tank bund you soon come to the extensive pleasure gardens. This royal park, known as the "Park of the Goldfish", covers 14 hectares (35 acres) with pavilions and two ponds skillfully designed to fit around the huge boulders that stand in the park. The ponds have adjacent changing rooms, fine reliefs of elephants on the sides of the ponds, and it was here that Prince Saliya was said to have met Asokamala. From atop the rocks there was once a platform intended for looking out over the tank.

Mirisavatiya Dagoba Continuing around the tank bund you pass behind the rest house and then turn off the bund track to this huge dagoba. There are various legends associated with this dagoba which was the first to be built by Dutugemunu after he defeated Elara and captured the city. One is that he was bathing in the tank and had left his sceptre, containing a relic of the Buddha, implanted in the ground. When he returned he found it impossible to pull his sceptre out and taking this as an auspicious sign had the huge dagoba built. Notice the plain guardstones around the dagoba, quite unlike later carved ones. North-east of the dagoba was the monk's refectory complete with the huge stone troughs, in which the faithful placed boiled rice, as found in other locations around the city.

The Tanks
Apart from the numerous ponds, wells and small tanks — many of which have been filled in to reduce the risk of malarial mosquitoes — Anuradhapura has three great tanks. Nuwarawewa covers about 1200 hectares (3000 acres) and is the largest of the three. It was built around 20 BC and is well away from the old city, the new town of Anuradhapura stands on its banks. The 160 hectares (400 acres) Tissawewa is the southern tank in the old city — the Isurumuniya Temple stands on its bank and the Tissawewa Rest House backs on to it. The northern tank is the 120 hectare (300 acre) Bassawak Kulama — the Tamil word for tank, wewa in Sinhala, is kulam. This is the oldest tank, probably dating from around the 4th century BC.

Other
The remains of two stone bridges can be seen not too far from the Twin Ponds. They once crossed the Malvatu Oya and the Yoda Ela and were so substantial that it is conjectured they were used for taking elephants across. On your way to the bridges you can inspect the remains of the Vijayarama shrine with its 12 viharas. Just north of the Archaeological Museum is a smaller Folk Museum — it's open from 9 am to 5 pm except on Fridays and admission is Rs 1. Slightly south-east of the Ruvanvelisaya you can see yet another monk's refectory — keeping so many monks fed and happy was a full time job for the lay followers. This whole area around the Ruvanvelisaya, Sri Maha Bodhi and Brazen Palace was once probably part of the Maha Vihara — the "Great Temple". Close to the Ratnaprasada, in the north of the city, is the Lankarama, a 1st century BC vatadage.

South of the Isurumuniya there are the extensive remains of the Vessagiriya cave monastery complex which dates from much the same time as the Isurumuniya. Situated off to the north-west of the Bassawak Kulama are the ruins of the Western Monasteries. The monks here had totally forsaken the luxurious life their brother monks often lived — their contempt was evidenced in the squatting plates seen in the Anuradhapura Museum. Here they dressed in scraps of clothing taken from corpses and lived only on rice.

Accommodation in Anuradahapura — the bottom end
Nothing, apart from one of the two rest houses, is very convenient in Anuradhapura. The town is divided into an old (the sacred) area and a new area — with an expanse of fields and the river separating them. Only the Tissawewa Rest House is in the old town-sacred area. All the other places are in the new town and generally not very close to the centre.

There are three popular centres for the shoestring travellers in Anuradhapura — two are a km or two out of town on one side, one on the other. Pick of the bunch is the *Shanthi Guest House* (tel Anuradahapura 515) at 891 Mailagas Junction, about two km from the new town centre. To get there take a Wijepura bus to the Mailagas Junction which is right beside it. Or you can walk from the New Bus Depot but it's a long, sweaty walk if you're carrying much gear. There are a whole series of rooms ranging from Rs 20 for the simple doubles in a separate building (which surprisingly has less mosquitoes than the main house), through Rs 40 for a bigger room with fan on up to Rs 60 for a room with own bathroom. The rooms are comfortable and spotlessly clean but it's the friendly atmosphere, pleasant lounge and extensive menu (with lots of those standard "travellers' eats") which makes all the difference. If only their bicycles were as well kept as the owner's 1931 Austin 7.

On the other side of town, at the junction where the Jaffna road joins the Mihintale road, is *Travellers' Halt*, another in the island wide network and probably the best known since it's often a first stop for travellers arriving from the Indian ferry. Doubles here cost from just Rs 15 and there are dorm beds for Rs 6.50. The third cheapie is the *King's Dale* which is about a hundred metres away on the Mihintale road. If you're coming in from Trincomalee by bus get down outside it or at the junction for the Travellers' Halt. Do not go on into town.

There's a fourth possibility but the *Paramount Hotel* is really for emergencies only since it's rather a grubby dive. Singles Rs 15, doubles Rs 25 and it does have the advantage of being quite central and having a reasonable (if sometimes terribly slow) restaurant downstairs. We had a rather useless and slow dinner and a surprisingly fast and tasty breakfast here. There is not much else by the way of low cost eateries in Anuradhapura. Just across from the market there's an ice cream specialist, *Eskimo House*, which usually seems to be out of ice cream, and a similar place by the Old Bus Depot.

Accommodation in Anuradhapura — the top end

Anuradhapura has two very pleasant rest houses and three hotels which are all clumped together. Plus a couple of up-market guest houses. The *Tissawewa Rest House* (tel Anuradhapura 522) is really quite delightful and has the considerable advantage of being right in there with the ruins. This does have the minor drawback, for some people, that since it is in the "sacred area" they can't provide alcohol — although you can bring your own with you. It's one of those elderly places with class that the Sri Lankans seem to be able to do so well. A big spacious verandah looks out on the garden in the front and it backs on to the Tissawewa Tank. There are 25 rooms and singles/doubles costs from Rs 100/140 room only or Rs 175/275 all inclusive.

The *Nuwarawewa Rest House* (tel Anuradhapura 565) is the second rest house and is fairly convenient for the New Town area. It backs on to the Nuwarawewa Tank and while it is not as "olde worlde" as the Tissawewa

Rest House it is still very pleasant in its own way. In what seems to be Rest House fashion there is an open air verandah dining area. There are 60 rooms and costs are slightly higher than the Tissawewa Rest House. At Mihintale, about 14 km out of Anuradhapura, there is another, smaller, rest house.

The clump of hotels also sits on the edge of the tank, but rather further around and less convenient for the New Town centre. The *Miridiya Hotel* (tel Anuradhapura 212 and 519) is the top Anuradhapura establishment. There are 50 rooms with room only singles starting around Rs 125 and all inclusive costs from around Rs 200/260 for singles/doubles. The *Rajarata Hotel* (tel Anuradhapura 578) is also on Rowing Club Rd and has 51 rooms. Singles start from around Rs 120 (non-airconditioned) or Rs 150 with air-conditioning. All inclusive singles/doubles are around Rs 240/320. Finally there is the *Samara Hotel* (tel Anuradhapura 234) with just 11 rooms and singles from Rs 70 room-only, singles/doubles at Rs 125/200 all inclusive.

Amongst the more expensive guest houses the *Monara Guest House* is at 63 Freeman Mawatha, has nine rooms and costs from Rs 40 single, Rs 75 double for room only.

Anuradhapura — Getting There & Getting Around
Anuradhapura is on the railway route between Colombo and Talaimannar or Jaffna. There are two trains a day running through the city for Talaimannar and four for Jaffna, plus one that terminates or starts in Anuradhapura. The trip takes four to five hours Colombo-Anuradhapura or Anuradhapura-Jaffna, three to four hours Anuradhapura-Talaimannar. Colombo-Anuradhapura costs Rs 8.50 3rd class, Rs 16.90 2nd class and Rs 25.40 1st class — plus the usual sleeper, berth, etc, supplements. By road there are about a dozen buses Colombo-Anuradhapura each day, the trip takes about 6½ hours. There are also about a dozen buses making the five hour trip to Kandy and three or four on the six hour trip to Jaffna.

As in Polonnaruwa the city is too spread out to investigate comfortably on foot. A quick taxi tour would cost about Rs 75 but a bicycle is the nicest way to explore the ruins in a leisurely fashion although concentrated groups are pleasant to walk around. It's a fairly short bus ride out to Mihintale, a taxi there and back with two hours to climb the stairs would cost about Rs 60. As an Anuradhapura taxi driver disarmingly explained it the price is actually lower for tourists than Sinhalese — "because tourists just rush up and down, Sinhalese spend ages".

MIHINTALE
Situated 11 km north-east of Anuradhapura on the road to Trincomalee, Mihintale is of enormous spiritual significance to the Sinhalese because this is where Buddhism originated in Sri Lanka. In the year 247 BC, King Devanampiya Tissa of Anuradhapura was deer hunting around the hill at Mihintale and met Mahinda, son of the great Indian Buddhist-Emperor Ashoka and was converted to Buddhism. Each year a great festival is held at

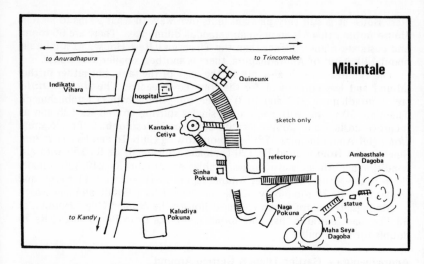

Mihintale on the full moon night of Poson (usually June). Exploring Mihintale involves quite a climb so you are wise to visit it early in the morning or late in the afternoon to avoid the midday heat.

The Stairway
A ruined "hospital" and the remains of a quincunx of buildings, laid out like the five dots on a dice, flank the roadway before you reach the base of the steps. In a series of flights, 1840 ancient granite slab steps lead majestically up the hillside. The first flight is the widest and shallowest, higher up the steps are narrower and steeper.

Kantaka Cetiya
At the first landing a smaller flight of steps leads off to the right to this partially ruined dagoba. Standing 12 metres high and measuring 130 metres around its base it was built sometime before 60 BC. It is particularly notable for its altar piece panels with their excellent sculptures of dwarves, geese and other figures. The dagoba, which at one time was probably over 30 metres high, was only discovered in the mid-1930s and you can see a reconstruction of its interior design in the museum in Anuradhapura.

Monk's Refectory
At the top of the next flight of steps you reach the monk's refectory where there are huge stone troughs which it was the lay-followers responsibility to keep filled. There are also two 10th century AD stone slabs inscribed with the rules and regulations of the monastery. They were erected during the reign of King Mahinda IV. Looking back from here you get an excellent view of Anuradhapura.

Ambasthale Dagoba

The final, narrow and steep, stairway leads to the place where Mahinda and the king met. The dagoba was built over the spot where Mahinda stood and nearby stands a statue of the king at the position where he stood. The name Ambasthale means "mango tree" and refers to a riddle about mango trees which Mahinda used to test the king's intelligence.

Maha Seya Dagoba

A path to the right leads to a higher dagoba which is thought to contain relics of Mahinda. Again there is an excellent view of Anuradhapura from the dagoba.

Mahinda's Bed

Above the Ambasthale Dagoba is the huge stone slab said to be the "bed" on which Mahinda waited for his meeting with the king.

Naga Pokuna

Half way down the top, steep flight of steps a path leads off to the left and cuts around the side of the hill which the Maha Seya Dagoba tops. Here you will find the Naga Pokuna or "snake pool" — so called because of the five headed cobra which is carved in low relief on the rock face of the pool. Its tail is said to reach right down to the bottom of the pool. You do not need to retrace your path to the steps, if you continue on you will eventually loop back to the second landing.

Sinha Pokuna

Just below the monk's refectory on the second landing is a small pool surmounted by a rampant lion said to be one of the best pieces of animal carving in the country. There are also some fine freizes carved around this pool. Do not go back down the main steps, continue on beyond the lion pool and follow the gently sloping track down to the road.

Kaludiya Pokuna

If you turned left on the main road and walked a little southward you will soon come to the turnoff to the Kaludiya Pokuna or "dark-water pool". This artificial pool was carefully constructed to look like a real one and features a rock carved bath-house and the ruins of a small monastery. It's a peaceful, quiet and beautiful little escape. Back towards the village of Mihintale you could search for the hermit caves in the "royal cave hill" or divert into the ruins of the Indikatu Vihara.

Tanks

A casual glance at the map of Sri Lanka would immediately indicate that the island is dotted with lakes, even in the dry northern area. It's a false impression for lake-like though they may be most of them are in fact artificial "tanks". Many of them are around two thousand years old and virtually all of them are over a thousand years in age. Even today they would be quite considerable engineering projects — for their time they are simply fantastic. The tanks were constructed by the great kings of ancient Ceylon to provide irrigation water for the growing of rice; particularly in the dry northern region. They are in many ways a more lasting reminder of their power and ability than the great cities they also built; for the cities reverted back to the jungle whereas the tanks have become part of the landscape. Useful though they may have been, and indeed still are, one suspects that tank building was not purely an altruistic activity for the great kings. Like many other dryland rulers the Sinhalese kings seem to have taken a considerable interest in water and its enjoyment — as the many pools and ponds at Anuradhapura and Polonnaruwa will testify. Two of the greatest tank builders were Mahasena (276-303 AD) and Dhatusena (459-477 AD) who is better known for his death at the hands of his son Kasyapa, the architect of Sigiriya.

POLONNARUWA

When Anuradhapura became too exposed to attack from south India the reluctant decision was made to shift south. In actual fact the Indian Chola dynasty had already established a city at Polonnaruwa but from the time Vijayabahu I (1111-1132) defeated the invaders Anuradhapura was abandoned in favour of the new, more remote, centre. It was Parakramabahu I (1153-1186) who raised Polonnaruwa to its heights, erecting huge buildings, planning beautiful parks and as a crowning achievement building a tank so large 2400 hectares (5940 acres) that it was named the Parakrama Samudra — the "Sea of Parakrama". The present lake incorporates three older tanks so it may not be the actual tank he created.

Parakramabahu I was followed by Nissanka Malla (1187-1196) who succeeded in virtually bankrupting the kingdom in his attempts to match his predecessors's achievements. By the early 1200s Polonnaruwa was beginning to prove as susceptible to Indian invasion as Anuradhapura and despite two further centuries of efforts to stand strong, eventually it too was abandoned and the Sinhalese capital shifted to the very south of the island.

Polonnaruwa stands 104 km (65 miles) south-east of Anuradhapura and 213 km (133 miles) north-east of Colombo. Although it is now nearly a thousand years old it is still much younger than Anuradhapura and its monuments are generally in much better repair. Furthermore they are arranged in a more compact area and their development is easier to follow. All-in-all if you're something less than a professional archaeologist you'll probably find Polonnaruwa the easier of the ancient cities to appreciate. Like Anuradhapura there is a new satellite town built well away from the ancient ruins but Polonnaruwa also has a fair size town right in amongst the ruins.

The ruins at Polonnaruwa can be conveniently divided into five groups: a small group near the rest house on the banks of the tank; the royal palace group a little to the east of the rest house; a very compact group just a short distance north of the royal palace group — usually known as the quadrangle; a rather spread out group further north — the northern group; a small group far to the south towards the new town — the southern group. There are also a few scattered ruins outside these groups.

Rest House Group

The rest house is delightfully situated on a small promontory jutting out into the Topawewa tank. It's a delightful place for a refreshing post-sight-seeing lemonade. The small archaeological museum is slightly to the east of the rest house, above the canal. It's not of great interest but is the place you have to go for photographic permits. Concentrated a few steps to the north of the rest house are the ruins of Nissanka Malla's royal palace — they are not in anywhere near the same state of preservation as that of the Parakramabahu palace group.

The royal baths are nearest to the rest house. Furthest north are the King's Council Chamber where the king's throne in the shape of a stone lion once stood — it is now in the Colombo Museum. Inscribed into each column in the chamber is the name of the minister whose seat was once beside it. The mound nearby becomes an island when the waters of the tank are high — on it are the ruins of a small summer house used by the king.

The Royal Palace Group

Across the main road from the rest house and museum, to the north of the moat, this group of buildings dates from the reign of Parakramabahu I. There are three main things to see in this group:

The Royal Palace Parakramabahu's palace was a magnificent structure, measuring 31 by 13 metres (102 by 42 feet) and was said to have had seven stories. The three metre thick walls certainly have the holes to receive the floor beams for two higher floors but if there were a further four levels they must have been constructed of wood. The roof in this main hall, which had 50 rooms in all, was supported by 30 columns.

Audience Hall The pavilion used as an audience hall by Parakramabahu is particularly notable for the frieze of elephants around its base — every elephant is in a different position.

Bathing Pool In the south-east corner of the palace grounds the Kumara Pokuna, or Prince's Bathing Pool, still has one of its crocodile mouth spouts remaining.

Quadrangle

Only a short stroll north of the Royal Palace ruins, the area known as the Quadrangle is literally that — a compact group of fascinating ruins, in a raised up area, bounded by a wall. It's the most concentrated collection of buildings you'll find in the Sri Lankan ancient cities.

Vatadage Standing right by the quadrangle entrance the Vatadage is a typical "circular relic house", there are similar structures at Medirigiriya and Anuradhapura (the Thuparama). The outermost terrace of the Vatadage is 18 metres (58 feet) in diameter and the second terrace has four entrances flanked by particularly fine guardstones and with a moonstone at the northern entrance which is said to be the finest in Polonnaruwa, although not of the same standard as some of the best at Anuradhapura. The four entrances lead to the central dagoba with its four seated Buddhas. The stone screen is thought to be a later addition to the Vatadage, probably made by Nissanka Malla.

Thuparama Situated at the southern end of the quadrangle the Thuparama is a *gedige*, an architectural style which reached its perfection at Polonnaruwa and this is one of the best. It's the smallest gedige in Polonnaruwa but the only one with the roof still intact. The building shows strong Hindu design influence and is thought to date from the reign of Parakramabahu I. A stairway, built into the extremely thick walls, leads to the roof. There are several Buddha images in the inner chamber.

Gal-Potha The stone-book, standing immediately east of the Hatadage is a collosal stone representation of a palm-leaf *ola*-book. It measures nearly nine metres long by 1½ metres wide and from 40 to 66 cm thick. The inscription on it, the longest such stone inscription (of which there are many!) in Sri Lanka, indicates that it was a Nissanka Malla production. Much of it extols his virtues as a king but it also includes the footnote that the slab, weighing 25 tons, was dragged from Mihintale nearly 100 km away!

Hatadage Also erected by Nissanka Malla this tooth-relic chamber is said to have been built in one day — or 60? — or contained 60 relics?

Latha-Mandapaya The busy Nissanka Malla was also responsible for this unique structure. It consists of a latticed stone fence, a curious imitation of a wooden fence with posts and railings, surrounding a very small dagoba surrounded by stone pillars. The pillars are shaped like lotus stalks topped by unopened buds. Nissanka Malla is said to have sat within this enclosure to listen to chanted Buddhist texts. It stands outside the quadrangle enclosure.

Satmahal Prasada This curious building, about which very little is known, has a very clear Cambodian influence to its design. It consists of six diminishing storeys (there used to be seven) like a stepped pyramid.

Atadage This tooth-relic temple is the only surviving structure in Polonnaruwa dating from the reign of Vijayabahu I. Like the Hatadage it once had an upper wooden storey.

Siva Devale No 1 Southernmost of the quadrangle buildings this Hindu temple indicates the Indian influence that persisted throughout Polonnaruwa's period as capital. It is notable for the superb quality of its stonework which fits together with unusual precision. The domed brick roof has collapsed but when this building was being excavated a number of excellent bronzes were discovered and these are now in the museum in Colombo. The building dates from the 13th century, one of the latest Polonnaruwa structures and actually stands just outside the raised quadrangle platform.

Close to the Quadrangle
Continuing along the road north from the quadrangle a gravel road branches off to the right, just before you reach the city wall. It leads to the oldest Polonnaruwa building:

Siva Devale No 2 Similar in style to No 1, at the quadrangle, this is the oldest structure in Polonnaruwa and dates from the brief Chola period when the invading Indians established the city. Unlike so many buildings in the ancient cities it was built entirely of stone so the structure today is seen much as it was when first built, one does not have to imagine the now missing wooden components.

Parakramabahu Vihara Also known as the Pabula Vihara this is a typical dagoba from the period of Prakramabahu. It is the third largest stupa in Polonnaruwa.

The Northern Group
The northern structures are much more spread out — while you could easily walk around the royal palace and quadrangle buildings you will need a bicycle or other transport to comfortably explore these ruins, which are all north of the city wall. They include the Gal Vihara, probably the most famous Buddha images in Sri Lanka.

Rankot Vihara After the three great dagobas at Anuradhapura this is the next biggest in Sri Lanka. Built by Nissanka Malla, in clear imitation of the Anuradhapura style, it stands 55 metres (180 feet) high. It is situated to the left of the road, about half way from the quadrangle to the Alahana Parivena buildings.

Lankatilaka Built by Parakramabahu, and later restored by Vijayabahu IV, this huge *gedige* has walls still standing 17 metres (55 feet) high although the roof has now collapsed. The cathedral like aisle leads to a huge, but now headless, standing Buddha image. The outer walls are decorated with bas reliefs showing typical Polonnaruwa structures in their original state. The group of buildings around here are part of the Alahana Parivena group — the name means crematory college since the temples and monasteries stood in the royal cremation grounds established by Parakramabahu.

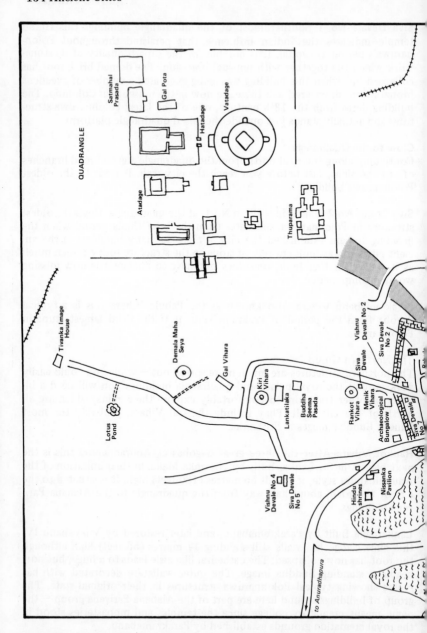

QUADRANGLE

Satmahal Prasada

Gal Pota

Hatadage

Vatadage

Atadage

Thuparama

Tivanka Image House

Demala Maha Seya

Lotus Pond

Gal Vihara

Kiri Vihara

Lankatilaka

Buddha Seema Pasada

Rankot Vihara

Menik Vihara

Siva Devale

Vishnu Devale No 2

Siva Devale No 2

Archaeological Bungalow

Siva Devale No 7

Vishnu Devale No 4

Siva Devale No 5

Hindu shrines

Nissanka Pavilion

to Anuradhapura

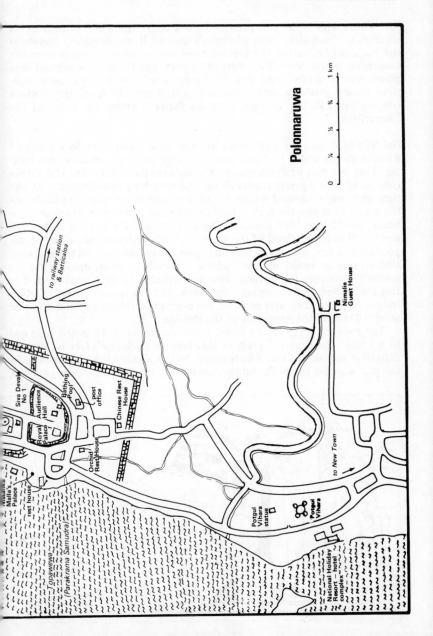

Polonnaruwa

0   ¼   ½   ¾   1 km

Kiri Vihara This is the best preserved unrestored dagoba in Sri Lanka and is credited to Subhadra, Parakramabahu's queen. It was originally known as the Rupavati Cetiya but the present name means milk-white since when the overgrown jungle from 700 years of neglect was cleared the original lime plaster was found to be still in perfect condition. There is also a fine *mandapaya* (raised platform with decorative pillars) and the monastery abbot's convocation hall in this same Alahana Parivena group but south of the Lankatilaka.

Gal Vihara Across the road from the Kiri Vihara you come to a group of Buddha images which probably mark the high point of Sinhalese rock carving. They are part of Parakramabahu's northern monastery. The Gal Vihara consists of four separate images all cut from one long slab of granite. At one time each was enshrined within a separate enclosure — you can clearly see the sockets cut into the rock behind the standing image, into which wooden beams would have been inserted. The standing Buddha is seven metres tall and is said to be the finest of the series. It stands with the arms in an unusual position and this, plus the sorrowful expression on the face, led to the theory that it was an image of the Buddha's desciple Ananda, grieving for his master's departure for nirvana since the reclining image is next to it. The fact that it had its own separate enclosure, and the later discovery of other images with the same arm position, has discounted this theory and it is now accepted that all the images are of the Buddha.

The reclining image of the Buddha entering nirvana is 14 metres long and to my mind the beautiful grain of the stone of the image's face is the most delightful part of the Gal Vihara group. Notice also the subtle depression in the pillow under the head and the sun-wheel symbol on the pillow end. The

other two images are both of the seated Buddha, one is smaller and of inferior craftsmanship within a small cavity in the rock. The other is, like the standing and reclining images, out in the open.

From the Gal Vihara you can cut back around the hill to rejoin the northern road further along on foot. With wheels you have to follow the road along and turn right to reach the final spread out series of ruins.

Demala Maha Seya A typical Parakramabahu truncated dagoba, now largely overgrown, it stands to the right of the road. You pass by the base of this huge structure if you walk from the Gal Vihara.

Lotus Pond Further north a track to the left leads to the unusual Lotus Bath — nearly eight metres in diameter, the bath is in the shape of an eight petalled lotus blossom. You descend into the empty pool by stepping down the five concentric rings of petals.

Tivanka Image House The northern road ends at this image house — the name means "thrice bent" and refers to the fact that the Buddha image within is in a three-curved position normally reserved for female statues as opposed to the more upright male form. The building is notable for the energetic dwarves who cavort around the outside and for the fine frescoes within. Some of these date from Parakramabahu III's later attempt to restore Polonnaruwa but others are far earlier.

Southern Group
The small southern group is close to the compound of new "top end" hotels. By bicycle it's a pleasant ride along the bund of the Topawewa tank over the ancient spillway.

Potgul Vihara Also known as the library dagoba this unusual structure is a thick walled, hollow, stupa-like building which may have been used to store books. It's effectively a circular *gedige* and four smaller solid dagobas arranged around this central dome form the popular Sinhalese quincunx arrangement.

Statue There are various other lesser ruins in the southern group but most interesting is the statue at the northern end. Standing nearly four metres high it's an unusually lifelike representation, in contrast to the normally idealised or stylised Buddha figures. Exactly whom it represents is a subject of some controversy. Some say that the object he is holding is a book and thus the statue is of the Indian religious teacher Agastaya. The more popular theory is that it is a rope representing the "yoke of kingship" and the bearded stately figure is of Parakramabahu I.

Accommodation in Polonnaruwa — the bottom end
There is one very pleasant place out in the New Town, not so bad if you

have a *good* bike to get into the old town with, and a couple in the Old Town bazaar. *Nimalia Guest House* is at No 2 Channel, New Town — double rooms at Rs 30 and also some dormitory accommodation. To get there take an 847 bus from the railway station or the Old Town bus halt. At the junction beyond the New Town statue a sign directs you — it's about a km walk. Good food here, but poor bikes. It's part of the travellers' halt network.

In the Old Town area there is the *Chinese Rest House* with rooms at Rs 20 all the way to Rs 60 depending on the facilities. There is also the rather primitive *Orchid Rest House* with singles at Rs 10 up to the better doubles at Rs 30.

Accommodation in Polonnaruwa — the top end
You've got a choice here of the extremely conveniently and attractively situated rest house or a complex of three recently constructed tourist hotels. The *Polonnaruwa Rest House* (tel Polonnaruwa 515) is on a promontory right by the tank, it's small (just 10 rooms) with room-only costs of around Rs 100 (single or double) or Rs 150 with air-conditioning. Add Rs 70 per person for all meals.

The three hotel complex, known as the National Holiday Resort, is located slightly beyond the Potgul Vihara ruins. Here you'll find three very similar standard hotels — the 21 room *Amalian Nivas* (tel Polonnaruwa 605), the 30 room *Araliya Hotel* (tel 627) and the 40 room *Hotel Seruwa* (tel 667-8). All have rooms (single or double) at around Rs 150 plus about Rs 75 to 100 per person for all meals. All rooms are air-conditioned, the complex overlooks the tank and there is an outdoor swimming pool.

At Giritale, overlooking the Giritale Tank about 12 km from Polonnaruwa, there is another modern hotel complex consisting of the 54 room *Royal Lotus Hotel* (contact tel 24916-7) with all the usual mod-cons and singles or doubles at around Rs 200 room only. Or the 42 room *Giritale Hotel* (contact tel 25984) which is a little cheaper. Also in Giritale, but on the Polonnaruwa road, is the small 10 room *Hotel Hemalee* with singles/doubles at Rs 75/125.

Polonnaruwa — Getting There & Getting Around
Polonnaruwa is on the Colombo-Batticaloa rail line, shortly after the junction where the line to Trincomalee splits off. There are two trains daily in either direction, the train from Colombo splitting into a Trinco and Batti train at the junction. From Colombo the day train takes about five hours but the night train takes seven or eight. Fares are Rs 10.80 3rd class, Rs 21.60 2nd class and Rs 32.30 in 1st. Batti is only about an hour and a half from Polonnaruwa by train. From Colombo there are four or five buses a day, via Dambulla, the trip takes about six hours. There are also five buses daily to Anuradhapura, six to Batticoloa and seven to Kandy (again via Dambulla).

Bicycles are the ideal transport for Polonnaruwa's not too widely scattered monuments. A number of bicycle shops in the old town centre, or in guest houses, hire out bikes — going rate is around Rs 2 per hour or Rs 15 per day. Some of the bikes are the usual Sri Lankan old nails, caveat emptor, etc! Arriving in Polonnaruwa by rail it costs 50c for an 847 bus from the station to the old town and then 30c from the old town to the new town. A car can be hired for three hours for around Rs 75, long enough to have a quick look around the ruins.

MEDIRIGIRIYA

The Mandalagiri Vihara, a vatadage virtually identical in design and measurement to that of Polonnaruwa, is about 40 km from Polonnaruwa and takes a little effort to get to. You may feel it worthwhile for whereas the Polonnaruwa vatadage is crowded amongst many other structures the vatadage here stands by itself. Furthermore it tops a low hill and this adds to the eerie, lost city feel of the remote ruin.

An earlier structure may have been built around the 2nd century AD but the one that stands there today was constructed in the 8th century. A granite flight of steps leads up the hill to the vatadage which has concentric circles of pillars around the central dagoba. The circles have 16, 20 and 32 pillars respectively. Four large seated Buddhas, one of which is still in good condition, face the four cardinal directions. The vatadage is notable for its ornamented stone screen.

Getting to Medirigiriya

Without your own transport, getting to Medirigiriya can be a little time consuming and, as usual on Sri Lankan buses, tiring. Medirigirya is about 24 km north of Minneriya which is on the route between Polonnaruwa and Anuradhapura or Dambulla. To get there by bus involves at least one change — you can bus to Giritale or Minneriya then catch another bus from there to Medirigiriya. From Polonnaruwa the bus fare is Rs 1.20 to Minneriya and another Rs 2 to Medirigiriya. The surprise comes at Medirigiriya because the vatadage is not actually there — it's three km away along a road where buses rarely run. We walked all the way there and three quarters of the way back before a bus came by, fortunately we were able to stow our bags in a tea boutique first. From Minneriya on to Dambulla the bus fare is Rs 2.50.

DAMBULLA

The great rock caves of Dambulla are situated 100 to 150 metres above the road and the village of Dambulla. The first part of the climb up to the cave temple is along a vast, sloping rock face. From the caves you have a superb view over the surrounding countryside, Sigiriya is clearly visible to the northeast, only 19 km away. The caves history is thought to date back to around the 1st century BC when King Valagam Bahu was driven out of Anuradhapura and took refuge here. When he regained his throne he had the caves converted into a magnificent rock temple. Later kings made further improvements including King Nissanka Malla who had the temple interior gilded, earning it the name of "Ran-Giri" — the Golden Rock.

There are five separate caves, the largest of which is over 50 metres long and about 6 metres high. In this cave there is a 15 metre long reclining Buddha. The second cave has many large images of Hindu gods and all the caves are full of Buddha images in a variety of positions and are decorated in glowing colours with frescoes showing scenes from the Buddha's life and events in Sinhalese history. The frescoes are comparatively modern and not of particular significance. As dusk draws in hundreds of swallows swoop and dart around the cave entrances. The temple closes at 7 pm.

Accommodation in Dambulla

There's a fairly limited selection of places to stay in Dambulla and most of them are not great value. The *Dambulla Rest House* is probably the best value although it is the most expensive at Rs 50/75 for singles/doubles room only. It has very pleasant gardens and a cool, breezy verandah where you can sit and sip an evening drink — it's also the most conveniently situated for the caves. Dambulla consists of two parts — one is on the Kandy road where you'll find the caves and the Rest House, then there's about a km of open country before you reach the junction with the Colombo road and the rest of the town.

Right by that junction is the *Rangiri Rest House* where plain and spartan doubles run around Rs 25, it's probably the closest to charging what the rooms are worth, of the Dambulla cheapies. A bit further down is the rather grubby and rather expensive for what you get (Rs 25 to Rs 50) *Motel*. Then the *Wahaveli Restaurant* whose Rs 20 doubles are the cheapest in town and certainly look it.

Finally, and you're now about three km from the cave entrance, there is the *Sayonara Lodge* behind the cinema. It's the nicest place in town after the Rest House but the prices are way out of line for what you get. The rooms are clean and fresh looking and do have mosquito nets but a basic, fanless double costs Rs 40 while the better rooms with fan and attached bathrooms are up to Rs 90 (including breakfast) plus 10% service charge! So, the Rest House apart, Dambulla's not a great place for cheap accommodation.

Getting to Dambulla

Dambulla is 72 km north of Kandy on the main road from there to Anuradhapura, Polonnaruwa and Trincomalee. The road from Colombo intersects the Kandy road about a km north of Dambulla village which actually consists of two parts — the village proper around the bottom of the cave hill and another part around the Colombo-Kandy road junction. Buses pass through Dambulla with the usual Sri Lankan inconsistent frequency but the nearest railway station is at Habarana, 22 km to the north.

SIGIRIYA – THE ROCK FORTRESS

The rock fortress of Sigiriya is one of Sri Lanka's major attractions — it takes a little effort to get there but the experience is well worthwhile. In 473 AD King Dhatusena was overthrown by a palace revolt led by his son Kasyapa. The king, so one of the many legends goes, was walled up alive by his ungrateful son. Kasyapa was the son of Dhatusena and a palace consort while his half-brother Moggallana, who fled to India swearing revenge, was the son of the king and his true queen. Fearing an invasion by his half-brother, Kasyapa decided to build an impregnable fortress on the huge rock of Sigiriya. When the long expected invasion finally came, 18 years later in 491, Kasyapa did not simply skulk within his stronghold but rode out at the head of his army on an elephant. In attempting to outflank his half-brother Kasyapa took a wrong turn, became bogged in a swamp, his troops deserted him and, finding himself alone, he took his own life.

Sigiriya later became a monastic refuge but eventually fell into disrepair and was only rediscovered by archaeologists during the British era. Describing it as merely a fortress does Sigiriya no justice. Atop the 200 metre high rock (377 metres above sea level) Kasyapa built a 5th century penthouse — a rock-top pleasure garden. It is hard to imagine Sirigiya at the height of its glory but at one time it must have been something akin to a European chateau, plonked on top of Australia's Ayers Rock!

The base of the rock, which rises sheer and mysterious from the surrounding jungle, is ringed by a moat and rampart. To the west of the rock an extensive garden was laid out, you can clearly trace its pattern from the top of the rock. A switchback series of steps leads to the western flank of the rock and then ascends it steeply.

Frescoes – the Sigiriya Damsels

About half way up the rock a modern spiral stairway leads up from the main route to a long sheltered gallery in the sheer rock face. Painted in this niche are a series of beautiful women — similar in style to the rock paintings at Ajanta in India, these 5th century pin-ups are the only non-religious paintings to be seen in Sri Lanka. Although there may have been as many as 500 portraits at one time only 22 remain today — several were badly damaged by a vandal in 1967. Protected from the sun in the sheltered gallery they remain in remarkably good condition, their colours still glowing.

Mirror Wall with Graffiti

Beyond the fresco gallery the pathway clings to the sheer side of the rock and is protected on the outside by a three metre high wall. This wall was coated with a mirror smooth glaze on which visitors of over a thousand years ago felt impelled to note their impressions of the ladies in the gallery above. The graffiti were principally inscribed between the 7th and 11th century and 685 of them have been deciphered and published in a two volume edition — Sigiri Graffiti (Dr S Paranavitana, Oxford University Press, 1956) They are of great interest to scholars for their evidence of the development of the Sinhalese language and script. A typical graffiti reads:

> The ladies who wear golden chains on their breasts beckon me. As I have
> seen the resplendent ladies, heaven appears to me as not good.

or a female graffitist;

> A deer-eyed young woman of the mountain side arouses anger in my
> mind. In her hand she had taken a string of pearls and in her looks she
> has assumed rivalry with us.

Lion Platform

At the northern end of the rock the narrow pathway emerges onto a large
flat platform from which the rock derives its name of Sigiriya — the lion
rock. In 1898 H C P Bell, the British archaeologist who was responsible for
an enormous amount of archaeological discovery in Ceylon, was excavating
on this platform and discovered two enormous lion paws. At one time a
gigantic brickwork lion sat at this end of the rock and the final ascent to
the top commenced with a stairway which led between the lions paws and
into its mouth! Today this once sheltered stairway has totally disappeared
apart from the first steps and to reach the top means clambering across a
series of grooves cut into the rock face. Fortunately there is a stout metal
hand rail but those who suffer from vertigo are strongly advised not to look
down. Still, sari-clad Sri Lankan women manage it even on windy days so it
can't be that bad.

The Summit

The top of the rock covers 1.6 hectares (four acres) and at one time must
have been completely covered with buildings, only the foundations of which
remain today. The design of this rock-top palace, and the magnificent views
it enjoys even today, makes one think that Sigiriya must have been much
more palace than fortress. There is a pond, scooped out of the solid rock
and measuring 27 metres by 21 metres. It looks for all the world like a
modern swimming pool although it may have been used merely for water
storage. Also on the summit is the stone throne, also cut from the solid rock,
which faces towards the rising sun. You can sit here and gaze across the surrounding jungle, as no doubt Kasyapa did 1500 years ago, and watch for an
invading army, complete with elephants.

Other

At the base of the rock there is a small archaeological museum and nearby
there are the ruins of associated monasteries and dagobas. If you would like
to know a lot more about Sigiriya including the many points of interest on
the route up the rock, I suggest you try and find a copy of R H de Silva's
booklet *Sigiriya* published by the Department of Archaeology in Colombo,
1976.

Accommodation in Sigiriya

As in nearby Dambulla the *Rest House* is the nicest place to stay. It's right opposite the entrance to the rock and has the usual pleasant Rest House setting. There are 17 rooms, two of which are air-conditioned. Nightly cost is Rs 100 for a single or double, Rs 150 for the air conditioned rooms. Breakfast is Rs 15, or you can stay all-inclusive for 175 single, Rs 250 double. This is one of the nicest rest houses and is a popular meal or snack stop for tour buses visiting the rock — they make excellent sandwiches.

The other upper bracket place is the *Sigiriya Hotel*, about a km around the rock on the other side of the tank. There are 31 rooms which cost Rs 125 single, Rs 130 double, room-only. It has a pleasant open air bar/restaurant and the mighty rock is in clear view but it is not so conveniently close as the Rest House.

For the shoestringer there is not an awful lot of choice. Close to the Rest House there is the *Archaeological Circuit Bungalow*. The rooms are pretty simple but do have mosquito nets and they cost just Rs 10 if there's space available. Or there's the *Sigiriya Camp Site* which is one of those nice ideas which appears to have fallen flat on its face. The site is a long way (over a km) to walk beyond the rock and there you will find a number of "tents" (they're wood and canvas and on permanent bases) which cost Rs 20 and sleep as many as you care to squeeze in. There's an outhouse for each "site" and there are some Rs 30 rooms in the office building. It's so far off the beaten track that nobody appears to use it.

At Habarana, *The Village* is a new top end hotel intended to be at a mid-point location for all the ancient cities — it's nearest to Sigiriya. There are 100 rooms — simple and straightforward, prices from around US$20 for a room-only double. Contact phone numbers are 21101 and 27206.

Getting to Sigiriya

Sigiriya is about 10 km (6 miles) off the main road between Dambulla and Habarana. The turn off is at Inamaluwa, but buses are not terribly frequent, nor do they seem to run very much to schedule. If you are not lucky enough to grab one at the appropriate time the best idea is probably to take a bus to the Inamaluwa junction then wait for something to come by. You may be lucky with a ride or, if worst comes to worst, the Sigiriya bus will eventually turn up. Closer to Habarana there's a collection of tea houses, a popular bus halt, from where you can clearly see the rock a few km away — you could try walking it if you didn't fancy your chances with the buses.

AUKANA

The magnificent 12 metre (39 feet) high standing Buddha of Aukana is believed to have been sculptured during the reign of Dhatusena in the 5th century AD. The Kalawewa Tank, one of the many gigantic tanks he constructed, is only a couple of km from the statue and the road to Aukana from Kekirawa runs along the tank bund for several km. Aukana means "sun-eating" and dawn is the best time to see it — when the sun's first rays light up the huge, but finely carved, statue's features. Unfortunately, after many years of standing out in the open, an ugly (even if it is authentic) brick shelter has recently been constructed over the image. Note that although the image is cut out of the rockface, and still narrowly joined to it at the back, the lotus plinth on which it stands is a separate piece.

The Aukana Buddha is well known and frequently visited despite its relative isolation. Few people realise that 11 km to the west there is another image, also standing 12 metres high although of inferior workmanship. The Sasseruwa image was not completed and is now virtually forgotten in its jungle setting. A legend relates that the two images were carved at the same time in a competition between a master and his pupil. A bell would be rung to signal the completion of the first image — carving them took several years but it was the finer Aukana image, the work of the master, which was finished first and the Sasseruwa image was abandoned by the pupil.

Getting to Aukana

Not easy! It's out in the jungle, not too close to anywhere apart from the Colombo-Gal Oya railway line. There is an Aukana railway halt only a short walk from the Buddha statue but it's unlikely that express trains will halt there — apart from the special rail tour trains that is. Kalewewa station is, however, only about four km away and trains do halt there. You could get an early morning look at the Buddha then catch the 9.48 train from Colombo or the 9.35 to Colombo. By road Kekirawa is the jumping off point on the main Dambulla-Anuradhapura road. Buses run through there with reasonable frequency and from there to Aukana with somewhat less regularity. Supposedly there is one at 8 and 9.20 am though. Hiring a car from the Kekirawa sharks will set you back Rs 50 for a Kekirawa-Aukana-Kalewewa (or back to Kekirawa) circuit.

YAPAHUWA

This rock fortress, rising 100 metres from the surrounding plain, is similar in concept to the much better known Sigiriya. It is only four km from Maho, the railway junction where the Colombo-Trincomalee line splits from the Colombo-Jaffna line, but a long way from anywhere else. Yapahuwa, the "excellent mountain" was originally constructed in the early 1200s as a fortress against the invading Kalingas of south India. For a very brief period between 1272 and 1284 it was the Sinhalese capital under Bhuvanekabahu I and it is believed that it was from Yapahuwa at that time that invading

A elephant bas relief at Isurunumiya, Anuradhapura
B Potgul Vihara statue, Polonnaruwa
C wall painting, Sigiriya

Indians carried away the sacred tooth-relic (now in Kandy) only for it to be recovered in 1288 by Parakramabahu I. A building to the east of the main fortifications is possibly the tooth-temple. Some of the buildings on the rock top are of much more recent construction but Yapahuwa's magnificently carved ornamental staircase is its best point. The porch on the stairway had very fine pierced stone windows, one of which is now in the museum in Colombo.

ALUVIHARA

The rock monastery of Aluvihara is beside the Kandy-Dambulla road just beyond the town of Matale — about 29 km from Kandy and 45 km before Dambulla. The monastery caves are situated in rocks which have fallen in a jumble from the mountain sides high above the valley. It's an extremely picturesque setting — in fact it has even been described as "theatrical". Some of the caves have fine frescoes, there is a 10 metre long reclining Buddha image and one cave is dedicated to the Indian Pali scholar Buddhagosa who is supposed to have spent several years here. It is said that the doctrines of the Buddha were first recorded here, in the Pali script, around the first century BC.

East Coast Beaches

Compared to the beach strip stretching south of Colombo on the west coast, the east coast is relatively undeveloped. The only real beach resort developments are at Nilaveli, just north of Trincomalee, and at Passekudah, a little north of Batticaloa. The east coast's big attraction is that it is at its best when the monsoon is making things unpleasant on the west coast. Apart from beaches there are also two important wildlife sanctuaries and the interesting towns of Trincomalee and Batticaloa.

A   elephant bath time at Katugastota, Kandy
B   Adam's Peak shadow at dawn
C   Kandaswamy Kovil, Jaffna

TRINCOMALEE

The major east coast port of Trincomalee (or "Trinco") has the most convoluted post-European history of any place in Sri Lanka. The Dutch (or rather the Danes because the Dutch sponsored visit actually used Danish ships!) first turned up here in 1617 but their visit was a brief one. At that time Portugal was the dominant European power in Ceylon but they did not arrive in Trinco until 1624 when they built a small fort. The Dutch took it from them in 1639 but promptly handed it over to the King of Kandy with whom they had a treaty. In 1655, treaties conveniently forgotten, they took it back but in 1672 they abandoned it to the French who promptly handed it back to the Dutch. Finally it was the British turn and they took it from the Dutch in 1782 but promptly lost it to the French who turned round and gave it back to the Dutch a year later! Much of this back and forth trading was a result of wars and political events in Europe of course. In 1795 the British were back again and the Dutch, months away from the latest news in Europe, were totally uncertain whether to welcome them as allies in their struggles with the French or fend them off as enemies of themselves and their friends, the French. After a bombardment lasting four days the British kicked the Dutch out and Trincomalee was once again the first British possession in Sri Lanka. Much of the interest in Trinco was due to its immense harbour, hailed by Lord Nelson in 1770 (at that time still a lowly midshipman) as "the finest harbour in the world." The river Mahaweli, Sri Lanka's largest river, which starts near Adam's Peak and flows through Kandy, reaches the sea at Trinco's Koddiyar Bay.

Fort Frederick

Originally constructed by the Portuguese the fort, which stands on the spit of land pointing out into the sea, is still used by the military today. Parts of it are off limits but you are quite free to enter it and follow the road through the fort to Swami Rock at the seaward end of the spit. Close to the gate there is said to be a stone slab, inscribed with the double fish emblem of the south Indian Pandyan empire and with an inscription said to predict the "coming of the Franks". This was just one of several Trinco "sights" which we were totally unable to locate despite a number of enquiries!

As you follow the road through the fort about a hundred metres from the gate a large building with a verandah stands on your right. This is Wellesley Lodge (although nobody in Trinco seems to know it!) where the Duke of Wellington, the "Iron Duke" of Waterloo fame, recovered from an illness in 1799 after taking on Tippu Sultan in India. The boat he should have taken went down with all hands in the Gulf of Aden so his poor health was fortunate for him but not so for Napoleon.

Swami Rock

At the end of the road through the fort you come to Swami Rock, also known as "lover's leap". Since a Hindu temple occupies the end of the spit you must leave your shoes at the gate house. When the Portuguese arrived here in 1624 there was an important Hindu temple perched atop the rock so with typical religious zeal they levered it over the edge. Little wonder that E F C Ludowyk wrote of the Portuguese:

> They laid forcible hands on everything. There was nothing they touched that they did not destroy.

Skin divers have found traces of the temple under the waters over 100 metres below and the temple lingam was recently recovered and is now mounted in the new temple precincts. The present temple is a comparatively recent construction since the British would not allow local people within the fort for many years. There is a *puja* here every evening to which visitors (barefoot of course) are quite welcome; it's especially colourful on Fridays.

The "lover's leap" label came from a story of a Dutch official's daughter who, watching her faithless lover sail away, decided to make the fatal leap. In actual fact the official erected the pillar in his daughter's memory simply because he was rather fond of her — eight years after her supposed romantic demise and the column's erection she married for the second time.

Fort Ostenberg & Admiralty House

You will need special permission if you wish to visit this restricted area. On the lawns of Admiralty House, another British construction, there is a huge Banyan tree said to be large enough to shelter 1000 people. Amongst the British admirals who have stayed there was Sir Charles Austen, younger brother of novelist Jane Austen.

Other

Trinco has one of the few Vishnu temples to be seen in Sri Lanka. It also has a large Chinese population, another rarity outside of Colombo. If you can find St Stephen's Cemetery (we weren't sure if we could or couldn't) then you might also be able to find the grave of P B Molesworth the first manager of Sri Lanka's railway systems who, in his spare time, dabbled in astronomy and while living in Trinco discovered the famous Red Spot on Jupiter — didn't know that did you? Across the other side of Koddiyar Bay a stone at the foot of an old tree near Mutur announces:

> This is the White Man's Tree, under which Robert Knox, Captain of the ship *Ann* was captured AD 1660. Knox was held captive by the Kandyan king for 19 years. This stone was placed here in 1893.

In actual fact it was Robert Knox's father (Robert Knox Snr) who was captain of the *Ann* and Robert Knox Jnr who spent 19 years in Kandy — see "Books" for more information. There is a reasonably regular launch service from Trinco to Mutur where there is also a good rest house. A short distance

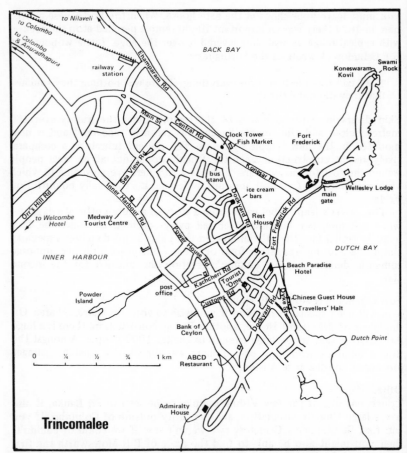

Trincomalee

beyond Mutur you come to Seruwawila dagoba dating back to the third century BC. Legend also relates that the Kanniyai hot springs, only eight km out of Trinco, were placed there by Vishnu to distract the demon king Ravana who named them after his mother, thinking that she had died.

The lighthouse at the southern point of Koddiyar Bay, Foul Point, affords a fine view over the bay. Getting round to this side of the bay involves either a boat trip or a long series of ferry crossings by land. There are a number of pleasant islands in the bay, particularly Sober Island which is popular locally for picnic excursions, and a number of good beaches. Dutch Bay, right in Trinco, can suffer from a very dangerous undertow so take great care if swimming there. The best beaches in the Trinco area are north of the city, particularly at Nilaveli.

Accommodation in Trincomalee — the bottom end

Trinco has a lot of cheap places but few in the middle range. If you're looking for a double room in the Rs 20 to Rs 50 range (and the Rs 50 places are not much better than the Rs 20 places) there's plenty to choose from particularly near Dutch Bay. Almost next door to the Rest House on Dockyard Rd there is *Beach Paradise* where reasonably clean, if rather spartan and drab, doubles cost Rs 20. The engagingly named, if very unspecial, *Tourist 'Ome* is a little back off the main road.

If you carry on another hundred metres or so, keeping close to the waterfront on Dyke Rd, you will come to the *Chinese Rest House* which has a variety of rooms — doubles, again fairly spartan, cost Rs 25. Almost next door, and also backing on to the beach, is the *Travellers' Halt* where dorm beds cost Rs 5, doubles Rs 20. Unlike the Chinese Rest House it does not do food.

More cheapies can be found scattered around Trinco — particularly near the bus station and over on Inner Harbour Rd on the inner harbour side where the *Medway Tourist Centre* has doubles for Rs 30 — pleasant rooms with mosquito nets but a rather run down (if reasonably clean) toilet block.

There is not a great choice of food places although the Medway has the *Sunlaing Restaurant* with not too special food. The *ABCD Chinese Restaurant* looks good but on one try the food certainly wasn't. On the other hand the *Beach Paradise Hotel* had surprisingly good food in their restaurant — the Rs 10 boiled crab is a real taste treat. A couple of other places are good for a snack — ice cream and milk shakes in a duo of snack bars on Dockyard Rd towards the bus station; good curd and honey at the Sirasera store just down from the ABCD. And plenty of local boutiques for a cheap rice and curry near the bus station.

Accommodation in Trincomalee — the top end

Top end accommodation in Trinco is really out at the beach at Nilaveli, 15 or so km away. If you want to stay in the town, or at least closer to it, you have two choices. The *Welcombe Hotel* (tel 373) on Orr's Rd used to be a British Officer's club in the days when this was a big British naval base. There are 36 rooms with singles at around Rs 100 room-only, doubles at Rs 150. The other hotel is the new 75 room *Hotel Club Oceanic* (tel 600) on the beach at Uppuveli, about six km out of the city. Rooms, single or double, start at around US$28.

Getting to Trincomalee

There are two daily trains to Trinco from Colombo, taking about nine hours if you travel overnight or six to seven if you take the early morning departure. Fares from Colombo are Rs 12.30 3rd class, Rs 24.50 2nd class and Rs 36.70 in 1st. By bus it takes about seven hours and there are four buses each day. Buses run frequently from Trinco to Anuradhapura, fare is Rs 7. The short bus ride up the coast to Nilaveli costs just Rs 1.50 but short though it is (or should be) that went down as another Sri Lankan bus disaster when we did it — even the bus driver was complaining about his vehicle's grossly over-loaded condition.

NILAVELI

The beautiful beach of Nilaveli stretches for quite a distance north of Trincomalee. The village itself is found around the 9th milepost but the places to stay are concentrated around the 11th milepost (the more expensive ones) and the 13th milepost (the cheaper ones). Nilaveli has three more expensive places, a handful of high-medium price places, and a dea th of cheap accommodation. A stay at Nilaveli is really just a pleasant spell of suntan collecting. You can hire a boat (around Rs 35 per person, minimum of three people, from one of the hotels) and get out to Pigeon Island. It used to be used for gunnery practise in the British Navy but today is better used for skin diving and spear fishing. You could probably negotiate with one of the local fishermen to be taken out rather more cheaply.

Accommodation in Nilaveli — the top end

The two premier places share a common turnoff at about the 11th milepost. The road runs about a km and a half from the sea at this point so it is a long way down to these two side-by-side and very similar beachfront hotels. The *Nilaveli Beach Hotel* (tel Nilaveli 05) has 39 rooms, all the usual conveniences, and costs from around Rs 180 for a single, room-only up to around Rs 250/380 for an all-inclusive single/double. Since there is no other place to eat out here apart from at the hotels visitors virtually have to opt for the all-inclusive tariff. The *Moonlight Beach Lodge* (tel 25894) has 32 rooms and is slightly more expensive — room only single for Rs 225, singles/doubles at around Rs 280/380 all-inclusive.

The third, more expensive place is a couple of km further on where the road crosses a large lagoon. Here you'll find the *Blue Lagoon Hotel*, just before the bridge. Doubles cost Rs 120 or with full (and filling) board it is Rs 250. The hotel consists of a number of two roomed units — each with its own verandah. There are big, mosquito netted beds (Nilaveli has powerful mosquitoes) and each comfortable room has its own bathroom — only four of the rooms have fans though. The Blue Lagoon Hotel has the best of both worlds, the beach right in front of it and the calm waters of the lagoon to one side. It's a pleasant, relaxing place to stay and the food is quite good and certainly filling!

Accommodation in Nilaveli — the bottom end

If you crossed the lagoon bridge, just after the Blue Lagoon Hotel, about a hundred metres on your right is virtually the only real cheapie in Nilaveli. The *Trails End Rest House* at Kumburupiddy (the actual village of that name is a couple of km inland) has room for about seven or eight people in friendly if a little cramped and spartan conditions for just Rs 7.50 per bed.

It's a washing-from-the-well style of life but if you can face that then it's a very pleasant and relaxed place to drop-out for a while. There really is nothing much else to do at Nilaveli apart from laze on the beach.

There are a number of guest house places along the beach but none of them are terribly good value. *Siesta Cottage* is Rs 125 for a double. The *Beach Bungalow* has a six bed unit at Rs 100 or a four bed room at Rs 50. The *Night Jar* is only available if you book the whole place — it takes eight to twelve people at Rs 50 per person bed & breakfast.

KALKUDAH-PASSEKUDAH
The major tourist development on the east coast is at Passekudah Beach, about 30 km north of Batticaloa or 65 km south of Trincomalee — if you could easily travel down the coast. Due to all the ferry crossings just south of Trinco the usual road route turns inland at Kalkudah to the railway station at Valachchenai. The beach at Passekudah is less than a km off the road from the junction at Kalkudah.

There's a fine beach at Kalkudah too, but it's not the wide, reef protected sort of bay you find at Passekudah. The Kalkudah headland juts out to separate the Kalkudah Beach from the golden sweep of Passekudah where the reef turns the bay into a calm, blue, shallow swimming area.

This region was badly hit by the late '78 cyclone and although the resort was rapidly rebuilt it will be a long time before the tree cover regenerates. Until then natural shade will be at a premium on the beach. The intention here is to have a high class development to attract the big-spending European package tourists but there are also plenty of cheaper places to stay, particularly back from the beach. This package orientation has another benefit for the independent traveller — since the "season" officially starts on the first of April the resort is virtually deserted prior to that date; even though the monsoon can be finished much earlier and the weather may be just fine.

Accommodation in Kalkudah — the bottom end
There's a neat division here; the cheap places are in Kalkudah while the expensive ones are at Passekudah. There is quite a selection of cheapies although not so conveniently situated for the beach. About a km (probably less) along the Kalkudah-Batticaloa road, close to the beach, you will find *Sandyland* where rooms run from Rs 20 up to a pleasant cabana with its own bathroom for Rs 35 — probably rather more at the height of the season. Lots of villagers around the Kalkudah junction have rooms on offer but other guest houses are all strung along the Kalkudah-Valachchenai road.

First of all there's the fairly primitive *Mala Guest House* right on the corner — rooms and a cabana for Rs 15 and Rs 20. A km or so along the road there's the similar *Honalulu Travellers' Halt* (that's how it's spelt) on the left and the very pleasant *Safari Cottages* on the right. Individual little

cabanas around a swimming pool, moderately priced at the latter.

A bit less than a km further you come to the *Kalkudah Hotel*, part of the Travellers' Halt network. Dorm beds from Rs 10, rooms from Rs 20 to Rs 35. Virtually next door is the spotlessly clean and very well run *Sunflower Guest House* with excellent rooms at Rs 30, 40 and 50. Very good food here too and, like other places, you can hire bikes.

If you are shoestringing it at one of these places you will be wise to take your own refreshments if you head off to Passekudah beach for the day — you will find drinks at the beach hotels are rather expensive.

Accommodation in Passekudah — the top end

All the Passekudah hotels were badly damaged by the cyclone — particularly the *Rest House* (which is actually on the Kalkudah corner) which looked like being out of operation for some time to come. There are three upper-bracket places, all fronting right on to the excellent beach — all three were badly damaged by the cyclone but quickly repaired. At the Kalkudah end of the sweep of beach you will find the 16 room *Sun Tan Beach Hotel* — separate cabanas costing Rs 250 single, Rs 350 double.

The other two hotels are more or less in the centre of the bay — side by side and rather similar in design and feel. The *Imperial Oceanic Hotel* is the larger of the two with 66 rooms priced at Rs 300/350 singles/doubles room only or up towards Rs 500 all inclusive. Like the smaller, but similarly equipped and priced, *Sun and Fun Hotel*, it's open and airy making maximum use of white paint and tiled floors.

Transportation — Trincomalee-Kalkudah-Batticaloa

On the map there's a straightforward route down the coast between the two major east coast ports. In practise the coastal route is rarely used and you'll have to loop inland to the ancient city area, then back to the coast, whether you travel by bus or rail. The reason for this roundabout route is the series of lengthy, time consuming ferry crossings you would have to make if travelling by road. They're all close to Trincomalee but effectively discourage a straight through bus connection. The road does run along the coast between Kalkudah and Batticaloa though.

If you're going to pause in Kalkudah you'll find it initially a rather confusing place. Buses terminate in Valachchenai, about three or four km from Kalkudah. So heading south you then have to take another bus on to Batticaoloa, or even the few km to Kalkudah. Some of the cheaper hotels are found along the Valachchenai-Kalkudah road so if you're heading north from Batticaloa don't hop off the bus at Kalkudah, unless you're planning to

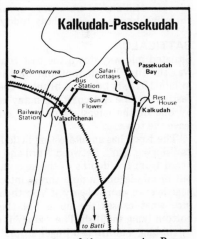

Kalkudah-Passekudah

to Polonnaruwa
Safari Cottages
Bus Station
Passekudah Bay
Rest House
Kalkudah
Sun Flower
Railway Station
Valachchenai
to Batti

stay at one of the expensive Passekudah hotels. The cheapies are generally a km or so after the Kalkudah corner. If you arrive in Valachchenai by train you'll find yourself a couple of km from the bus station so that much further away from Kalkudah.

There are three buses and two trains a day between Batti and Polonnaruwa — coming from Colombo the trains divide at Gal Oya for Batti or Trinco; in the other direction the Batti and Trinco trains join here. Valachchenai-Polonnaruwa train fare is Rs 4.90, third class.

●

A cyclone devestated the Batticaloa area on 23 November 1978. The winds started building up in the afternoon and soon after 6 pm trees started to fall, the wind grew steadily worse until at 9 to 9.30 pm the eye of the storm passed over. An hour or so later the eye had passed and the winds started again with equal ferocity but in the opposite direction and continued until 4 am after which it tapered off. A Batticaloa resident told me how his family sheltered under a central arch in their house — protecting their heads from flying tiles with umbrellas and pillows after the roof flew off. His 84 year old grandfather said it was the worst storm in his life. In Kalkudah his brother sheltered with 60 to 80 local residents under the concrete roofed verandah of an estate house (now the *Sun Flower Guest House*) after all the other neighbouring houses had been flattened. Electricity was not restored to Batticaloa until February 1979 and rebuilding will be a long, slow process. Millions of trees were uprooted, depriving thousands of people of their livelihoods — particularly toddy tappers.

●

BATTICALOA

Situated mid-way down the east coast road Batticaloa (Batti to its friends) was the first Dutch foothold on the island in 1602. Much more recently, in late 1978, it bore the brunt of the disastrous cyclone that devastated the east coast. The east coast has many lagoons and Batti is virtually surrounded by one of the largest. You must cross bridges and causeways to enter or leave the town.

The town has an interesting little Dutch fort but Batti is most famous for its "singing fish". Between April and September a distinct, deep note can be heard from the depths of the lagoon. It is strongest on full moon nights and out in mid-lagoon a pole thrust into the lagoon bottom will permit you to hear it even more clearly if you then hold the pole to your ear. Nobody is sure what causes the noise but theories range from shoals of catfish to bottom lying shellfish. The "song" is described as the type of noise produced by rubbing a moistened finger around the rim of a wineglass.

Accommodation in Batticaloa

The November '78 cyclone virtually shut down Batti; it was well into '79 before electricity and water supplies were restored and both the larger places to stay were badly damaged. On Trincomalee Rd, between the railway station and the bus halt, the *Orient Hotel* was de-roofed by the storm. It has 12 rooms and costs about Rs 30 per person, room only.

The *Rest House* is situated right beside the old Dutch Fort on the bus stand side of the river. It was virtually demolished by the cyclone and will require more-or-less a total rebuild. The smaller *Grand Eastern Hotel* survived relatively unscathed — it's the cheapest of the three places in Batti and can be found directly across the river from the bus halt. For food in Batti the Orient Hotel's downstairs restaurant (which also survived the storm) is a good bet.

ARUGAM BAY & POTTUVIL

The coastal road runs a little further south from Arugam Bay but effectively this is the end of the east coast road. From Pottuvil you have to head inland to Badulla and the hill country or skirt round the Yala park to rejoin the coast at Hambantota. Pottuvil is the junction town but it's a dreary little place and Arugam Bay 2½ km to the south, is the place to stay. There's a wide, sweeping beach with crashing surf that can be dangerous for the unwary swimmer. A small fishing village can be visited just south of the lagoon mouth. Arugam Bay is a good base for visits to the Lahugala wildlife sanctuary.

Accommodation in Arugam Bay

Arugam Bay is about 2½ km (1½ miles) from the town of Pottuvil and unless you have been fortunate enough to arrive at an appropriate time for one of the Panama buses (or have your own transport) you may well have to walk it. The bay itself is backed by a huge, flat, shallow lagoon which is separated from the sea by a narrow strip of sand. On the Pottuvil side of the bridge across the lagoon mouth there are three places to stay.

First of all there's the *Cuckoo's Nest Rest House* where a dorm bed (supply your own sleeping bag, it's bed only) costs just Rs 5. It's a fairly primitive, electricity-less place. Right next door there's the very comfortable *Arugam Bay Rest House* which has five rooms and costs Rs 30 per person room only — for foreigners, locals pay just Rs 7.50. It's very pleasantly situated and comfortable although a little lacking in the friendliness that seems to characterise most Rest Houses. Food can be a little variable too although one possible taste treat here is wild boar — they are said to be far too numerous in the Arugam Bay area.

Finally, another hundred metres along, there's the *Seasands* where rooms cost Rs 50 single, Rs 90 double for room only — meals are available. If you crossed the bridge you would find yourself in the small fishing village where, if you don't mind the discomfort of not having electricity or running water, you can get a room in a village house for Rs 10 or less.

Transportation — Batticaloa-Arugam Bay

The road hugs the coast from Batticaloa south to Potuvil (just before Arugam Bay) where it turns inland to Badulla and the hill country. At times it actually runs on causeways along narrow sand spits separating the sea from the vast lagoons that are found all along this coast. There are a number of small villages, a fair size town (Akkaraipattu) and some wide open stretches of beach along the 107 km (67 mile) trip. If you want to stop there are on-the-beach rest houses at Kalmunai and a little south of Akkaraipattu. Bus fare for the trip is Rs 5.40, it should take about four hours. There are four buses daily, from Arugam Bay they're all before noon.

LAHUGALA SANCTUARY

Only 15 km inland from Pottuvil, Lahugala is renowned for its superb variety of birdlife and its equally crowded elephant herds. The lush green pastures watered by the Mahawewa and Kitulana tanks attract elephants at any time of year but around August, when the dry season drought has dried out surrounding areas, the elephants start to move in, eventually forming the largest concentrations to be seen anywhere in Sri Lanka. With the October rains most of them drift back to their regular haunts but throughout the year you can see herds of elephants here even from the main road as your bus passes by. Lahugala also has the ruined Magul Maha Vihara, one of the most evocatively "lost in the jungle" ruins in Sri Lanka. It's located about four km back towards Pottuvil and a km south of the ruins you can see the remains of a circular structure which may have been an elephant stable.

Jaffna & the North

The North

The North of Sri Lanka is the least visited region of the entire country. It's a contrast to the rest of the country both in the general landscape, the people and their religion. Although the south Indian Tamils can be found all over Sri Lanka, this is the region where they predominate. For the visitor the north means basically just two areas: the Jaffna peninsula at the extreme northern tip and the island of Mannar which is the ferry arrival and departure point from India.

Jaffna

The Jaffna peninsula is a considerable contrast to the rest of Sri Lanka both in its climate and landscape, and in its people and culture. Whereas the south of the island is lush and green the Jaffna region is dry and sometimes barren. Where the Sinhalese of the south are Buddhists and easy-going, sometimes almost to an extreme, the Tamils of the north are Hindus and industrious, often to the annoyance of the Sinhalese! The population of the peninsula is about 750,000 and it is the least visited region of Sri Lanka.

The peninsula is actually almost an island, only the narrow causeway known as Elephant Pass, for once elephants did wade across the shallow lagoon here, connects Jaffna with the rest of Sri Lanka. Jaffna is low lying, much of it covered by shallow lagoons, and has a number of interesting islands dotted offshore. In all it covers 2560 square km (999 square miles).

Jaffna has always been greatly effected by its proximity to India and Indian culture still has a strong influence on the region. Jaffna was the last Portuguese stronghold on the island and they only lost it to the Dutch after a long and bitter struggle in 1658. As elsewhere on the island the Portuguese had made themselves less than popular with the local population and a disgruntled local leader brought the Dutch forces by an overland route to the town of Jaffna. The Portuguese, expecting an assault from the sea, were taken by surprise and 4000 of them squeezed into their fort, designed to hold only 200. Despite lack of space and provisions they held out against the Dutch seige for over three months — until one in every three was dead and every cat and dog had been eaten. Even on surrender they insisted that they should depart with banners flying, muskets loaded and with a field piece. But, reported a Dutch observer, they were so weakened by their long ordeal that: "the enemy found themselves unequal to dragging the desired gun".

Jaffna Fort
The fort, built in 1680 by the Dutch, is perfectly preserved and is probably the best example in Asia of the typical Dutch fortification pattern of that period — a grass covered mound, surrounded by the moat, from which the fort rises. It was a grander and more heavily armed fort than that of their headquarters in Batavia (Jakarta), Indonesia. The star-shaped fort occupies a total of 22 hectares (55 acres) and was built over the earlier Portuguese fort. The outerworks were constructed over a century after the innerworks, just three years before it was quietly handed over to the British in 1795.

Jaffna Fort is not a walled city like Galle in the south, it was built purely and simply as a fort and most of the buildings within are much as the Dutch left them. They include the now deserted and little used Groote Kerk dating from 1706. If you ask in the Jaffna Archaeological Museum someone will accompany you across to the old church and unlock the doors. Inside the floor is paved with tombstones, some as old as 1606. Close to the church, but up on the outer fort wall, is a small house dating from the British period in which Leonard Woolf, Virginia Woolf's husband, lived for some time. It features in his autobiography *Growing*. Also within the fort the King's House, one time residence of the Dutch commander, is an excellent example of Dutch architecture of the period.

Archaeological Museum
Jaffna has an interesting little museum (itself a fine old Dutch building) on Main St, no distance at all from the rest house. Amongst the exhibits are some from the archaeological excavations currently taking place at Kantaro-

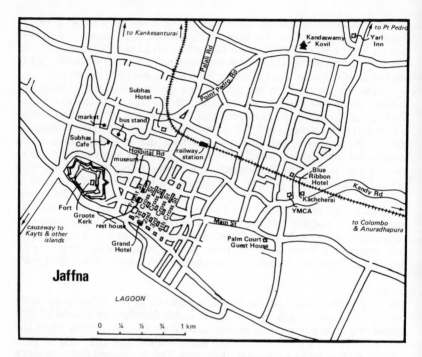

dai about 16 km out of Jaffna. Here "a miniature Anuradhapura, buried in the Tamil country" has been discovered, fascinating evidence of a Sinhalese-Buddhist culture pre-dating the Tamil-Hindu period. There are also interesting exhibits connected with Jaffna Tamil life and culture. Main St is also interesting for the amazing number of undertakers who seem to operate from it!

Hindu Kovils (temples)

Jaffna has many kovils but most of them are of comparatively recent construction. The destructive Portuguese tore all the earlier ones down and while the Dutch were more tolerant they certainly did not encourage their reconstruction so most of them date from the British era. The architecture is generally typical of the south Indian Dravidian style and each temple will have its gigantic wooden festival cars — the "juggernauts" from which the word is derived. The most spectacular car festival is held from the Kandaswamy Kovil in Nallur during July or August of each year. Evening *puja* services are held each day and visitors are generally welcome.

The original Kandaswamy Kovil has been variously described as dating from the 15th, 10th or even an earlier century. Its modern successor is topped by a typically Dravidian gopuram — the tall "spire", alive with a technicoloured Disneyland of Hindu characters. Other important kovils are generally outside the city limits.

Other
Jaffna has an active little market — with plenty of the mangoes for which the peninsula is famous, in season. Also plenty of Palmyrah cane ware including delightfully cheap straw hats. The shady Honduras mahogany trees, which dot many parts of Jaffna, were introduced by Percy Acland, a British administrator who was nicknamed the "Rajah of the North". He also designed the Jaffna kachcheri which is, unfortunately, now falling apart. There is much more to the Jaffna peninsula than just the town of Jaffna — other attractions are covered under "Around the Peninsula" and "Islands".

AROUND THE PENINSULA
The peninsula country looks quite unlike other parts of Sri Lanka — the intensive agriculture is all a result of irrigation and for the southern coconut palms Jaffna substitutes the stark looking palmyrah. Fear not toddy addicts, there is a palmyrah toddy too — it's said to be best on the island of Delft.

The peninsula is famous for its tidal wells — it rests on a limestone platform and deep wells of water rise and fall, though seemingly out of harmony with the tides. The deepest of these wells, at Neerveli, is fresh for the first 15 or so metres but salt for the balance of its 45 metre depth. At Keerimalai on the north coast of the peninsula there is a fresh water spring right by the beach. Manalkadu, at the eastern end of the peninsula, is a unique mini-desert with shifting sand dunes and occasional sand storms. Further east still there's the relatively inaccessible Chundikkulam wildlife sanctuary which is noted for its rich birdlife.

Jaffna has a number of good beaches although it's a long, long way from being the sort of beach resort centre you find on the east and west coasts in the south. Popular beaches include Kalmunai Point near Jaffna and Palm Beach on the north coast but Casuarina on the island of Karaitivu is best known although the water here is very shallow and you have to walk a fair distance out from the shore. And, of course, there are kovils dotted around the peninsula. The Kandaswamy Kovil at Maviddapuram, 15 km north of Jaffna near Keerimalai, has a car festival rivalling that of its namesake temple in Jaffna. Dutch kirks can be seen at Achchubeli and Vadukkodia, two Dutch toll-gates at Point Pedro, and the ruins of Portuguese churches at Myliddy and Chankanai. Erected in 1641 the Chankanai church is still in reasonably good repair.

ISLANDS
The islands off the peninsula are virtually as well known as Jaffna itself, particularly the island of Delft. Three of the major islands — Kayts, Karaitivu and Punkudutivu — are joined to the mainland by causeways over the shallow

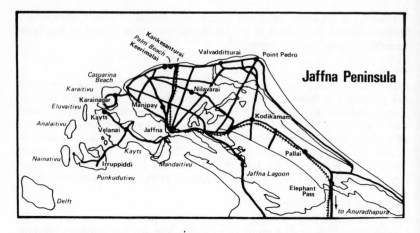

waters around the peninsula. Close to the town of Kayts, at the northern tip of the island of Kayts, stands the island fort of Hammenhiel which is accessible by boat from Kayts. Ask for the fort caretaker in Kyats. The name means "heel-of-the-ham" and relates to the Dutch view that Sri Lanka was shaped rather like a ham. There are other Dutch forts at Velanai on Kayts, on the island of Delft and at Elephant Pass on the mainland. The Delft and Velanai forts were built over earlier Portuguese ones.

Delft, named after the Dutch town of that name, is about 15 km out and reached by boat services from Siriputu whereas most other ferry services run from Kayts including the very short hop across to Karaitivu which is joined to the mainland by a causeway but not, as maps seem to indicate, to Kayts. The island is noted for the locally bred Delft ponies (of which very few are now left), for traces of the Portuguese and Dutch eras (such as the Dutch garrison captain's country-house with a stone pigeon-cote) and for its bleak, windswept beauty.

The usually uninhabited islands of Kachchativu and Palativu host major Roman Catholic festivals during the months of February or March each year. At Nagadipa on the island of Nainativu there is the most important Buddhist shrine in Jaffna — it commemorates a visit the Buddha is supposed to have made to this region of Sri Lanka. Nainativu also has a stone inscribed edict from the 12th century Polonnaruwa king Parakramabahu which announces rules for the disposal of shipwrecks, and is the site for a colourful annual Hindu festival at the Nagaposhani Animal Kovil.

Accommodation in Jaffna — the bottom end

It must be a faded memory now but a framed picture shows the manager of the *Grand Hotel* receiving an award for the best hotel in Jaffna in 1969. These days a single costs Rs 10, a double Rs 20 — the rooms are clean, plain, flimsily walled and wide open to the mosquitoes, of which Jaffna has a great number. If you order so much as a cup of tea here, first ascertain the price or be prepared to engage in a little price-bending come departure day. The Grand is within walking distance from the train or bus station, or about a Rs 3 taxi ride.

The *Blue Ribbon Hotel* is similarly priced, near the *YMCA* which costs Rs 12.50 per person but is open to men only. The Y is quite a modern establishment. Jaffna also has a *Rest House* which costs Rs 40 for a double and is very centrally located but is a rather grubby and rundown shadow of other Rest Houses around the island.

Accommodation in Jaffna — the top end
Top of the top end in Jaffna is the *Subhas Tourist Hotel* (tel Jaffna 7228) at 15 Victoria Rd. It's big (45 rooms) with a balcony-restaurant and only a short distance from the railway station. Room only costs range from around Rs 60 for the cheapest non air-conditioned single up to Rs 250 for an air-conditioned double. Bed and breakfast and all-inclusive tariffs are also available.

The pleasantly relaxed *Palm Court* is not quite so central at 202 Main St (tel Jaffna 244 and 628). There are just 10 rooms and costs are around Rs 50/75 for singles/doubles or Rs 125/250 all-inclusive. Finally there's *Yarl Inn Guest House* at 241 Point Pedro Rd (tel Jaffna 7674). That's slightly beyond the Kandaswamy Kovil, coming from the railway station. It has just five rooms starting from around Rs 25 for room-only singles.

Places to Eat
Jaffna has a few places to try for a meal apart from the hotels. Right by the bus station there's the *Subhas Cafe*, a three part complex with ice cream and refreshments in one air-conditioned section, meals in another. The food here is quite good and the ice cream is excellent — it qualifies as Jaffna's taste treat. *Ricoh*, only a couple of doors away, is another ice cream specialist and also has a good selection of Indian sweets in the front window. In the modern bazaar complex there are a number of food counters with appetizing looking short eats. While you're there try a Jaffna mango too. They're reputed to be the finest in Sri Lanka and I'm in definite agreement!

TALAIMANNAR
The island of Mannar (Talaimannar literally means "Mannar Head") is a place many visitors pass through, for this is where the India ferry from Rameswaram arrives, but few linger. Mannar is probably the driest and most barren area in Sri Lanka and the landscape is chiefly notable for the many baobab trees — a native of Africa and Madagascar, the Mannar baobabs were probably introduced by Arab traders many centuries ago. They're a most peculiar looking tree with a girth that often exceeds their height. The jungle shrine of Madhu (see "Festivals" in the introduction) can also be found on

the island.

Mannar, the major town on the island, is at the landward end of the island — close to the three km long causeway across which the railway runs. It's uninteresting apart from its picturesque Portuguese/Dutch fort. The town of Talaimannar is about three km before the pier — the ferry departure point for India. A little further west an abandoned lighthouse at South Point marks the start of Adam's Bridge, the chain of reefs, sandbanks and islets that almost connects Sri Lanka to India. This is the series of stepping stones which Hanuman used to follow Ravana, the demon king of Lanka, in his bid to rescue Sita.

Wildlife Parks

It's perhaps a little astonishing that Sri Lanka — small and densely populated as it is — manages to set aside 10% of its total area for wildlife sanctuaries. Some of these are designated as Strict Natural Reserves where no visitors are allowed — they're for the animals only. Others are Nature Reserves — populated but animal and bird life is protected. Or simply Jungle Corridors — seasonal migrating paths such as those that elephants might follow as their usual water sources dry up. For the overseas visitor the most interesting are the National Parks where you can see animals in their natural habitat.

Sri Lanka has a wide variety of wildlife but the two that attract most attention are the elephants and the leopards, both of which a park visitor stands a very good chance of seeing. Less exotic animals you may well come across include the mongoose, wild buffalo, mouse deer, sloth bear, loris, sambhur, jackal, monkey and wild boar. The latter animal is one that hunters are still welcome to take a shot at since the Sri Lankans reckon there are far too many of them! Reptile life includes a wide variety of goannas, lizards, snakes including some very fair size pythons, and crocodiles — so watch where you swim. Bird life is even more abundant with hornbills, flycatchers, bee-eaters, minivets, orioles, woodpeckers, flamingoes, pelicans, fishing eagles, a varied assortment of storks, spoonbills, coots and many others.

There are a number of national parks, each with specialities for certain animals or birds, but the best known and most visited are Wilpattu and Ruhunu, better known as Yala. Entry into these parks is strictly regulated — visitors are only allowed in vehicles, a park warden must accompany them, and except at certain designated spots you are not allowed to leave your vehicle. There are jungle bungalows where you can stay for more extended study of the wildlife — they can be booked through the Wildlife Conservation Department, 54 Chatham St, Colombo 1 (tel 24208). At Wilpattu and Yala park, entry (including a warden to accompany you in your car) costs Rs 10 per person. To hire a jeep or Land-Rover for a half day costs in the region of Rs 600 or 700 including fuel. Car rental companies normally stipulate that their vehicles cannot be taken into the parks — many of the park tracks require four-wheel drive in any case.

WILPATTU

Covering 1085 square km, the Wilpattu National Park is on the north-west coast, directly west of Anuradhapura which is the usual jumping off point for park visits. Jeeps can easily be hired in Anuradhapura or at the park turn-off at Wilpattu. From Anuradhapura it is only about 30 km to the park turn-off (at milestone 27) and from there it is another 22 km to the park entrance.

The park gets its name from the many *villus*, small seasonal lakes, which dot the generally dry landscape. Between the lakes the park is generally grassy plains, sand dunes and forestland — particularly in the eastern part of the park where there are also a number of ancient Sinhalese ruins. Approximately 270 km of jeep track loops confusingly through the park, it would be easy to get lost. Wilpattu is best known for its leopards, you have the best chance in Sri Lanka of seeing leopards here. Other animals you may see are spotted deer, wild boar, wild buffalo and the mongoose. In the *villus* you have a good chance of spotting crocodiles and large goannas will often scuttle out of your path. Wilpattu has much bird life with certain of the

lakes absolutely alive with birds during the November, December and January nesting time. There are a number of bungalows in the park.

●

A Visit to Wilpattu

Two or three other people at our guesthouse had been to the park and seen leopards so we were easily persuaded to join a group and hire a Land-Rover. Between six of us it cost Rs 650, including the driver and admission to the park. Sandwiches packed the night before, we got up at 4 am, an ungodly early hour in easy-going Sri Lanka. With a little persuasion and a push-start our vehicle got moving and we trundled off, all a little bleary eyed. Early morning or around sunset are the best times to visit the park since so many of the animals are nocturnal and sleep during the heat of the day. It can also get very hot for bumping around in an open jeep later in the day.

By the time we'd got to the park, signed in and collected our guide it was closer to 6 am. We'd already seen a mongoose before we arrived in the park and our second rushed across the road as soon as we entered. With the canvas roof rolled back we all stood in the back, scanning the trackside for signs of movement and shivering since it was still rather cold at this time of morning. We soon came across storks, pelicans, goannas, many deer and some wild buffalo but naturally it was a leopard we all wanted. We paused at one waterhole and were rewarded with the sight of a crocodile yawning widely, inviting some foolish bird to hop inside.

Several times we met other jeeps but each time the answer was the same — no leopards. When the king of the Sri Lankan beasts did deign to show his spotted face it was totally unexpected. Suddenly the jeep stopped and there he was, lapping water from a stream only a short distance from the track. We'd all been busy watching the lake on the other side. Hardly daring to breathe (but cameras clicking) we watched him finish his leisurely pre-breakfast drink and then, with scarcely a disdainful glance in our direction, stroll back into the jungle. Perhaps looking for a deer or something to really get his teeth into.

We drove on to a jungle bungalow and stopped for our sandwiches and tea but afterwards it was simply more of the same, no more leopards. By 10 am it was getting uncomfortably hot so we were glad to drop our guide off, roll the roof back into place and head back to Anuradhapura in time for lunch.

●

Wilpattu Accommodation

Outside the park there's the *Hotel Wilpattu* (tel 24625, 21101 and 27206) at Kala-Oya. There are 35 rooms with all-inclusive costs around Rs 300 for a double. Inside the park there are seven jungle bungalows with daily costs of Rs 8 per person. A cook is provided but you must bring your own bedding and food.

YALA

The 1249 square km of the Ruhunu National Park lies on the south-eastern corner of the island — it's generally known as Yala. You can approach Yala either from the south coast or the hill country — Tissamaharama and Kataragama are the usual jumping off points for the park. Yala is a mixture of scrub, plains, brackish lagoons and rocky outcrops. Part of the park is a Strict Natural Reserve and the easternmost section, Kumana, is particularly good for bird life. Visits to Kumana are usually made from Pottuvil on the east coast rather than from Tissamaharama. Jeeps for visiting the park can also be hired at Hambantota. Yala has much the same variety of wildlife as Wilpattu but it is particularly known for its elephant population. As at Wilpattu the best time for seeing the animals is October through December.

Yala Accommodation

Outside the park there is accommodation at Kataragama, Wirawila, and at Tissamaharama. The 45 room *Kataragama Rest House* (tel Kataragama 27) has a room-only cost of Rs 45 for a single or double. Shoestringers can try staying at the *Ramakrishna Mission Madam*. Kataragama is not, of course, just an entry point to the park — this is also an important pilgrimage point particularly for Hindu penitents during July and August.

At Tissamaharama the *Rest House* (tel Tissamaharama 95) has 38 rooms and costs Rs 150 in the non air-conditioned rooms, Rs 200 with air-conditioning. The *Yala Safari Beach Hotel* (tel 33143-4-5) has 50 rooms with all inclusive costs from around Rs 250 a double. Or there is the small, five room *Piyankara Tourist Guest House* on Kataragama Rd where room-only doubles cost from Rs 75.

Wirawila has two accommodation centres — the *Ibis Safari Lodge* (contact tel 82069) has just five rooms with bed & breakfast doubles at around Rs 125. Or there is the 40 room *Sanasuma Holiday Resort* (contact tel 071 7472) which costs around Rs 175 for a room-only double.

Within the park there are six bungalows and two more over in the Kumana region, known as Yala East. As at Wilpattu the nightly cost is Rs 8 per person and you must provide your own bedding and food.

OTHER PARKS

The great majority of visitors head for either Wilpattu or Yala but there are a number of others. The Gal Oya park covers about 540 square km, a little inland from the east coast. It has a huge tank, the Senanayake Samudra, and March to July is the best time to see wildlife here. Elephants are the main attraction, as in Yala. Accommodation is available at the 22 room *Inginiyagala Safari Inn* (tel Inginiyagala 26) where doubles cost around Rs 200.

The Lahugala Sanctuary is a very small park also renowned for its seasonal elephant population. Situated near Pottuvil on the east coast it is covered in the "East Coast" section. There are many smaller bird sanctuaries including the Chundikkulam Sanctuary near Jaffna.

Glossary

Adam's Bridge — chain of sandbars and islands that almost connects Sri Lanka to India.

Ambalamas — wayside shelters for pilgrims.

Amudes — loin cloths worn by gem miners, very similar to the G-strings worn by tourists at Hikkaduwa!

Arrack — distilled toddy, often very potent indeed.

Avalokitesvera — one of the Buddha's most important disciples.

Baas — skilled workman.

Banian — long, loose sleeved, over-shirt.

Banyan tree — a type of Bo-tree.

Baobab — strange water-holding African dry land trees which were introduced into the northern regions of the island by Arab traders.

Beedis — small hand rolled cigars.

Bel Kalla — a "Bell Fragment", name given to a newly discovered archaeological find, after H C P Bell the first British Government Archaeologist.

Betel — nut of the betel tree chewed as a mild intoxicant.

Bhikku — Buddhist Monk.

Bodhisattva — follower of the Buddha.

Bo-tree — *Ficus religiosa* — large spreading tree under which the Buddha was sitting when he attained enlightenment.

Bund — built up bank or dyke around a tank.

Burgher — Eurasians, generally descended from Portuguese or Dutch-Sinhalese inter-marriage.

Choli — short jacket worn with a sari.

Coir — matting or rope made from coconut fibres.

Copra — dried coconut kernel, used to make cooking oil.

Crore — 10 million (of anything).

CTB — Ceylon Transport Board, responsible for Sri Lanka's terrible bus system.

Culavamsa — the "Genealogy of the Lesser Dynasty" continues the history of the Mahavamsa right up to 1758, just 40 years before the last King of Kandy, Sri Wickrema Rajasinha, surrendered to the British.

Curd — yoghurt, usually buffalo-curd and always delicious.

Dagoba — Sinhala word for Buddhist religious monument composed of a solid hemisphere containing relics of the Buddha, known as a pagoda, stupa or chedi in other countries.

D-form — currency exchange form on which you must record all foreign currency transactions.

Dhal — a thick soup made of split lentils.

Dharma — Buddhist teachings (Sanskrit word, in Pali it is Dhamma).

Dhobi — laundryman.

Dravidian — southern Indian race which includes Tamils.

Ganga — river.

Gedige — ancient Sinhalese architectural style, extremely thick walls and a corbelled roof.

Groote Kerk — the old Dutch church in Jaffna and Galle.

Guardstone — carved ornamental stones that flank doorways or entrances to temples.

Hopper — popular Sri Lankan snack meal — either string hoppers or egg hoppers.

Illama — gem bearing strata in gem fields.

Jaggery — hard, brown, sugar-like sweetner made from kitul palm sap.

Juggernauts — huge, extravagently decorated temple "cars" which are dragged through the streets during Hindu festivals.

Kachcheri — government secretariat or residency.

Kharma — law of cause and effect (Sanskrit word, in Pali it is Khamma).

Kitul — one of the Sri Lankan palm trees, used to make jaggery and treacle.

Kotte — the most important southern Sinhalese capital after the fall of Polonnaruwa — today it is Colombo.

Kovil — Hindu temple.

Kul — spicy chowder dish, popular in Jaffna.

Lakh — 100,000, a standard large unit in Sri Lanka and India.
Laksala — government run arts and handicrafts shop.
Loris — small, nocturnal tree-climbing animal.

Maha — the north-east monsoon season.
Mahavamsa — "Genealogy of the Great Dynasty", a recorded Sri Lankan history running from the arrival of Vijaya in 543 BC through the meeting of King Devanampaya Tissa with Mahinda and on to the great kings of Anuradhapura.
Mahaweli Ganga — Sri Lanka's biggest river, starts in the hill country near Adam's Peak, flows through Kandy and eventually reaches the sea near Trincomalee. The only river which flows north from the hill country.
Mahayana — large vehicle Buddhism.
Mahinda -- son of the Indian Buddhist-Emperor Ashoka, credited with introducing Buddhism to Sri Lanka.
Mahout — elephant rider/master.
Mawatha — Avenue.
Moonstone — semi-precious stone or a carved stone "doorstep" at temple entrances.
Mouse deer — very small variety of Sri Lankan deer.

Nibbana — pali word for nirvana.
Nirvana — the ultimate aim of Buddhist existence, a state where one leaves the cycle of existence and does not have to suffer further rebirths.

Pagoda — see dagoba.
Pali — the original language in which the Buddhist scriptures were recorded, scholars still look to the original Pali texts for the true interpretation.
Palmyrah — tall palm trees found in the dry northern region.
Paranibbana — the transition stage to nibbana, as in the reclining Buddha images where the Buddha is in the state of entering nirvana.
Perahera — procession, usually with dancers, drummers and even elephants.
Pettah — bazaar area of Colombo.
Plantains — bananas, come in many varieties in Sri Lanka.
Pola — special food market on certain day of the week.

Pooja — religious service.
Poya — full moon holiday.

Rawana — the "demon king of Lanka" who abducts Rama's beautiful wife Sita in the Hindu epic the *Ramayana*.
Relic Chamber — chamber in a dagoba housing a relic of the Buddha but also representing the Buddhist concept of the cosmos.
Ruhuna — ancient southern centre of Sinhalese power which stood even when Anuradhapura and Polonnaruwa fell to Indian invaders, it was located near Tissamaharama.

Sadhu Sadhu — "blessed, blessed", the words pilgrims cry out as they climb Adam's Peak.
Sambhur — species of deer.
Sangamitta — Mahinda's sister, she brought the sapling from which the sacred Bo-tree has grown.
Sangha — the brotherhood of the Buddhist monks.
Sanskrit — ancient Indian language, the oldest known language of the Indo-European family.
Sari — traditional female garment in Sri Lanka and India.
School pen — ballpoint pen.
Singing fish — mysterious "fish" which sing from the lagoon in Baticaloa.
Sinhala — language of the Sinhalese people.
Sinhalese -- majority population of Sri Lanka, principally Sinhala speaking Buddhists.
SLFP — Sri Lanka Freedom Party.
Sloth bear — large, shaggy, honey-eating Sri Lankan bear.

Tamil — people of Indian descent who comprise the largest minority population in Sri Lanka.
Tank — artificial water storage lake, many of the tanks in Sri Lanka are both very large and very ancient.
Tantric Buddhism — Hindu influenced Buddhism with strong sexual and occult overtones, Tibetan Buddhism.
Taylor, James — not the rock singer, this one set up the first tea plantation in Ceylon.
Thambili — king coconut, makes a very refreshing drink.

Theravada — small vehicle Buddhism as practiced in Sri Lanka.

Tiffin — lunch, a colonial English expression.

Tiffin boys — they pick up city workers' tiffins from their homes and transport them into the city.

Toddy — mildly alcoholic drink tapped from the palm tree.

Toddy tapper — the people who perform acrobatic feats in order to tap toddy from the tops of palm trees.

Tripitaka — the "three baskets", one of the classical Buddhist scriptures.

UNP — United National Party, first Sri Lankan political party to hold power after independence.

Vanni — the northern plains, the tank country.

Vatadage — ancient Sinhalese architectural style, extremely thick walls and a corbelled roof.

Veddah — the original people of Sri Lanka prior to the arrival of the Sinhalese, still struggling on in isolated pockets.

Villus — small seasonal lake-lets found in the Wilpattu park.

Yala — the south-west monsoon season.

UPDATE

We've had so much feedback from travellers in Sri Lanka that we've decided to add this update supplement to this February '81 reprint. The most overwhelming report from Sri Lanka is that prices have rocketed. Many travellers asked how many years ago the information was gathered for this book — the information was up to date, prices have simply shot up. I'd particularly like to thank David Stanley, Conny Van Manen, Jeanne Paterson, S K H Karunathilaka, Mrs R Amerasinghe, E Slansky, Mrs S W Herath, Richard Eiger, K C Blacker, P B Woodal, John & Claire Owen, Lorne Goldman, P Jackson, T B Singalaxana and The Australian office of the Sri Lanka Tourist Board for their assistance in this update supplement.

GENERAL INFORMATION

Costs Prices, particularly of accommodation, have zoomed in Sri Lanka. Biggest increases have been posted at the "international standard" hotels and at some of the more popular rest houses. Increases in these places are often of the order of 50% to 100% compared to the prices quoted in the book!

Visas Visa extensions are now more of a hassle, you may only get one two-week extension after your initial month.

Photography Note that permits for taking pictures in the ancient cities are not available on Saturdays. A permit now costs Rs 45 and only covers Anuradhapura, Polonnaruwa and Sigiriya. You're up for a further Rs 10 at Minintale and Aukana. There is also a Rs 30 entrance charge for Signiya and Polonnaruwa and Rs 10 for each car! Note that the charge only allows one visit.

What to Bring A sink plug.

Swimming Several warnings about tricky currents at Hikkaduwa and Trinco — there are strong ocean currents, no lifesaving protection and a few tourists have been drowned. I've got to agree — while I was in Sri Lanka a Canadian drowned in Trinco, a French woman in Hikkaduwa.

Beer The tax on liquor has been increased and a beer now costs upwards of Rs 15 and sales hours are restricted to 11 am-2 pm and 5-10 pm.

Other Drugs The Sri Lankan police are starting to get into the drug busts game and, as you might expect, Hikkaduwa is the first target. Take care.

Crafts Complaints about poor quality — jewellery is set very poorly (have to agree) and clothes (in Hikkaduwa) are badly made.

Begging That "give me school pen" annoyance certainly seems to annoy a lot of other people too! "Most people approached us not for friendliness but for some gain," commented one visitor.

Matches "Good, no-nonsense" Chinese matches are now available. Hopefully Chinese drinking straws will follow?

GETTING THERE

Air Lanka, carefully run with Singapore Airlines' Supervision, is now in full swing and there are a lot more flights to Sri Lanka. In particular the connections

169

from India are now much easier, since the overload on Indian Airlines has been eased. They also operate a Tristar to Europe. Connections and prices between Australia and Sri Lanka are no better but the introduction of cheap Apex fares to South-East Asia makes getting to Sri Lanka a whole different story. The most economical way will probably be to Apex to Singapore or Bangkok then buy a ticket from there to Colombo or talk to some Australian travel agents — deals are being made.

Talaimannar Ferry Sri Lanka harbour tax is now Rs 10. When travelling Sri Lanka-India you should ignore the hustlers who tell you that the bank at the pier will not change Sri Lankan rupees into the Indian variety. They will.

The *Travellers' Rest* at Mannar costs Rs 12 per person. From there plenty of buses go to Anuradhapura or Sangupiddy (for Jaffna) on the next morning. The ferry departs from India at 2 pm on Mondays, Wednesdays and Fridays. From Sri Lanka it's 10 am on Tuesdays, Thursdays and Saturdays. The Sri Lankan customs and immigration officials are getting into hassling "hippies" and making them return to India.

Airport Arrival & Departure Airport departure tax is now a hefty Rs 100, just like India and Nepal. They're all getting into this one. You can count on around Rs 180-200 for an airport taxi now (or Rs 90 from Negombo) but there is now a bus from the Taprobane in Colombo for all flights at a cost of Rs 55.

GETTING AROUND

There have certainly been some changes in this department. There are now a lot of private buses running in competition with the CTB buses. They cost about twice as much as the CTB buses although some travellers add that you should check prices before departure and be prepared to bargain. Another says that they are noted for bad tyres and high accident rates — "not much different from the CTB". Still they do appear to always have seats available (because the locals can't afford them) and even if they are "just as uncomfortable as the CTB buses" they don't make lengthy stops every hundred metres. "A good alternative for those whom reckless speed doesn't faze", adds another letter. Colombo to Kandy is Rs 15 — from the Fort Station, they

depart when full. There are also buses to Nuwara Eliya (Rs 30) and Hikkaduwa from Colombo.

Colombo also has a fleet of three-wheeler taxis which are cheaper than the regular car taxis. Petrol is now a very expensive Rs 40+ per gallon.

One traveller commented that the Railtours office was very helpful and friendly but the package tours only operated during the October peak season. It's difficult to make any rail bookings outside Colombo as all bookings are mailed to Colombo and confirmation (or otherwise) is mailed back! You're not supposed to make bookings more than 10 days ahead and from rural depots not more than five days in advance.

COLOMBO

Note that the National Museum is closed on weekends. A general warning about Colombo public swimming pools — poorly chlorinated, risk of infections.

The Hotel Intercontinental's pool is open to non-guests — at Rs 50 per day! Flag fall on the metered three-wheelers is Rs 1.40. Beware of money dealers — one traveller was ripped off by a Sri Lankan asking him to change US$10 into rupees. Colombo General Hospital is a "festered pesthole" — the writer went on to recommend Dr Theva A Buell, 31/2A Guildford Crescent, Colombo 7 (tel 92417) — near the Lionel Wendt Centre. The doctor says Sri Lankan medical care is getting worse since it is hard for people to study abroad now that English isn't taught like it once was.

Cheap Accommodation   Some varied comments on the Colombo cheapies: *Perpetual Tourist Lodge* is now "perpetually closed" — yes? *Seabreeze* is "noisy and a brothel in the afternoon" while *Sea View* "certainly doesn't have any view" and is "over-priced and filthy". To each their own! On the other hand the *Guest House* (tel 81527) at 492½ Galle Rd, south end of Welligama, is "moderately priced" at Rs 60 single and Rs 120 double and "very clean, restful". Or Number 6, 2nd Lane, Dehiwala has a "homey atmosphere, good food, the landlady likes quiet, non-alcoholic types." The downtown *YMCA* now costs Rs 90 for a double. See what I mean about the prices rocketing. Even the *Horton Youth Hostel* now costs Rs 60 for a double or Rs 70 with a wash basin.

More Expensive Accommodation A rave for *Hotel Nippon,* 125 Kumaran Ratnam Rd, Colombo 2. A large room with antique furniture, fan and bathroom is Rs 95 on the second floor or Rs 105 on the first. The price includes a full breakfast. There are also rooms with balconies but they don't have private bathrooms. Jerry Raymond, the manager of the Nippon's kitchen, is a "fine and informative man". It's "the best bargain in Colombo and the best located". The Nippon's restaurant and bar are supposed to be good — Indian, Japanese and Chinese food. Take a 138 bus from Port or about Rs 6 by three-wheeler. Truth to tell I looked in at the Nippon and thought it was quite nice but somehow missed it out when I wrote Colombo up.

At Nugegoda, on the outskirts of Colombo, the guest house run by Dr & Mrs W A Karunaratne combines "Sri Lankan flavour with high standards of western plumbing. Comfortable and impeccably maintained, very clean, marvellous food which you can eat outdoors overlooking a superb garden. For travellers who want 5-star luxury at 2-star prices." The address is *Amra,* 1 Dias Place, Pepiliyana Rd, Nugegoda (tel 073-3315). Prices without breakfast are US$7.50/9 single/double or US$9/12 with air-con, plus 10%.

Places to Eat The *Park View Club,* 70 Park St, near Viharamahadevi Park and the Chinese Embassy (and the Horton Youth Hostel) is good for Chinese food. A meal costs from Rs 7.50 to Rs 25 but you get so much food that two people can order one meal and split it up.

Taprobane Hotel gets a couple of raves — one writer comments (in glowing detail) on their Rs 85 (plus 10% service) businessman's buffet lunch. All you can eat and all sorts of food. Worth starving for — "roast leg of beef, lots of cold cuts, curried crab, fried string hoppers with cashews, pepper beef, yellow rice with peanuts, all kinds of good salads, cold chicken and seer fish with nice sauces, great soup, cheeses, a whole table full of desserts, French pastries, chocolate eclairs, various cakes, puddings, fruit, tortes." Good grief, what sort of food trip were they on! Every day except Sunday from noon to 3 pm. Down in the basement the Blue Leopard night club does an excellent lunchtime curry-buffet on weekdays for Rs 22.

WEST COAST

INDURUWA

This quiet fishing village is eight km south of Bentota. At the *Ripples Tourist Inn* there are eight rooms in what was once a private villa. Basic, but adequate, rooms cost Rs 100 with private bath, Rs 50 without. Meals are in the Rs 35 range for an "astoundingly good dinner of freshly caught fish; lunch and breakfast correspondingly less." The manager, Richard Pieris, is an excellent fish chef who worked for the Australian High Commission for 25 years. There's a secluded, palm-fringed beach, small fishing colony and toddy tappers. "A real find."

HIKKADUWA

A number of letters commented on how pleasant Hikkaduwa is during the monsoon season. Less crowds, prices drop dramatically, weather is OK and within the reef you can still swim — although another letter commented "surf is good but swimming not much cop."

A recommendation for the "Tourist Library" (it's on the Hikkaduwa map) where a local watchmaker lends out paperbacks he's collected. You have to leave a Rs 15 refundable deposit but the writer adds "I think it's a nice idea donate your deposit."

Accommodation During the monsoon rates can drop to less that 25% of the high-season rates. This is your chance to stay in the flashy hotels at knock down rates. *Blue Corals, Darshana Guest House, Coral Front Inn* and *Ozone Tourist Rest* are all recommended as special bargains in the off-season although one writer added that the manager of the *Blue Corals* is an "unpleasant sod"!

Dr Suriarachchi's guest house at 42 Baddegama Rd, just 150 metres from the railway station, is recommended as being clean, friendly, with all facilities, good food and you can have free medical attention! Rs 200 a double in season. The

Pink Guest House is "good for long-term stays". *Curio Shop and Guest House* is cheap, good security (seem to be a lot of thefts at Hikkaduwa now) and *Lions Paradise* is cheaper still.

Places to Eat Mainly confirmation of my original comments — *Rangith's Snacks* is still popular, *Hotel Francis* for food is "a little more expensive, but good value", *Sun Sea Sand* has "excellent breakfasts and a very clean kitchen, the manager takes real pride in offering only good meals." Good food at *Hotel Paradiso* too.

GALLE

A rave recommendation for R K Kodikara's guest house at 29 Rampart St, Fort Galle which is friendly and cheap — doubles from Rs 30, Rs 40 with fan. Singles at half that price. The *Sydney Hotel*, right beside the bus stand and very near the railway station, has singles for under Rs 20. The *New Oriental* gets a rave: "best value for money in Sri Lanka — space, antique opulence and cheerful service". Downstairs singles are Rs 120, upstairs Rs 140 or doubles for Rs 200-240. "A substantial Rs 20 breakfast and the only un-musty rice I tasted."

Sharly Guest House, 9 Rampart St, is about a minute to the right inside the main gate. Small restaurant has good cakes, four or five rooms from Rs 60. The *Orchard Holiday Home,* at 61 Light House St (tel 09 2370), is recently opened and the manager has written to say what a great place it is.

MATARA

The *SK Guest House* has more than just accommodation, it also has a batik studio and showroom and a pleasant garden. In the fort Asoka de Silva, 6 Middle St, has a nice and giant sized bungalow where you can get a double for Rs 25.

TANGALLA

The *Rest House* is next to the Fish Co-Op writes one unhappy traveller — his room had no water, a too small mosquito net and a fan "like a hurricane". Plus accommodation costs have zoomed up to Rs 150 per person and that included only breakfast. And the service was bad! To add to the gloom *Peace Haven* would not give room-only prices, room plus breakfast and dinner was Rs 265 a double, cheaper rooms Rs 215 although the cabanas may be cheaper still. J Ranaweera, Marakailliyas, Tangalla has a house on the beach — lovely food, good accommodation and Rs 30 a double. Take the road from the town centre to the Rest House and it's on the left before the fish factory. Avoid Mrs Fernando's guest house nearby, the same writer added. Some plus recommendations also came in for the *Tangalla Beach Hotel* and the *Magic Circle Guest House*.

HAMBANTOTA

The *Rest House* is now "very expensive" but there is M Razeek's guest house at 13 Philip St where you can get a double at Rs 30 and food if required.

TISSAMAHARAMA

On the coast, eight km from Tissamaharama, the small village of Kirinda has a fine beach and a small Buddhist shrine on the rocks. Next to the dagoba there is a statue of Queen Viharamahadevi who, according to legend, landed at this place after being sent to sea by her father King Kelanitissa. The king sent his daughter to sea as a penance for killing (injuring?) a monk. The daughter landed unharmed and subsequently married the local King Kavantissa. Her statue is also in Tissamaharama and her son was the famous King Dutugemunu. The village was used as a land base by Arthur C Clarke and others when diving for the Great Basses wreck — see Clarke's *The Treasure of the Reef.*

THE HILL COUNTRY

KANDY

More price increases — the Botanical Gardens and the Museum now cost Rs 10 and Rs 20 respectively for foreigners, discount to students with ISIC cards. Note that at the time of the Perahera, Kandy is booked out long in advance and everything is *very* expensive. Kandy is recommended by one writer for good brassware at low prices. The pool at the *Hotel Suisse* cost Rs 10 per day and "it's clean".

Accommodation The *Traveller's Nest* now has 12 rooms and a dorm and a 12-seater van for sightseeing. The telephone no. is 2633, not as in the main text. *Hotel Woodstock* has "the best location in town". Follow the sign for the Hotel Constellation, beside the Temple of the Tooth, veer left up the steep dirt path and the hotel is at the top of the path and some steps. You get a wonderful breeze and a great view of the temple and lake. It's run by a nice Buddhist family and costs from around Rs 15 or 20 per bed, the octagonal room at the front is a bit more expensive at Rs 65.

Blue Star at 30 Hewaheta Rd, Talwatte (08-4392) has rooms and cabanas, it's clean and relaxed, the food (eat with the family) is fantastic and room only costs are Rs 100 to 150 for a double, Rs 240 to 290 with half-board. Plus 10%. Or Mrs N de Almeida, 83 Mangala Mawatha, Watapuluwa H/S is also recommended. *Olde Empire* is "a clean place", doubles at Rs 55 in the front, Rs 50 in the back. *Travellers' Halt* at Katugastota is "one of the nicest youth hostels in all of Asia". Ask directions for the railway bridge at Katugastota, cross the bridge and the YH is the second house on the left (no sign). Rs 12.80 for a bed and big breakfast — "like being one of the family".

NUWARA ELIYA

Hill Side Guest House does appear to have closed down. A shame. And *Molesworth* gets some really negative reports — even people who think it's OK report that the rooms are "dank and musty". Doubles cost Rs 35 to 50. The *Municipal Rest House* now costs Rs 48 but add on Rs 7.50 if you want a heater at night. Note that Nuwara Eliya can get very cold at night. One writer reports you can buy second hand coats and sweaters from the street stalls — NE's own version of an Australian or New Zealand "Op Shop". Dinner at the *Hill Club* now costs Rs 66 including service but it's still a great experience. Mrs Lane, behind Cargill's Department House charges Rs 15 a bed in double rooms.

ANCIENT CITIES

KANDY TOUR

"Mary's tour" from Kandy through the ancient cities starts at the Goodshed Bus station, east of the railway station on the opposite side of the road to Peradeniya. Take a bus to Dambulla (Polonnaruwa, Anuradhapura and Trinco buses all go that way). Get off at the first stop opposite the pink gate to the cave. Leave your bags at one of the local tea stalls while you explore the caves. The Sigiriya bus starts from this same point, every two hours or so, the tea stall owner recommended the 4 pm bus as being least crowded. Get off at the Nilmari Lodge, a little before the ruins' entrance in Sigiriya. You take a bus to the main road (Polonnaruwa Junction) and from there it's 2½ to three hours by CTB bus or preferably, a mini-bus (since you'll get a seat) to Polonnaruwa.

ANURADHAPURA

The map on 120-121 shows the Mahaweli Ganga when it should show the Malwatu Oya (Flower Garden River). *Shanthi Guest House* room prices appear to have

WORLD'S END

Note that when you've got to the end of the road you've still got a two hour walk to *Farr's Inn.*

HAPUTALE

If you're visiting the monastery at Adisham note that the father "doesn't like hippies" and that you should call or write for reservations if you intend to stay. Rs 125 all inclusive and the food is "terrible"!

RATNAPURA

The Gem Museum also has a very fine art gallery of mostly silver objects designed by the owner, Purandara Bhadya Marapana. The art objects are "top class, he uses traditional elements in a very creative manner."

doubled but they do have new bikes. There are *Railway Retiring Rooms* at Rs 77 (only half that for locals) but choose a road side room rather than a railway side. *Tissawewa Rest House* has an annexe with rooms at Rs 132 (other rooms are Rs 214) but you have to press the man at the desk to get him to admit they exist. They seem to be "reserved for Sri Lankans and local Britishers."

POLONNARUWA

It now costs Rs 30 to enter the ruins but it can "easily be avoided". If you hire a car it's another Rs 10 to take that into the ruins. One writer got a car from the Orchid Rest House for Rs 65 — to see the ruins and be taken to the train station, five km away. The *Orchid Rest House* gets a number of bad notices. "Filthy and fly-ridden" according to one correspondent. "Don't trust the staff, things disappear from your room," added another.

The *Chinese Guest House* is also not so good from one letter, with quite poor food, served in an uncaring manner," the room wasn't as bad as the indifferent attitude which greets you here". But then somebody else wrote that it was "good with good food", but added not to rent bikes here, the bike shop across from the Orchid has fairly good bikes. And somebody else simply said it "is the best". *Nirmalia Guest House* has "lovely food but it's a hassle unless you fancy jungle walks". *Rest House* prices have escalated — now Rs 300 to 385 for a double with all meals.

A new addition is *Jenica Tourist Guest House,* five minutes walk from the police station along New Town Road. Singles/doubles with shower, attached bathroom and mosquito nets cost Rs 15/20. There's also a dorm, restaurant, bike and motorcycle hire and parking space for vans. Solo-women should be careful walking around the more remote ruins. One lady was assaulted but managed to fight off her attacker.

DAMBULLA

There's a Rs 3 entry charge to the cave temple plus Rs 15 for your camera. Just before the *Rest House* on the Kandy road there's a *Tourist Welfare Centre* — it's a rock bottom place, without electricity, but it is friendly and food is available. A dorm bed is Rs 10, single Rs 15 and a double Rs 20.

SIGIRIYA

The Lodge at Nilmari, just before the ruins' entrance on the right hand side of the road, is "the place for shoestringers". Rs 30 a double, very basic, no electricity, but clean toilet and shower. There are three rooms (two doubles, one triple). The owner, Lionel, is a very helpful local man and his wife prepares excellent food. Dinners around Rs 12.50. The Archaeological Bungalow no longer rents rooms. It now costs Rs 30 to go up on the rock, plus there is the photography charge, get tickets from the Department of Archaeology or you'll have to climb back down again from half-way up. No student concessions and no chance of sneaking in like you can in Polonnaruwa.

ALUVIHARA

In one of the monastic caves there is a horror chamber with colourful statues of devils and sinners showing various forms of punishment. The writer "particularly liked" the punishment of a sexual sinner who had his skull cut open and was having his brain ladled out by two demons while he wept bitterly. At Matale, near Aluvihara, the *Salgado Hotel & Bakery* has a few rooms at Rs 20.

EAST COAST

TRINCOMALEE

Some good news, some bad. If you want to visit Admiralty House you have to get permission in Colombo. The *Rest House* costs Rs 150 and has good food. *Tourist 'Ome* appears to have been renamed *Guest 'Ome!* The *Travellers Halt* scores a number of bad reports — dirt, rats and dishonesty seems to be the order of the day. The adjacent *Chinese Guest House* doesn't appear to be much better. On the other hand *Votre Maison,* 45 Green Rd (behind the Nelson Cinema), is a "really nice place". Dorm beds for Rs 10 and more rooms soon. Good food at cheap rates — "can't beat their big glass of curd for Rs 3". *Mohamed's Place,* opposite the general hospital, costs Rs 10 for a bed in the dorm or in a two-bed cabana. The bakery near the Travellers Halt does hoppers, dal and a pint (!) of tea for Rs 3 to 4.

NILAVELI

The *Blue Lagoon* has some plain doubles at lower prices — no fan or mosquito net. Eat at the stalls near the bridge on the main road, delicious vegetable and egg rotis, curd, baked goodies and fruit. Near the Blue Lagoon, on the same side of the bridge, is the *Doola Eella Guest House,* three doubles available at Rs 35 each but expansion is planned and prices will, no doubt, rise — particularly if they put electricity in.

Beware of the currents near the lagoon mouth, in fact all along the beach. Pigeon Island, near Nilaveli, has a good coral reef for diving and swimming is said to be safe there.

TRINCOMALEE-KALKUDAH
"We travelled along the coastal route and it's a better way to go. There are now only three ferry crossings. The first requires a change of bus, the second takes the bus across, and the third is the ferry from Mutum across the harbour to Trinco — which takes 1½ hours and costs Rs 3."

KALKUDAH
Now almost fully recovered from the cyclone — the hotels and rest houses are back in operation. Beware of theft while you're on the beach if you're staying in a local house — "small boys systematically go through the luggage, threatening to go to the police has some effect." Sunflower Guest House has been renamed *Sandy's Place* and costs around Rs 30 a double.

BATTICALOA
The *Rest House* has been rebuilt and now costs Rs 108.

ARUGAM BAY
Seasands now costs Rs 175 a double for room only. *Crosswinds* costs Rs 80 per night (shower but no electricity) and is very friendly, does good meals.

JAFFNA & THE NORTH

JAFFNA
The *Paradise Hotel,* in the middle of town is very cheap, (Rs 10 a single) and has good, inexpensive food downstairs. *Kumaran Tourist Inn,* five minutes walk from the bus station at 67 Stanley Rd, costs Rs 40 a double. The vegetarian restaurant at 112 Hospital Rd, close to the bus station, does good meals for Rs 5.

WILDLIFE PARKS

KATARAGAMA
A short bus ride from the centre (three km) you'll find Shelton de Silva on Sella Kataragama Rd, off Milagama Rd, Milagama. He's pleased to put people up at his house/farm on the bank of the Menik Ganga and on the edge of the jungle. It's beautiful, isolated, peaceful, has nice food and is very basic. Rs 50 for a double includes three meals. He's well known so easy to find or you can contact him through his friend Dasa at the Premisin Hotel, New Town Kataragama, opposite the bus station and YMBA. Dasa also puts people up overnight for about Rs 20, his sign is in Sinhalese.